*Reinvention of the Public Library
for the 21st Century*

REINVENTION OF THE PUBLIC LIBRARY FOR THE 21ST CENTURY

Edited by

William L. Whitesides, Sr.

1998
LIBRARIES UNLIMITED, INC.
Englewood, Colorado

Libraries Unlimited, Inc.
P.O. Box 6633
Englewood, CO 80155-6633
1-800-237-6124
www.lu.com

Production Editor: Kay Mariea
Copy Editor: Carmel Huestis
Proofreader: Eileen Bartlett
Indexer: Kay Meredith Dusheck
Design and Layout: Pamela J. Getchell

Library of Congress Cataloging-in-Publication Data

Reinvention of the public library for the 21st century / edited by
    William L. Whitesides, Sr.
        xxvi, 302 p. 17x25 cm.
        Includes bibliographical references and index.
        ISBN 1-56308-628-X (cloth)
        1. Public libraries--United States--Administration.   2. Public
    libraries--Aims and objectives--United States.   I. Whitesides,
    William L., Sr.
    Z731.R423   1998
    025.1'974--dc21   98-29869
                                                                        CIP

CONTENTS

9 THE TECHNOLOGY: WILL THE END JUSTIFY THE MEANS?

10 TECHNOLOGY AND SERVICES FOR THE SPECIAL POPULATION

APPENDIX
Outlook for Gale Research/*Library Journal* "Libraries of the Year" and Other Selected Libraries in the Twenty-First Century

CHICAGO PUBLIC LIBRARY

FOREWORD

As a student of library sciences three decades ago I had the good fortune to read journalist Hawthorne Daniel's small volume entitled *Public Libraries for Everyone*—borrowed, incidentally, from a neighborhood branch library. The plastic-covered jacket on the book stated that the contents included "a profile of the perfect administration of public funds" and "the story of the National Library Services Act." In that time of promise, few would have suggested that the public library would need "rethinking" or "reengineering." Public library services were discussed in the context of development, growth, and opportunity. Survival was not a question.

Now, as we approach the twenty-first century, students of library and information science continue to consider both the past and the future of the unique institution we know as the public library. Social, political, economic, and technological factors have influenced the public library, and new approaches to prioritizing its roles, developing its resources, delivering its services, and financing its activities have resulted. The same influences have created competition for the public library's customers, its staff, and its financial support and have raised questions about the viability of the institution.

The present volume, planned and written by graduate students and edited by their instructor, suggests a future of continuing opportunity for the public library. The book is not a traditional textbook; rather, it identifies 12 important platforms from which discussions of public library priorities, policy, and practice can be launched. The reading lists and library profiles point to more resources for instructors, students, practitioners, and discussion leaders.

William L. Whitesides and his students have prepared the stage for continuing the discussion of what the public library will be in the next century.

Elizabeth S. Aversa
Dean, School of Library and Information Science
The Catholic University of America

PREFACE

After I was selected in 1996 to teach "The Public Library," a class offered by The Catholic University School of Library and Information Science through the University of Richmond, I tried to locate a suitable, current (or at least recent) textbook for a graduate level course on the subject. The faculty did not recommend a single text, and my search of the literature did not reveal anything of substance more recent than the early 1990s. Because I expected to have students anticipating a career in the twenty-first century, at the time a mere four years away, I decided, with Dean Elizabeth Aversa's support, to ask the class to write a book on the reinvention of the public library for the millennium.

The approach to "reinvention" that the class considered was similar to the Steve Cisler approach in "Weatherproofing a Great, Good Place: The Long-Range Forecast for Public Libraries: Technostorms, with Rapidly Changing Service Fronts"[1] adapted from a presentation he made for a public library symposium. His philosophy is that libraries that can combine the old and the new, print and electronic media, analog and digital, storytelling and multimedia, will continue to attract the widest range of users and survive the "technostorms" of today and tomorrow.

Some may believe that Michael Hammer's and James Champy's approach of "reengineering" is necessary for the twenty-first-century public library, and, in fact, some public libraries may require Hammer's more drastic approach. Reengineering is "the fundamental rethinking and radical redesign of business processes to achieve dramatic improvements in critical contemporary measures of performance, such as cost, quality, service, and speed."[2] Hammer's four key words, as applied to the business environment, are "fundamental," "radical," "processes," and "dramatic." Reengineering requires starting over with totally different approaches to the process structure of previous years.[3]

Another—and a more moderate—strategy is that described by David Osborne and Ted Gaebler in *Reinventing Government*. Their "map" includes ten principles, on the basis of which entrepreneurial governments (or in this case, public libraries) are emerging around the country. The principles, not listed here, are based on the following five fundamental beliefs (I have substituted the word *library* for *government*): "We believe in libraries"; "we believe that civilized society cannot function effectively without effective libraries"; "we believe that the people who work in libraries are not the problem; the systems . . . are the problem"; "neither traditional liberalism nor traditional conservatism has much relevance to the problems our libraries face today"; and "we believe in equity—in equal opportunity for all Americans."[4]

And still other practitioners may adopt the philosophy of Peter Drucker, the sage of management theory, or of W. Edward Deming of TQM (Total Quality Management) fame. The update of "the planning process," with a subtitle "a transformation process," discussed later in this preface, is another approach to "reinvention."

After the first session of the class, we lost four enrollees who could not, for several reasons, undertake the effort to research and write one of the chapters. Of those willing to try, a few agreed to work as teams. Although the team approach may be effective in the work environment, team cooperation and sustained mutual effort in a commuting-student situation presented problems. The students who survived did a masterful job researching print and electronic resources, and I graded their chapters and reviews accordingly.

We are indebted to George M. Eberhart's *Whole Library Handbook 2*,[5] which was the textbook we used for background, statistics, illustrations, documents, and ephemera on public libraries.

One of the students recommended at the first class meeting that we analyze the Gale Research/*Library Journal* Public Library of the Year Awards for the last five years regarding each library's reinvention for the twenty-first century. Each student selected one award or runner-up library for a review of the library's attempts to reorganize itself. Since there was not a sufficient number of award libraries, some other notable libraries were selected by some students. Students interviewed the director or another member of the staff to update the material in each *Library Journal* article. These analyses appear in the appendix and are referred to where appropriate in the chapters.

In addition to the references cited for each chapter, we have included additional readings that may be helpful for practitioners, researchers, and fellow students of other library and information programs. For the professors and perhaps leaders of continuing education events, there are also discussion questions at the end of each chapter.

As the millennium approaches, circumstances are bound to change and other publications will have appeared. We hope this edition will contribute to further discussion and a fuller understanding of some of the issues. We did not undertake the soft management issues such as library conflict resolution, supervisory skills, or personnel management that may be learned on the job or in staff development opportunities. We did not cover materials for a public library, as that subject is covered elsewhere in "Collection Development" courses. We believe, however, that we covered most of the topics appropriate for a semester graduate course on the public library, for continuing education courses and discussions, and for general knowledge sought by administrators, staff, trustees, and Friends.

The students' research and rewriting of chapters were completed in 1997. One notable publication which can contribute greatly to the ongoing discussion arrived in early 1998. It is the current revision of "the planning process" by Ethel Himmel and William James Wilson with the Revision Committee of the Public Library Association entitled *Planning for Results, a Public Library Transformation Process*, ALA, 1998.[6]

On behalf of the School of Library and Information Science of The Catholic University of America, I want to thank the graduate students whose names appear as authors of the individual chapters for doing the research and writing, and for rewriting their work as a result of class discussions. I also want to thank Fran White and John and Emily Salmon for their respective contributions in editing the final manuscript.

William L. Whitesides, Sr.
Editor

Notes

1.   Steve Cisler, "Weatherproofing a Great, Good Place: The Long-Range Forecast for Public Libraries: Technostorms, with Rapidly Changing Service Fronts," *American Libraries* 27, no. 9 (October 1996): 42–46.

2.   Michael Hammer and James Champy, *Reengineering the Corporation: A Manifesto for Business Revolution* (New York: Harper Business, 1993), 32.

3.   Ibid., 49.

4.   David Osborne and Ted Gaebler, *Reinventing Government* (New York: Penguin Books, 1993), xvii–xix.

5.   George M. Eberhart, comp. *Whole Library Handbook 2: Current Data, Professional Advice, and Curiosa About Libraries and Library Services* (Chicago: American Library Association, 1995).

6.   Ethel Himmel and William James Wilson, *Planning for Results, a Public Library Transformation Process* (Chicago: American Library Association, 1998).

INTRODUCTION

REINVENTING LIBRARIES:
Responding to the Forces of Change

 *Lisa Crisman*

Have you visited your local public library lately? If you haven't, you should plan a visit soon. You may not recognize what you see. Libraries across the nation are responding to a variety of social, economic, and physical pressures. This introductory chapter will address some of the issues facing libraries in the United States today as they attempt to "reinvent" themselves to remain viable participants in the vast information universe of the twenty-first century.

As communities vary, so do the libraries that serve them. In areas where population and economy are declining, public libraries are scrambling to find ways to remain open, keep up with technology, and ensure access for all patrons. Burgeoning neighborhoods are adding new library branches or remodeling older facilities. These new spaces tend to be technological wonders, completely wired and ready to connect to the "information superhighway." Most library systems fall somewhere in the middle, adjusting to budget constraints while answering the call for equal information access in all forms, often while personnel are redistributed.

History of Libraries and Their Ethical Responsibility

Libraries generally began as social concerns funded by generous benefactors. Throughout ancient Greece and Rome there are records of rulers consolidating funds to construct buildings to house public records. In England, a public library was founded in the seventeenth century through private donations. In America, during the mid-nineteenth century, several public libraries were founded, including the Boston Public Library and the Enoch Pratt Free Library in Baltimore. These institutions began through the generous support of wealthy benefactors. In most cases, the underlying goal of the institution was to ensure free public access to a wide variety of historical and cultural information.

These original libraries evolved into the public library systems we know today. The question is: What role do we now expect libraries to fill? This book addresses this and other questions concerning libraries' relations with individuals and communities as well as the social responsibility of the institution. Included are examples of how some libraries are fulfilling their goals and how this vision follows the American Library Association's Library Bill of Rights.

The Public Library As "Place"

The foundation of any library is its mission statement; its policies arise from that base. In framing the public library today and in the future, librarians must consider an abundance of underlying factors, many of which are beyond their control. Political regulations, budget constraints, and public perception of the library all affect the vision of the library. Chapter 3 addresses these concerns and offers some suggestions for consideration.

The public library ecosystem is affected by several factors. The first is the political environment, including policies enforced at the federal, state, and local levels. These policies tend to shape many of the decisions regarding the public library and its physical space. In the new information economy, federal regulations are affecting library policies toward Internet access.

The economic environment directly affects the type of service given by the library as well as the standard of living of its patrons. The development of a practical library budget is crucial to maintaining a viable standard of service. Blurring the lines is the growing practice of private funding for public library programs and services. Is this practice in line with the principle of free library access to all? And what of the issue of "fee vs. free"? Many systems are faced with the pressure of connecting to the "information highway" without adequate funds or equipment. What services must be cut in order to meet this need? Chapter 9 introduces these considerations and, although not solving the problems, offers suggestions to consider.

One of the most critical factors is the perception of the public library by librarians and also by the public. A determining factor is the economic background of its community. The needs of a library's "public" shape the vision of the library's service to the community. If the library's main goal is equal access for all, will it be possible to avoid an information gap between those with direct access to technology at home and those who rely solely on the library? Chapter 3's appendix offers a variety of models to consider from literacy center to virtual library.

People and Libraries

In the phrase "public library," the first word is "public." Without people, the public library would cease to exist. The original goal of the public library was not to provide additional information to the wealthy who often had their own well-stocked libraries; rather, its goal was to provide free access to information for all people on an equal basis, regardless of social or economic background. The other half of this equation is the library personnel. Like their patrons, librarians and the paraprofessionals who assist them are diverse. Chapter 5 addresses the issues affecting library personnel and their relationships with their public.

The demands that librarians face today and tomorrow are very different from those addressed by their forebears. The introduction of technology demands that librarians continually develop new techniques and knowledge. Traditional methods must be maintained at the same time new ideas are introduced. It is no longer acceptable for librarians to be proficient in one area and have little knowledge of the other parts of the library. They increasingly need to learn a variety of aspects of the library's management in order to present a seamless transition from one department to another. Communication between departments is the key to presenting a unified staff. Support of paraprofessionals and involvement in professional organizations are also critical issues for librarians.

In addition to the library staff, other persons who directly affect the smooth operation of the library include volunteers, the library board of directors, and the Friends organization; all must be considered when adopting policies. The management team and its management style are crucial to the leadership of the library and where the library will stand in the next century.

Finally, the community at large is the library's reason for existence. It is the public library's responsibility to meet the needs of its patrons by designing programs and services to match those needs. It is imperative that the library be a visible force in the community, participating in community meetings, decision making, and support of the people in the area. Services for adults, young adults, children, disabled patrons, new immigrants, and senior citizens are all essential components of the library program. Connecting all patrons with new technologies and a variety of information formats can ensure that the "highway" will not bypass the library. The American Library Association's suggestions for addressing the issues of diverse segments of the population are included in this book.

Technology: Pros and Cons

Webster's New World Dictionary of the American Language defines technology as "a method, process, etc. for handling a specific technical problem" and "the system by which a society provides its members with those things needed or desired." The roots of the word come from the Greek *technikos*, which is derived from *techne*, meaning art or artifice. Its Indo-European base, *tekth-*, to weave, build, or join, aptly describes the challenges facing libraries and librarians today when adopting the newest technologies. It is critical that the traditional services of the library be maintained and seamlessly woven into the fabric of the twenty-first-century library.

Automation has created a practical alternative to the manual handling of circulation of items within the library system. Online catalogs allow access to databases and information in other library settings originally not available to the public library. Computers have helped to lessen the clerical responsibilities of librarians while freeing them to address the concerns of the public. Innovations are continually being introduced to allow increased information access to disabled patrons. Library patrons no longer have to visit their library physically in order to conduct library business. In short, computers have streamlined the business of librarianship.

In the process, the view of the library's mission has blurred. At risk is that a large segment of the population, through its economic or geographic situation, is left out of the information explosion. The public library's greatest challenge at this time is how to meet the technological needs of its patrons without leaving anyone out. And if the library's mission changes, how is the integrity of this public institution ensured? How will the library of the future continue to meet the needs and desires of its public? And where do books, knowledge, and literacy fall in this vision of the future?

The Bottom Line

Political regulations are not the only external considerations of the public library. Federal, state, and local funding create a universal cause-and-effect situation often completely outside of the library's control. Chapter 11 addresses the sources of funding for public libraries and some of the factors influencing these funds. Included are grants, endowments, and corporate funding as well as private contributions.

Libraries rely heavily on the support of the community—another reason to maintain an active presence within that community. Suggestions for a fund-raising campaign are outlined. The library director and staff must act like politicians. Librarians must go beyond the walls of the library and into the community to connect the library with public services if the public library is to remain viable. Bond referenda bring the library's concerns directly before the pocketbooks of its patrons. A year-round presence in all aspects of the community can ensure success when library funding is at issue.

Charges for services, Internet access costs, and collection development are all future considerations for the public library's budget committee. How will the library of the twenty-first century adapt to these increasingly expensive demands while maintaining a traditional approach to service to its patrons? Several examples are given in the appendix to illustrate what some libraries are currently doing to meet these challenges.

A Future for Public Libraries

Theorists are predicting the demise of the library as we know it today. The National Information Infrastructure is working toward the universal connection of every school and library by the year 2000. But what then? After we all get connected, who will be there to show us how to use what we find? Librarians.

Throughout history, increases in technology and knowledge have brought with them additional questions and concerns on how to adapt and use this new information. Libraries and librarians will continue to fulfill their role as an integral part of the assimilation of information. Along with that role will be the continued need for a human presence to guide users in education and in the introduction of new technologies and ideas. Libraries will continue to promote the integrity of information and sources. Through the cataloging of items from Internet sites to photographs to new articles, librarians will play an active role in helping to guide users to the answers.

This can be achieved only by the active participation of librarians in all stages of the process. Librarians must take on new roles as city planners, county commissioners, school board members, and business advisers. Librarians must continually advocate the role of the public library in the success of a community and be prepared to fight for funding. The public has shown that it wants and needs libraries. It will be the library's responsibility in the future to assess those needs and reflect its community presence through its mission and policies.

A BRIEF HISTORY OF PUBLIC LIBRARIANSHIP

Whitney M. Berriman

Librarians have always been an integral part of libraries; however, trustees, Friends, and users also play important roles. This chapter will focus on those figures considered influential in the establishment of public libraries: benefactors and librarians.

Greco-Roman Influences

In Greco-Roman times, libraries existed because of the generosity of benefactors. In 364 B.C., the Greek ruler Clearchus opened a public library at Heraclea in Bithynia. Roman ruler G. Asinius Pollio conquered Dalmatia and amassed great wealth circa 37 B.C. Pollio used this money to con- solidate several existing book collections in Rome. The consolidated collection became known as the Atrium Libertatis, which means "Temple of Liberty." The Atrium Libertatis was the first known public library in Rome.[1]

The public library located in the Temple of Apollo was one of two public libraries built under the direction of the Emperor Augustus. This public library was divided into two collections: Greek and Latin. The first librarian for this facility was Pompeius Macer. The second of the two public libraries was known as the Porticus Octaviae. Caius Melissus

1

served as its first librarian. Emperor Vespasian established a public library in 75 A.D. Emperor Domitian established a public library on the Capitoline Hill circa 81–96 A.D.[2]

European Influences

In Renaissance Europe, library benefactors and librarians were also important. In 1412, the title Protobibliothecarius Bodleianus was bestowed on the librarian at Oxford University. The title means "Bodley's librarian."[3]

In 1524, Martin Luther called for the establishment of a public library in order to spread Protestantism. In Bristol, England, circa 1615, the concerted efforts and donations of Robert Redwood and Dr. Toby Matthew made possible a city library. By 1653, Sir Humphrey Chetham had established a public library known as Chetham Library in Manchester, England. During the late seventeenth century, Dr. Thomas Bray furnished primarily theological works to ministers on a circulating basis. Also during this time, booksellers began to establish commercial circulating libraries.[4]

One of the most notable figures in public librarianship during the nineteenth century was Edward Edwards, a public library pioneer and library historian. Edwards also worked on the Committee on Public Libraries.[5]

During the early twentieth century, two figures emerged in support of the public library in Russia. Madame L. Haffkin-Hamburger fought for library service for the Russians before and during the Revolution. Afterward, she continued to work on behalf of libraries under the Soviets. In addition, Madame Lenin (Nadezhda Krupskaya) sponsored and encouraged libraries.[6]

American Influences

In 1833, the citizens of the Town of Peterborough, New Hampshire, allotted money from the State Literary Fund for the purchase of books in order to establish a free public library. The town postmaster acted as librarian.[7]

In 1852, the Trustees of the Boston Public Library issued its report that illustrated "the ideal conception of public library service."[8] The report focused on the history of printing and libraries and contained a forceful argument for the establishment of a public library in Boston:

> Reading ought to be furnished to all, as a matter of public policy and duty, on the same principle that we furnish free education, and in fact, as a part and a most important part of the education of all. For it has been rightly judged that—under political, social and religious institutions like ours—it is of paramount importance that the means of general information should be so diffused that the largest possible number of persons should be induced to read and understand questions going down to the very foundations of social order, which are constantly presenting themselves, and which we, as a people, are constantly required to decide, and do decide, either ignorantly or wisely.[9]

As a result of the report, the Boston Public Library was established in 1854. Charles Coffin Jewett, known as "one of the greatest bookmen in American library history," served as the first superintendent of the Boston Public Library from 1858 to 1868.[10]

Women entered the profession in 1856. The first-known female librarian was Mrs. A. B. Harden who served at the Boston Athenaeum.[11]

Another little-known but important figure in public librarianship was Justin Winsor, who was a prominent historian and literary figure. Winsor's contributions to public librarianship included the establishment of branch libraries and selected reading lists of popular items (now known as reader's advisory services). In addition Winsor promoted the concept of the public library to the public.[12]

A more well-known benefactor of public libraries was Andrew Carnegie. In 1881, Carnegie donated funds for the establishment of a public library in Pittsburgh.[13] Discussing his concern for public improvement, in 1900, Carnegie stated:

> I choose free libraries as the best agencies for improving the masses of the people, because they give nothing for nothing. They only help those who help themselves. They never pauperize. They reach the aspiring, and open to these the chief treasures of the world—those stored up in books. A taste for reading drives out lower tastes.[14]

By 1920, Carnegie had donated approximately $50 million in funds for 1,697 library buildings.[15]

Throughout civilization, it is obvious that public libraries, librarians, and benefactors were important. Figure 1.1 depicts the growth of public libraries in the United States 1850-1994.[16] As the twenty-first century approaches, public librarians have the opportunity to direct and influence the future of the public library just as the librarians of past centuries directed and influenced the public library we know today.

Discussion Questions

1. How has public librarianship changed over the years?
2. What are some of the skills that may be required of public librarians in the twenty-first century?
3. What role will the public librarian play in the public library of the twenty-first century?
4. What will constitute some of the ethical and legal considerations for twenty-first-century public librarians?

Notes

1. Michael H. Harris, *History of Libraries in the Western World* (Metuchen, N.J.: Scarecrow Press, 1984), 36, 50.
2. Ibid., 50, 51.
3. Josephine Metcalfe Smith, *A Chronology of Librarianship* (Metuchen, N.J.: Scarecrow Press, 1968), 36.
4. Harris, *History of Libraries in the Western World*, 141, 144.
5. Ibid., 143.
6. Ibid., 208.
7. Ibid., 227.
8. Ibid., 226.
9. Ibid.
10. Ibid., 228.
11. Smith, *Chronology of Librarianship*, 104.
12. Harris, *History of Libraries in the Western World*, 208.
13. Ibid., 229.
14. Ibid., 230.
15. Ibid., 229.
16. Michael Everette Bell, "Growth of Public Libraries in the United States, 1850-1994: A State-by-State Comparison" (original graphic).

Fig. 1.1 / 5

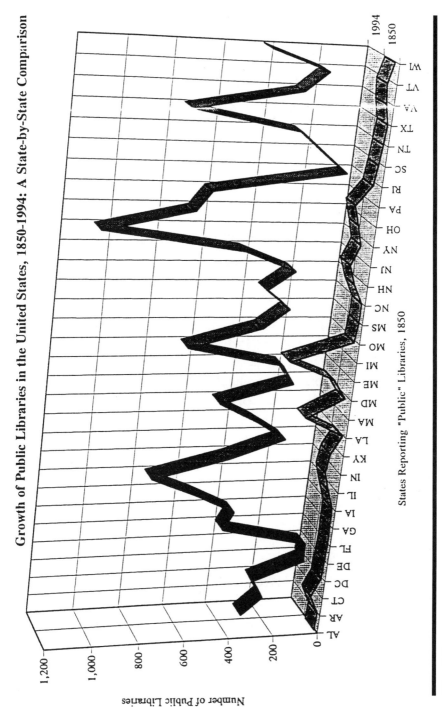

Growth of Public Libraries in the United States, 1850-1994: A State-by-State Comparison

Number of Public Libraries

States Reporting "Public" Libraries, 1850

Chart by Michael E. Bell.

Fig. 1.1.

THE VALUES
OF THE PAST

Charlene Chisek

Individual public libraries express their values in mission or vision statements, goals, and objectives. Instead of prescribing absolutes, this chapter reviews ideals from the past, and then, taking into account the rapid expansion of information technology, muses on possibilities for the future. In summary, the Library Bill of Rights repeats enduring values.

The Past

ALA

In 1987, the American Library Association (ALA) published *Planning and Role Setting for Public Libraries*. This manual introduced eight roles from which public libraries could choose in meeting a community's service needs.[1] According to the ALA, no one library can excel in all eight. In 1992, a Gallup Poll added two new roles, with the results shown in Table 2.1.[2]

Table 2.1.
The Public's Evaluations of the Importance of the Various Roles of the Public Library

Roles	%
Formal Education Support Center: the library provides students, both children and adults, with the books, magazines, and other services they need to do their schoolwork.	88
Independent Learning Center: the library provides adults who are not students with the materials and services they need to better themselves or to learn a new skill, such as how to read and write.	85
Preschoolers' Door to Learning: the library provides preschool children with picture books, story hours, and educational programs so that these children can have fun and learn to appreciate reading.	83
Research Center: the library provides scientists and scholars with the specialized research collections of books, magazines, and computerized information they need to conduct research or write books.	68
Community Information Center: the library provides people with information about their community.	65
Reference Library—Business: the library provides businesses in the community with the information they need to survive and prosper.	55
Public Workplace: the library provides people with a comfortable place to go when they need someplace outside of the house or apartment to read or think or work.	52
Popular Materials Library: the library provides people with a collection of current best-selling books and popular magazines, videos, and musical recordings for borrowing.	51
Reference Library—Personal: the library provides people with the information they need to answer personal and household questions.	48
Community Activities Center: the library serves as a neighborhood or community activity center—a place where organizations or clubs can hold meetings or present concerts and lectures.	41

Quite surprisingly, providing bestsellers rated low with the public at large. However, when patrons in another survey selected a reason for coming to the library, more opted "for its recreational role (popular materials library) than for any of the other *single* role descriptions presented."[3] This dichotomy may reflect the different expectations of nonusers and users. For example, in Connecticut, "low community awareness of particular services may provide a partial explanation for low usage."[4] Of course, these surveys left many questions unasked, such as: "Do you see an important role for the public library in protecting you from being overwhelmed by information in which you have an interest?"[5]

Individual Versus Community

The ALA's emphasis on serving communities irritates those who prefer to address individualized needs, all in the name of democracy. Since they are funded by taxpayers, libraries should serve each and every taxpayer. As Douglas Raber recounts:

> The need for an informed citizenry . . . is a functional necessity of a democratic society. The need for a means of self-improvement derives from the necessity of maintaining equal opportunity in democratic societies. The need for a means of personal enlightenment is closely associated with the spiritual celebration of the autonomous individual and mutual respect among individuals, both of which are regarded as central to the ultimate purpose of democracy itself.[6]

This has led to the debate in collection development between "Give them what they want" (community) and "Give them what they need" (individuals).

Instead of pitting the individual against the community, William F. Birdsall offers the image of a public library bridging the two. On one hand, library resources contribute to a shared culture and community of memory. On the other, these resources offer individuals "a window to the world of experience, ideas and values beyond the local."[7]

Social Activism, Conservatism, and Populism

Social activism takes public libraries even further: "to meet the information needs of marginal peoples and to break the cycles of oppression and exclusion created and sustained by the lack of access to information."[8] In other words, outreach to those who need the public library most takes prominence.

In response, conservatives design library service for "serious readers of any class for whom the educational purposes of libraries is central."[9] They claim that public libraries should concentrate on self-directed lifelong learning because other institutions supply social services and entertainment.

In contrast, populists believe libraries should "make the most wanted library materials readily available to the greatest possible number of community residents, as well as to serve as an access point to the most needed information."[10] Thus, the public library justifies funding as user-centered and output-oriented.

Distillation of Roles

Instead of limiting itself, the Denver Public Library recently distilled these roles into a familiar mission statement—"to inform, educate, inspire and entertain."[11] Four small words encompass the purposes described by the ALA and others. However, these words do not reveal what philosophical road Denver will travel in reaching these goals—the who, what, where, when, and how.

The Future

Customers, competition, and change demand flexibility and a quick response from public libraries in order for libraries to remain viable in the future. Library literature reveals no shortage of crystal-ball gazers who fall into three categories: pessimistic, neutral, and optimistic.

Pessimistic

Bruce Shuman's *Library of the Future* depicts nine scenarios which range from the demise of the public library to a fully automated, robotized environment where exotic adventures may be experienced in an easy chair via an electronic helmet. Along the way some libraries may become free only for poorer members of the community; everyone else has to pay. As the public library's importance to the community decreases, both taxpayers and governments cut costs to eliminate redundancy. For the pessimist the public library either dies through taxpayer and government neglect and downsizing or becomes a museum/monument out of nostalgia.[12] In any case, it loses its value to the citizenry.

Neutral

According to a 1996 *U.S. News*/CNN poll, "67% of American adults went to a public library at least once—up markedly from 51% in 1978."[13] Increased usage and robust building projects could lull some into satisfaction with the status quo. Others, however, want incremental changes.

Partnerships with schools and bookstores offer a win-win situation. For example, one district library "project involved linking the public library's CD-ROM network, Internet access, and online public access catalog to the Saline High School Library via fiber optic lines."[14] By sharing the cost and the resource, everyone in the classroom has access to information for a dreaded assignment, many simultaneously, but no one travels to the public library and the information never leaves the library. As a bonus, the public library added terminals that it might not otherwise have been able to afford.[15] In the same spirit, when super bookstores and public libraries cooperate to promote reading and books, they thrive instead of die. The Lisle Library District in Illinois has "set new goals, including piggybacking library programs with authors in store appearances to save money on transportation, speaker fees, and promotions costs; including cooperative literary events in Borders' newsletter; and receiving assistance from Borders in contacting authors directly."[16] Successful programs actually made the library more visible in the community. In both cases, by working toward a common goal, libraries remove duplication and provide better service that benefits all parties.

In Maryland, the public library took advantage of another opportunity to increase usage by instituting a Night Owl reference service Monday through Wednesday from 9 P.M. until 11:45 P.M., and Thursday and Friday from 5 P.M. until 11:45 P.M. Thus, the library meets customer expectations when "they need immediate answers to their questions. Later hours are the only time some callers have to help children with homework or to do personal projects or work brought home from the office."[17]

Still another forecaster predicts splitting the public library into two entities: an Information Center and a Community Resource Center. "Separation of the functions of information retrieval and of providing recreational reading material and lifelong learning opportunities must be regarded not as an attempt to fragment, but rather as an attempt to concentrate the services patrons need into efficient organizational structures."[18]

For some, competition with other agencies may put libraries in danger of losing funding and access. For example, the United States Postal Service (USPS) suggested a "program to put information kiosks in post offices to hook citizens into the National Information Infrastructure (NII) by delivering government forms, documents, and information to the public."[19] While the USPS sees its kiosk as complementary, even locating some in libraries, eventual access to the Internet would put the post office (which knows how to move paper) into the job of information provider without the professional expertise of the librarian.

Another suggestion evolves from the reliance on market forces to provide superior service at lower funding to government entities. "Each citizen gets information vouchers redeemable at bookstores, online services, magazine publishers, and even at poetry readings, video-rental outlets, storytelling sessions for children, and other cultural events. The public library would be forced to compete for the same vouchers."[20] This assumes that competition brings out the best, though it could also lead to serious cutbacks, with the following results:

- The library is a place where only the poorer sectors of the community may enter free of charge. Others pay admission charges.

- The library becomes a place where only a certain type of information or a certain type of service is available.

- The library is replaced by home access to information and entertainment.[21]

However, Librarian of Congress Dr. James H. Billington warns against too many compromises. First, a flood of infotainment that degrades knowledge also degrades democracy. Second, the United States may become divided into the information-rich and the information-poor. Third, home access detracts from the library as a gathering place.

Lastly, for some people, television has already replaced books; libraries suffer from the consequent passivity and devaluation of reading.[22]

Optimistic

Many optimists share a faith in the power of technology to change the nature of libraries and place a single-minded emphasis on information. In fact, Charles R. McClure, one of the authors of *Planning and Role Setting for Public Libraries*, has expanded the original roles to include network literacy center, global electronic information center, liason for government information center, center for electronic lifelong education, public access center and others.[23] His complete list is found on page 30. While some sound familiar, all reflect the effect of the global Internet connection.

On the other hand, the Carnegie Library of Pittsburgh has learned that libraries must become the publishers, editors, and distributors of local culture and local information to the world[24] that the Internet sorely lacks. As facilitators, libraries also offer web training to both public and private agencies and thus promote electronic self-reliance with the agency updating its own home page.

For Marilyn Gell Mason, technology only changes the way libraries deliver services. The mission of the library—to provide access to information for everyone in the community when and where the individual needs it—remains intact.[25] Bruce A. Shuman, on the other hand, allows for the possibility that technology could radically change the way libraries do business:

- The library becomes fully automated, handling requests for books, information, data, or answers in a conversational mode.

- The library becomes a place where wondrous and exotic adventures may be experienced while relaxing in an easy chair with an electronic helmet on one's head.[26]

Patterning libraries on the futurist Faith Popcorn's trends has led Marianne Roos even farther afield. To a stay-at-home public, the library offers next-day delivery of materials at home, or a cafe atmosphere in the institution. For citizens interested in small indulgences, the public library opens museum-quality gift shops. In an ergonomically sound environment, librarians customize service by tracking user preferences and notifying users of new arrivals. To employees who work at home, public libraries provide office and conference space, and so forth, for a fee. For others, the library lightens up life with colorful furnishings, poetry readings, drop-off babysitting, or ice cream sold on bookmobiles. For the vigilant consumer, the public library creates bulletin boards to comment on products and practices, or high-touch survey tools for ranking government programs. Lastly, libraries help save our society by sharing resources, encouraging the habit of lifelong learning, and retaining trust. In fact,

> we ought to be dreaming up ways to attract new library users and not be content merely to serve current users better. We must ensure that the political will to support *free* public libraries grows and is strengthened while we experiment with ways to meet the changing needs of our customers. Libraries are one of the few public institutions where people come gladly and willingly, where diversity is celebrated and encouraged, and where people are treated with equal respect and attention.[27]

To Marianne Roos, public libraries cannot circumvent personal services.

Bill of Rights

No matter how one decides to offer public library service better, faster, and cheaper, values endure in the Library Bill of Rights, most recently amended by the ALA Council in 1980.

The American Library Association affirms that all libraries are forums for information and ideas, and that the following basic policies should guide their services.

> I.   Books and other library resources should be provided for the interest, information, and enlightenment of all people of the community the library serves. Materials should not be excluded because of the origin, background, or views of those contributing to their creation.

II.   Libraries should provide materials and information presenting all points of view on current and historical issues. Materials should not be proscribed or removed because of partisan or doctrinal disapproval.

III.   Libraries should challenge censorship in the fulfillment of their responsibility to provide information and enlightenment.

IV.   Libraries should cooperate with all persons and groups concerned with resisting abridgement of free expression and free access to ideas.

V.   A person's right to use a library should not be denied or abridged because of origin, age, background, or views.

VI.   Libraries which make exhibit spaces and meeting rooms available to the public they serve should make such facilities available on an equitable basis, regardless of the beliefs or affiliations of individuals or groups requesting their use.[28]

From 1951 through 1996, the ALA Council adopted 16 interpretations of the Library Bill of Rights on the following topics: access for children and young people to videotapes and other nonprint formats; access to electronic information, services, and networks; access to library resources and services regardless of gender or sexual orientation; access to resources and services in the school library media program; challenged materials; diversity in collection development; economic barriers to information access; evaluating library collections; exhibit spaces and bulletin boards; expurgation of library materials; free access to libraries for minors; library-initiated programs as a resource; meeting rooms; restricted access to library materials; statement on labeling; and the universal right to free expression.[29]

Quite appropriately, this discussion of values ends on the note of intellectual freedom. At the ALA Midwinter Meeting President's Program on February 16, 1997, ten-year-old Vincent Dawkins proclaimed that he had a license to drive on the information superhighway and raised his Baltimore library card overhead in proof, much as an athlete clenches his fist in victory. On the same afternoon, U.S. Secretary of Education Richard W. Riley explained that he always tells children: "Empower yourself to be a citizen of the world. Get a library card."

Discussion Questions

1. What purpose does a public library serve?
2. What is the present and long-range effect on residents who have public library service available? Conversely, what is the effect where there is no library?
3. Does technology change the very definition of a public library?
4. What motivates people to participate or not in public library programs? What are the individual and social effects of use and nonuse? How can use be encouraged while recognizing the validity of individual preferences?
5. How much does the service of the staff add to the success and value of a public library?
6. Do patrons have access to the types of learning opportunities and information they consider valuable?

Notes

1. Charles R. McClure et al., *Planning and Role Setting for Public Libraries: A Manual of Options and Procedures* (Chicago: American Library Association, 1987), 28.

2. George D'Elia and Eleanor Jo Rodger, "Public Opinion About the Roles of the Public Library in the Community: The Results of a Recent Gallup Poll," *Public Libraries* 33, no. 1 (January/February 1994): 24.

3. Ibid., 138.

4. Alicia J. Welch and Christine N. Donohue, "Awareness, Use and Satisfaction with Public Libraries: A Summary of Connecticut Community Surveys," *Public Libraries* 33, no. 3 (May/June 1994): 150.

5. Herbert S. White, "How Many Priorities Are We Allowed to Have—and Who Sets Them?" *Library Journal* 120, no. 13 (August 1995): 50.

6. Douglas Raber, "A Conflict of Cultures: Planning vs. Tradition in Public Libraries," *RQ* 35, no. 1 (Fall 1995): 55.

7. William F. Birdsall, *Myth of the Electronic Library: Librarianship and Social Change in America* (Westport, Conn.: Greenwood Press, 1994), 142.

8. Douglas Raber, "ALA Goal 2000 and Public Libraries: Ambiguities and Possibilities," *Public Libraries* 35, no. 4 (July/August 1996): 225.

9. Ibid., 226.

10. Ibid., 228.

11. John N. Berry, "Denver's Daring Rededication," *Library Journal* 120, no. 7 (April 15, 1995): 6.

12. Bruce A. Shuman, *The Library of the Future: Alternative Scenarios for the Information Profession* (Englewood, Colo.: Libraries Unlimited, 1989), 118.

13. "News Briefs: Poll Finds Library Use on Rise," *American Libraries* 27, no. 2 (February 1996): 15.

14. Karen Commings, "Libraries of the Future: Public/School Library Co-operation Highlights Two Automation Projects," *Computers in Libraries* 16, no. 1 (January 1996): 14.

15. Michael Schuyler, "The View from the Top Left Corner: Libraries and Schools—The Technology of Cooperation," *Computers in Libraries* 16, no. 1 (January 1996): 44.

16. Susan Emmons-Kroeger and Jane Belon Shaw, "Professional Views: Super Bookstores and Public Libraries," *Public Libraries* 33, no. 2 (March/April 1994): 78.

17. Deborah C. Duke, "Night Owl: Maryland's After-Hours Reference Service," *Public Libraries* 33, no. 3 (May/June 1994): 148.

18. Leah K. Starr, "The Future of Public Libraries: Divided They Serve," *Public Libraries* 34, no. 2 (March/April 1995): 102.

19. Jean Armour Polly and Steve Cisler, "Internet@LJ: The Post Office and Public Libraries," *Library Journal* 120, no. 5 (March 15, 1995): 29.

20. Steve Cisler, "Weatherproofing a Great, Good Place: The Long-Range Forecast for Public Libraries: Technostorms, with Rapidly Changing Service Fronts," *American Libraries* 27, no. 10 (October 1996): 43.

21. Shuman, *Library of the Future*, 117.

22. Guy Lamolinara, "Digital Transformation: Dr. Billington Discusses Future of Public Libraries," *LC Information Bulletin* 55, no. 1 (January 22, 1996): 3.

23. Charles R. McClure, John Carlo Bertot, and John C. Beachboard, "Enhancing the Role of Public Libraries in the National Information Infrastructure," *Public Libraries* 35, no. 4 (July/August 1996): 234.

24. Bette Ann Hubbard et al., "Newest Members of the 'Net Set: Pittsburgh's Carnegie Cashes in on Community Info," *Library Journal* 121, no. 2 (February 1, 1996): 44–45.

25. Marilyn Gell Mason, "The Future Revisited," *Library Journal* 121, no. 12 (July 1996): 71.

26. Shuman, *Library of the Future*, 117.

27. Marianne Roos, "Tracking Trends for Public Libraries," *Virginia Librarian* 39, no. 3 (July/September 1993): 5–10.

28. American Library Association, Office of Intellectual Freedom, *Intellectual Freedom Manual*, 5th ed. (Chicago: American Library Association, 1996), 3–4.

29. Ibid., 20–121.

3 | THE POLITICAL, ECONOMIC, AND CULTURAL ENVIRONMENTS AND THE PUBLIC LIBRARY AS "PLACE"

 **Crista Lembeck**

Author's Note

Recently, I had the opportunity and good fortune to meet Dr. Charles R. McClure (he said to call him "Chuck"). Dr. McClure has written extensively on the fate of public libraries (see Additional Readings list). When I informed him that I was a Library Science student currently working on a paper concerning the economic, political, and social environments surrounding public libraries in the United States, he suggested that I examine two different sources. The first, a study entitled *Buildings, Books, and Bytes: Libraries and Communities in the Digital Age*, was funded by the W. K. Kellogg Foundation and prepared by the Benton Foundation. The study was prompted by the Kellogg Foundation's desire to inform its Human Resources for Information Systems Management (HRISM) grantees about where the public supports—or fails to support—libraries as they confront the digital world. The second source is the Fall 1996 issue of *Daedalus: The Journal of the American*

17

Academy of Arts and Sciences, which is entirely dedicated to libraries and the issues they are facing as they experience the technological revolution affecting our entire culture and society. I took his advice and uncovered a wealth of information, much of it directly relevant to this paper.

Although Dr. McClure believes that public libraries in America are in deep trouble, he also strongly believes that the individuals within the library community can and should play a major role in determining how libraries will develop in the twenty-first century. There are several things that Dr. McClure thinks public libraries must do in order to survive the changes taking place: "Public libraries need to align themselves with President Clinton's emphasis on technology in schools; they need to develop policies with respect to First Amendment rights and copyright infringement laws; they must determine a clear set of priorities; and, they must make the transition from tradition to modernity."

At the same time, Dr. McClure warns that "those who are too small to engage in politics are frequently punished by being governed by those who are dumber," and he stresses that the public library is "hampered by limited resources and a poorly defined federal policy environment."

Indeed, never before have the issues affecting public libraries been so widely discussed and become so controversial. Never before have the functions and values of the American public library been under such scrutiny. In this chapter, I share some of my findings and examine more closely the issues that concern our public libraries, taking into account the influence of surrounding political, social, and cultural environments. American public libraries and the environments in which they exist are currently in a state of flux—and change is inevitable.

Introduction

> As an integral institution in the intellectual community, the library responds to the same cultural, economic, and political forces that beset the rest of our institutions in troubled times.[1]

Libraries are rethinking themselves. There are environmental factors influencing the public library and the roles that public libraries play in any community. These factors include the economic, political, and sociocultural conditions surrounding public libraries.

Christine Borgman and Robert Gross see the current environment as unstable and "troubled."[2] Many people view any kind of change in this light. It is possible, however, to view change as progress or development. According to John N. Berry, "Total, cataclysmic change is not coming. The basic mission of the library, no matter what type of library it is, will remain. That mission remains to ensure that people get access to the opinion, information, and entertainment they need to function more effectively and enjoyably, regardless of the format in which that material is packaged."[3] The changes in the environmental factors surrounding public libraries will, without a doubt, affect public libraries dramatically. The goal for public libraries should be to embrace these inevitable changes and to emerge as stronger, more efficient, and more effective institutions. For libraries to support and serve the communities in which they exist, various environmental factors must first be recognized and understood, and then they must be reconciled with the concepts and beliefs of the public library communities that they serve.

The main catalyst for change has been the development of new information and communication technology during the twentieth century. With the rapid development of these technologies, the roles libraries play within our American society have also been changing. With the advent of new technological developments, libraries are being forced to reexamine how they store and retrieve information; in addition, as a result of these technological changes and their effect on the political, economic, and sociocultural conditions surrounding public libraries, it has become necessary to reassess the essential functions and purposes (missions) of our public libraries. The philosophy of librarianship is also being reevaluated.

Are libraries as we know them (i.e., paper or automated libraries) obsolete? Can (should) libraries exist without librarians? Should libraries only be sites (either physical or virtual) at which or through which people may access information—or do, and should, libraries play a larger role in our culture? How do we recognize and accept the fact that "just as important as our commitment to books is the realization that digital publications are also a part of our library collections"?[4] And should we be thinking beyond this fact in an effort to be proactive, rather than reactive considering the speed at which technology has been advancing our culture? (See chapters 8 and 9 for an in-depth discussion of the developments in technology and their effect on public libraries.)

There are those who argue that the essential purpose of the library has not changed; however, we cannot ignore the external (environmental) factors that are influencing public libraries as they enter the twenty-first century. These factors, along with the commitment of individuals concerned with and involved in the world of libraries, will determine the roles our public libraries will play in the coming century.

There is dissension even within the library community—while some believe that "total, cataclysmic change is not coming,"[5] others use stormy and turbulent metaphors to describe the current situation and the ever-changing environment surrounding public libraries. Steve Cisler claims that "the future is like a weather front,"[6] and that "the libraries that serve as bridges between the old and the new, the offline and the networks, the analog and the digital worlds, between storytelling and MUDS, will be those that attract the broadest groups of users and weather the storms of today and tomorrow."[7] Robert Gross and Christine Borgman claim that "in the current enthusiasm for the information superhighway, the larger purpose of libraries risks being lost."[8] By examining the discussions concerning the effect of the digital age on public libraries, it appears that a middle-of-the-road approach is the most successful for libraries attempting to ride the wave of rapid change and emerge relatively unscathed—or even stronger—as a viable public institution in the future. Yet a middle-of-the-road approach should not be mistaken for apathy or inactivity. As Dr. McClure and many others insist, the current environment surrounding public libraries (whether it be economic, political, or social) demands informed, yet cautious, activism.

Political Conditions

> Public Libraries are part of government; they are, therefore, political entities. Public librarianship is a political issue at the local, state, and federal levels. Library boards and library administrators are engaged in the governmental policy-making process, and are political participants in that process. . . . Politics and public libraries are interrelated.[9]

In order for public libraries to succeed in serving their communities, they "rely on public policies that support, or at least do not undermine or contradict"[10] their visions and missions. However, as David Shavit points out, libraries have placed themselves in a paradoxical position, and a popular myth has developed where libraries have been viewed by both the general public and librarians as apolitical.[11] We must recognize the links between the public library and politics if the public library is to emerge successfully in the twenty-first century. Unfortunately, it is clear that over the past 100 years of the history of the American public library "the patterns of library governance have been remarkably resistant to change."[12]

"Federal, state, and local governments are involved in the formulation and implementation of public policies. . . . Public policy is an authoritative and goal-directed governmental course of action that states an intention to do something about a public problem."[13] The topic of politics at the federal level that affects the public library has been addressed by Charles R. McClure, John Carlo Bertot, and John C. Beachboard, who received a grant from the National Science Foundation to study "Policy Issues in Assessing the Role of Public Libraries in the NII." One of the goals of this study was to "analyze the existing federal public library policy system to determine the degree to which that policy system might have to be changed to accomplish the administration's policy objectives regarding public libraries in the NII."[14] Politics (and policies) at the federal level certainly affect public libraries. In fact, "changing governmental priorities make it necessary for public librarians to adopt a more proactive role to ensure their patrons complete and unimpeded access to the information highway."[15]

"Most recently, the IITF committee on Applications and Technology stated that one of the national visions for the NII was to 'sustain the role of libraries as agents of democratic and equal access to information.' How these roles evolve, how the private sector, state and local governments, the education community, and libraries can work together to realize these visions, and how to determine the federal role in promoting these visions are critical concerns."[16] With this in mind, it must be recognized that public libraries, although noble in their intentions, do not always function as democratic institutions. In fact, if we examine some statistics (such as those presented in George M. Eberhart's *Whole Library Handbook 2*[17]), we find that patrons who use the library and patrons who do not are not equal in level of education, economic status, and other measures. The claim can be made, however, that everyone has equal access to the public library—but, again, it must be remembered that all libraries are not equal (in terms of the tax base that is funding them, in terms of the number of volumes they have in their collections, and so forth). Public libraries are affected by politics—federal, state, and local.

"In his January 23, 1996, State of the Union Address, President Clinton noted that we must connect every classroom and every library in America into the national information superhighway by the year 2000."[18] This policy demonstrates a commitment on the federal level to the connection between education (schools), public libraries, and the NII. What Beachboard and company argue is that federal policy alone is not and will not be enough to realize the vision of public libraries as major components of the National Information Infrastructure: "While federal policy visions for promoting access to and use of the Internet via public libraries continue to evolve, there has been an ongoing and serious erosion of support for libraries to accomplish the government's existing policy goals in this area. Indeed, the role of the federal government to coordinate policy, programs, and research and to develop initiatives supporting library-related efforts to enhance public access to the Internet continues to be fragmented and unclear."[19]

Other federal policies that affect public libraries include the Communications Decency Act (CDA), part of the Telecommunications Act of 1996. "The Federal Communications Commission (FCC) is working to implement the 'Snowe-Rockefeller' provision of the Telecommunications Act, which requires the FCC to ensure that public libraries, as well as schools and rural health care providers, can get telecommunication services 'at rates less than the amounts charged for similar services to other parties.' "[20] "At the federal level, one key component has been the transition of the Library Services and Construction Act into the Library Services and Technology Act (LSTA). According to its proponents, LSTA was designed to help libraries 'ensure that access is equitable, content is useful and usable, and expert help is available.' In the course of congressional consideration, this measure was folded into the omnibus appropriations bill for fiscal year 1997 and financed at $136.4 million a year."[21]

In many ways, state and local politics are more influential than federal politics on public libraries. "Almost all public libraries exist under provisions of state law. And library laws can and do change over the objections of a state's library community."[22] State and local politics are critical to public libraries because they can affect the quality and even existence of the public library more quickly and often more deeply than policies mandated at the federal level. "More than 90 percent of public libraries are governed by library boards. The vast majority of public library boards are appointed by elected officials."[23] (For a more in-depth discussion of library boards and other people who play a role in the management of our public libraries, see chapter 5, "People and Libraries.")

Local control is, and always has been, a central component of American politics. "The basic idea is that democracy thrives when citizens are in close control of their own institutions."[24] Of course this philosophy assumes equal opportunity, and yet it often ignores, or discounts, cultural, social, and economic segregation at the local level. Different communities have different economic bases and different power structures, as well as different values. These elements affect the strength of a public library. Keeping these factors in mind, "library professionals and advocates should pay attention to information policies as they develop at the state and local level. If libraries are to reflect and transmit American Culture in the digital age, they must ensure that their holdings and services can reflect a diverse set of views, images, and experience."[25]

Economic Conditions

> Public library funding has three components: tax revenue, fees, and private contributions. Opposition to fees makes them unlikely to become a significant source of revenue. Tax revenue will remain the major component, but its adequacy is declining. Therefore, directors and trustees have two options: provide a level of service that reflects decreased funding or increase funding through private means.[26]

Obviously the political and the economic environments surrounding public libraries cannot be separated; "how libraries are funded through federal, state, and local efforts will affect what services are offered and the boundaries on whom or on what community a library is expected to serve."[27] It is also clear that "almost all public library funding is local, usually coming from taxes paid by local residents for local services."[28] This means that the public libraries located in wealthy communities undoubtedly have access to more funds than public libraries located in poorer communities. This may be stating the obvious—but it is an important factor. Demographics, including average income level and average level of education, create and affect the economic conditions surrounding our public libraries.

Public libraries do not exist in a vacuum of the public sector when it comes to financing. In fact, "looking at library financing from a long-range perspective shows that libraries both profit and suffer from the economic cycles that affect the economy as a whole."[29] The economic conditions affecting American society as a whole have obvious effect on public libraries. In other words, "the fortunes of public libraries have waxed and waned with the general economic cycle."[30]

Economics affect the management of the public library, "as budgets tighten and taxpayers revolt, public library administrators must adopt management techniques that are creative, innovative, and economy-minded. There are plenty of ways to trim a budget, increase productivity, and maintain services without raising taxes."[31] These environmental factors have led to some exciting and innovative collaboration projects that have alleviated some financial burdens, generated enthusiasm, and developed local recognition. Some collaboration efforts are discussed in chapter 12, "The Future Is Now: Will Public Libraries Survive?"

"Nontraditional Funding Sources—Because of hard economic times and tight city budgets, library directors are increasingly seeking out funding from non-government sources. These funding sources include other nonprofit organizations, philanthropic foundations, and for-profit private sector companies desiring to fund new and innovative library services. It is not uncommon for groups of libraries to form interagency coalitions to collectively seek funding to provide specialized library services to selected user groups."[32] (A more in-depth discussion of public library funding may be found in chapter 11, "Sources of Funding for Public Libraries.") Internal and external economic factors affect our public libraries.

Sociocultural Conditions

Public libraries reflect the communities in which they exist. At their best, public libraries strive to serve the needs of the citizens within their communities, and thus they reflect the needs and desires of the people they serve. This is the nature of a public institution in a democratic society. A public library will fail if it does not serve the needs of the public. As our world changes, "the libraries of the world are changing, responding to new technologies, but also to new social and economic demands."[33] In order for public libraries to reflect the values and diversity of the societies in which they exist they must study their own communities. "The library's community study is related to the library's function and is necessary for its proper performance."[34]

Darlene Weingand provides the following list of "examples of secondary data that should be available locally"[35] when studying a community:

Age levels and groups: Number of children, young adults, older people, members of racial and ethnic groups, and non-English-speaking people

Education: Number of citizens with college or graduate degrees or at other educational levels, number of citizens attending special classes for additional education or retooling, and literacy levels of community

Economic facts: Occupational patterns, industries, small businesses, farms, and number of unskilled workers and professions

Schools and colleges: Existing educational facilities, including specialized, vocational, and remedial institutions, public and private

Community habits: Size and type of homes, and popular recreations and interests

Cultural opportunities: Regular concerts, theaters, lectures, amateur theater groups, and so forth

Civic interests and problems: Patterns of community growth, needs for expanded facilities, and matters of public concern

Churches: Number, denominations, and size; number having weekday group meetings, discussion groups, or summer programs for children

Clubs and organizations: Service clubs, special interest and hobby groups, book and current affairs discussion and action groups, civic groups, senior citizens, neighborhood clubs, and scout troops and other youth groups

Institutions: Hospitals and health and welfare institutions

Even with a close examination of such demographic information, disparity often exists between what librarians believe they and libraries should be to the community and what the community believes a librarian and library should be in the future. Apparently, "library leaders want the library of the future to be a hybrid institution that contains both digital and book collections," whereas "the public loves libraries but is unclear about whether it wants libraries to reside at the center of the evolving digital revolution—or at the margins."[36] "The public expects a major urban public library to continue its traditional role as a repository of knowledge and wisdom, providing access to information, knowledge, learning, and the joys of reading."[37]

The Benton Foundation reports findings about the ways in which "the intersection—and divergence—of library leaders' visions with those of the public hold lessons for everyone who values and wants to promote the public sphere of information and communications."[38] The study compared "library leaders' visions for the future with the public's prescription for libraries, derived from public opinion research."[39] "The results of a national poll indicate that in the opinion of the public the most important roles of the public library are to support the educational aspirations of the community, and to provide access to information. The role of the library as provider of popular materials for the community was ranked relatively low in importance. The difference between what the public actually uses is not necessarily contradictory but rather appears to be simply two different manifestations of public demand."[40]

> Library leaders are nearly unanimous in their belief that libraries, along with schools and the courts, are among our fundamental civic institutions. . . . Libraries are directly tied to a community's quality of life. . . . The digital library can be an extension of the traditional communal library. It is a new expression of the old American idea of providing the widest possible access to knowledge in the community. But some library leaders add a cautionary note. The digital library—and the digital age—can undermine the notion of library as a community institution and a building block of American culture. If the cost of technology becomes a barrier, entire segments of the community may be left out. If the desktop computer replaces the library as a community 'place,' the library's community functions may wither, and its traditional function as an identifier and shaper of the American experience may start to decline.[41]

An examination of the public library as place is important, taking into consideration these political, economic, and sociocultural environmental factors.

The Public Library As "Place"

> Is a library a collection of books, or is it a building? Historically, collections have needed buildings for storage, conservation, and access. The community has had need for a building—especially if it is a national library—to denote symbolically as well as literally the existence of a national published archive, announcing that the nation has a history of achievement, invention, exploration, and industry. But do libraries still need buildings?[42]

Libraries represent and define the communities in which they exist. Libraries can be symbolic of a culture; they can represent a history. The public library as we know it, a physical building—often a refuge for users—and definitely a site-specific facility designed not only for access to information but also for storage, and for preservation of culture and history, is changing with the advent of new technology. Public libraries should not be museums, and yet, we must strive to maintain the library as place at the same time that the advent of new technology threatens to cause the library to retreat from view on the American landscape.

While disparity exists between what librarians and other staff members believe they and libraries should be to the community and what the community believes a library should be in the future, there is consensus about libraries as buildings, as actual physical places. According to the Benton Foundation's study, "Americans value maintaining and building public library buildings. Americans support using library budgets to preserve and erect library buildings, placing this activity third in the poll's rankings of library services they would spend money on. . . . Clearly, the American public agrees wholeheartedly with the library leaders that the American public library building is an intrinsic part of the library's identity."[43] In addition, "The long-predicted obsolescence of the physical library, as a site and building, has been totally belied by the current boom in library building and the immense growth in the use of those new buildings when they open."[44]

The combination of a consensus between the public and library leaders and the boom in new library construction is a good sign, especially when many library leaders offer the pessimistic opinion that public libraries are doomed to becoming invisible as a result of pervasive technological advancements that will allow individuals to access and retrieve the information they seek directly from home, cyber bars, super bookstores, or even other public institutions such as post offices.

"As the electronic revolution accelerates, as books become bytes and digitizing the medium of choice, the library is in danger of disappearing from view."[45] This does not mean that libraries will not exist; however, libraries may not exist as we know them today—as actual, physical locations where paper is stored and retrieved in an effort to provide information, entertainment, and stimulation. Michael Gorman wrote in his "Foreword" for Michael Buckland's book, *Redesigning Library Systems: A Manifesto*, "The mix will be different and the library of the future may look different, but, as Michael Buckland points out, librarianship has enduring values and enduring ends."[46]

According to Steve Cisler: "Librarians must try to preserve their institution as a physical location and not just as an electronic distribution point."[47] And, "In *The Great Good Place*, Ray Oldenburg makes the case for preserving informal meeting places other than those where people live or work. The library is certainly one of these so-called Third Places, and it is crucial that we reaffirm the value of its corporeal existence to the communities that support it."[48]

"The librarian will be a kind of 'information engineer,' not just a simple keeper of books, a classifier, or a teacher displaced from the classroom. As an object, the book has changed. Library buildings have changed as operational spaces. The role of reading in a computerized society has gained new recognition. Librarians, as information engineers with broad humanist backgrounds, must change their way of thinking if they are to meet the challenges of the twenty-first century."[49]

Leah K. Starr offers a different view of the public library as place in the future: She proposes that public libraries divide the two functions of providing access to information and acting as a resource center and become separate entities. "Present-day public libraries are obliged to meet two objectives: to provide recreational reading and lifelong learning materials and services, and to provide electronic information services. In the future, the strain caused by attempting to meet these disparate goals and increased patron satisfaction may be accomplished by operating separate institutions for these separate functions."[50]

Starr proposes a model for public libraries in the future. "In this model of a possible future, the information seeker goes to the local Information Center (IC), where a wide range of information can be accessed electronically in addition to the many print sources that are still valuable."[51] She makes the analogy between the IC and "today's fast-food service business."[52] She maintains that "separation of the functions of information retrieval and of providing recreational reading material and lifelong learning opportunities must be regarded not as an attempt to fragment, but rather as an attempt to concentrate the services patrons need into efficient organizational structures."[53]

This author finds it very difficult to buy into Starr's proposal for the public library of the future, deeming it too extreme. For the public library to emerge as a strong and viable community institution in the twenty-first century, a balance must be achieved. This balance recognizes the necessity of the library as place, and it serves the changing needs and desires of the community in which it exists, as new technology is developed.

Most often, we have discovered that the users of the public library depend on its physicality. They need to know that a place is there for them and their children. This need presents an interesting dilemma for the librarian who is valiantly attempting to raise money to purchase computers, servers, and related equipment so that the library can be the community's on-ramp to the information superhighway. But the road that users are traveling is a dual-laned (or multilaned) expressway. Terminals are important, and everyone wants to be "connected." But the books and the library building are important, too, and the place the community calls the library still serves to draw the community to it and to pull the community together.[54]

Conclusion

The existing political, economic, and cultural environments surrounding public libraries affect the inherent structure and physical appearance of public libraries in the present and are influencing the roles libraries will play in our society and communities in the future. "These proposed roles suggest new directions for public libraries. . . . They will require a significant investment in the information infrastructure and new information technologies."[55] These roles will also require contributions and commitments from the political (both federal and local), economic (both public and private), and cultural (both popular and academic) realms or sectors surrounding public libraries.

In addition, note that the commitment must first come from the libraries themselves—meaning the individuals within libraries, the people who make libraries function. Without commitment from within, public libraries are certain to falter during such a tumultuous era. "The way that library leaders and visionaries respond to public opinion and the public policy context—as well as their own visions"[56] will determine the course of our public libraries.

Public libraries are not abstract entities that exist on their own. Public libraries cannot exist without people—people to run the libraries, be they digital, virtual, or physical locations—and people who desire to retrieve and use the library's materials.

Appendix: Possible Public Library Roles in the Electronic Environment As Proposed by Charles R. McClure

Network Literacy Center: The public library provides training and education for community members on how to access and use the Internet-global information network, how to identify and obtain electronic information resources, and how to transact electronic commerce and obtain electronic services.

Liaison for Government Information: The public library is the site of *first resort* for contact for accessing local, state, and federal electronic information services. A range of government-information resources and services is made available to the public directly through the public library.

Center for Electronic Lifelong Education: The public library is an electronic classroom that can provide community members with a broad range of educational opportunities as it uplinks and downlinks educational programming.

Electronic Information Access Center: The public library provides public access to terminals connected to the global information network and also provides dial-in capabilities for patrons at home to access the network.

Community Information Organizer and Provider: In collaboration with local government, the school system, and other local organizations, the public library is the hub for linking and managing local electronic information resources and services—via a community net or other techniques.

Economic Development Center: The public library supports local business and economic development through providing job/career information and skill assessments, small business support, network training, and by promoting liaisons and collaborations among local community services.

The Global Switching Station: The public library serves as the site of *first resort* to identify electronic information resources and connect the patron to those resources; in the vernacular of the Web, the public library is "hot-linked" to global electronic information services and resources.

The Electronic 24-Hr/Day Reference, Referral, and Reading Center: Librarians provide electronic reference and referral services. Many reference sources are now available in electronic format, from a single workstation at the library, or by remote access to the library. Those electronic reference and referral resources are made available to the community via dial-up.

The Profit-Making Information Store: The library either offers information services directly to patrons (local or remote) or serves as an outlet for other information providers and charges users for these services.

The Neighborhood Electronic Kiosk System: The library establishes multiple neighborhood electronic kiosks with public access both to the library and its electronic resources as well as to the global-information network.

The Virtual Library System: The public library becomes part of a "virtual system" with selected other public libraries and similar organizations located around the country or around the world.

The membership of the "virtual system" depends on the unique contributions that each library can bring to the system.[57]

Discussion Questions

1. Which environmental factor (political, economic, or cultural) do you view as being most influential on the public library? Why?
2. How do you envision the physical environment of the public library as a place in the twenty-first century?
3. What disparities exist between what public librarians see the role of the public library to be in the future and what the general public sees the role of the public library to be in the future?
4. How might a person who lives in a rural community use a library differently from a person who lives in an urban community?
5. How can the public library balance the obligation to collect information and preserve history with the need to provide access?
6. How is the public library diminishing from view or declining in visibility as a result of new advancements in technology?
7. "Are libraries, by their architecture and silences, 'holy places,' resisting the commercial civilization of a mall culture?" (Taken from "A Charge to Authors," *Daedalus* 125, no. 4 [Fall 1996]).
8. "Is it possible that we are confusing information with knowledge? Does a book create the possibility of continuous discourse, of a kind that can never be satisfied by a computer? Is all such talk of 'discourse' simply nostalgia for a world that is rapidly disappearing?" (Taken from "A Charge to Authors," *Daedalus* 125, no. 4 [Fall 1996]).
9. To what extent does the surrounding philosophical environment of a culture affect its libraries?
10. Deanna B. Marcum wrote, "One great advantage of public libraries is their neutrality within communities. They are public spaces that offer a place to learn on one's own about any subject and without review by any kind of authority figure. The library staff need not be consulted or involved in the pursuit of knowledge, unless the patron wishes." To what extent is a public library "neutral"?

Bibliography

Books

Buckland, Michael. *Redesigning Library Systems: A Manifesto*. Chicago: American Library Association, 1992.

Eberhart, George M., comp., *Whole Library Handbook 2: Current Data, Professional Advice, and Curiosa About Libraries and Library Services*. Chicago: American Library Association, 1995.

Shavit, David. *The Politics of Public Librarianship*. New York: Greenwood Press, 1986.

Weingand, Darlene E. *Administration of the Small Public Library*. 3d ed. Developed from previous editions by Dorothy Sinclair. Chicago: American Library Association, 1992.

Articles/Periodicals

Altman, Ellen, and Frank William Goudy. "Local Public Library Funding in the 1980s." *Public Libraries* 33, no. 1 (January/February 1994): 37–39.

Berry, John N. "Editorial: Just Take a Closer Look at the Library of the Present: The Future Is Here." *Library Journal* 122, no. 1 (January 1, 1997): 6.

Borgman, Christine L., and Robert A. Gross. "The Incredible Vanishing Library." *American Libraries* 26, no. 10 (October 1995): 900–904.

Carrigan, Dennis P. "Public Library Fund-Raising: A Report Based on a Survey." *Public Libraries* 33, no. 1 (January/February 1994): 31–36.

Cisler, Steve. "Weatherproofing a Great, Good Place: The Long-Range Forecast for Public Libraries: Technostorms, with Rapidly Changing Service Fronts." *American Libraries* 27, no. 10 (October 1996): 43.

Crowley, Bill. "Library Lobbying as a Way of Life." *Public Libraries* 33, no. 2 (March/April, 1994): 96–98.

D'Elia, George, and Eleanor Jo Rodger. "Public Library Roles and Patron Use: Why Patrons Use the Library." *Public Libraries* 33, no. 3 (May/June 1994): 138.

———. "The Roles of the Public Library in the Community: The Results of a Gallup Poll of Community Opinion Leaders." *Public Libraries* 34, no. 2 (March/April 1995): 94–101.

de Sant'Anna, Affonso Romano. "The Challenge of the Twenty-First Century." *Daedalus* 125, no. 4 (Fall 1996): 267–281.

Dowlin, Kenneth E., and Eleanor Shapiro. "The Future of Major Public Libraries." *Daedalus* 125, no. 4 (Fall 1996): 173–190.

Emmons-Kroeger, Susan, and Jane Belon Shaw. "Professional Views: Super Bookstores and Public Libraries." *Public Libraries* 33, no. 2 (March/April 1994): 78.

Kent, Susan Goldberg. "American Public Libraries: A Long Transformative Moment." *Daedalus* 125, no. 4 (Fall 1996): 207–220.

Lang, Brian. "Bricks and Bytes: Libraries in Flux." *Daedalus* 125, no. 4 (Fall 1996): 221–234.

Lehman, Klaus-Dieter. "Making the Transitory Permanent." *Daedalus* 125, no. 4 (Fall 1996): 307–329.

Marcum, Deanna B. "Redefining Community Through the Public Library." *Daedalus* 125, no. 4 (Fall 1996): 191–205.

McClure, Charles R., John Carlo Bertot, and John C. Beachboard. "Enhancing the Role of Public Libraries in the National Information Infrastructure." *Public Libraries* 35, no. 4 (July/August 1996): 232–238.

Sager, Donald J., contributing ed. "Professional Views: Super Bookstores and Public Libraries." *Public Libraries* 33, no. 2 (March/April 1994): 75–79.

Starr, Leah K. "The Future of Public Libraries: Divided They Serve." *Public Libraries* 34, no. 2 (March/April 1995): 102–104.

Electronic Sources

Buildings, Books, and Bytes: Libraries and Communities in the Digital Age. Funded by the W. K. Kellogg Foundation. Washington, D.C.: Benton Foundation, November 1996. Available: http://www.benton.org/Library/Kellogg/buildings.html (Accessed February 12, 1997).

Additional Readings

Books

Baker, Sharon L. *The Responsive Library Collection: How to Develop It and How to Market It.* Englewood, Colo.: Libraries Unlimited, 1993.

Birdsall, William F. *The Myth of the Electronic Library: Librarianship and Social Change in America.* Westport, Conn: Greenwood Press, 1994.

Crawford, Walt, and Michael Gorman. *Future Libraries: Dreams, Madness & Reality.* Chicago: American Library Association, 1995.

Davies, D. W. *Public Libraries as Culture and Social Centers: The Origin of the Concept.* Metuchen, N.J.: Scarecrow Press, 1974.

Shuman, Bruce A. *The Library of the Future: Alternative Scenarios for the Information Profession.* Englewood, Colo.: Libraries Unlimited, 1989.

Woodrum, Pat. *Managing Public Libraries in the 21st Century.* New York: Haworth Press, 1989.

Articles/Periodicals

Raber, Douglas. "ALA Goal 2000 and Public Libraries: Ambiguities and Possibilities." *Public Libraries* 35, no. 4 (July/August 1996): 224–231.

Sager, Donald J. "Professional Views: Doing Better: Reauthorizing the Library Services and Construction Act." *Public Libraries* 33, no. 1 (January/February 1994): 15–20.

———. "Perspectives: A Promising Frontier or the New Wasteland? Libraries and the Internet." *Public Libraries* 34, no. 2 (March/April 1995): 73–77.

Publications by Dr. Charles R. McClure

McClure, C. R. "Network Literacy in an Electronic Society: An Educational Disconnect?" In *Institute for Information Studies, The Knowledge Economy, The Nature of Information in the 21st Century, 1993–1994.* Annual Review of the Institute for Information Studies, A Joint Program of Northern Telecom, Inc. Queenstown, Md.: The Aspen Institute, 1993.

———. "Public Access to the Information Superhighway Through the Nation's Libraries." *Public Libraries* 34, no. 2 (March/April 1995): 80–84.

McClure, C. R., W. C. Babcock, K. A. Nelson, J. A. Polly, and S. R. Kankus. *The Project GAIN Report: Connecting Rural Public Libraries to the Internet.* Liverpool, N.Y.: NYSERNet, 1994.

McClure, C. R., J. C. Beachboard, and J. C. Bertot. "Enhancing the Role of Public Libraries in the National Information Infrastructure." *Public Libraries* 35, no. 4 (July/August 1996): 232–238.

McClure, C. R., J. C. Bertot, and J. C. Beachboard. *Internet Costs and Cost Models for Public Libraries*. Washington, D.C.: National Commission on Libraries and Information Science, 1995.

McClure, C. R., J. C. Bertot, and D. L. Zweizig. *Public Libraries and the Internet: Study Results, Policy Issues, and Recommendations*. Washington, D.C.: U.S. National Commission on Libraries and Information Science, 1994.

McClure, C. R., W. E. Moen, and J. Ryan. *Libraries and the Internet/NREN: Perspectives, Issues, and Challenges*. Westport, Conn.: Mecklermedia, 1994.

Notes

1. Christine L. Borgman and Robert A. Gross, "The Incredible Vanishing Library," *American Libraries* 26, no. 10 (October 1995): 904.
2. Ibid.
3. John N. Berry, "Editorial: Just Take a Closer Look at the Library of the Present: The Future Is Here," *Library Journal* 122, no. 1 (January 1, 1997): 6.
4. Klaus-Dieter Lehman, "Making the Transitory Permanent," *Daedalus* 125, no. 4 (Fall 1996): 314.
5. Berry, "Just Take a Closer Look," 6.
6. Steve Cisler, "Weatherproofing a Great, Good Place: The Long-Range Forecast for Public Libraries: Technostorms, with Rapidly Changing Service Fronts," *American Libraries* 27, no. 10 (October 1996): 42.
7. Ibid., 46.
8. Borgman and Gross, "Incredible Vanishing Library," 900.
9. David Shavit, *The Politics of Public Librarianship* (New York: Greenwood Press, 1986), xii.
10. Benton Foundation, *Buildings, Books, and Bytes: Libraries and Communities in the Digital Age*, funded by the W. K. Kellogg Foundation (Washington, D.C.: Benton Foundation, November 1996), preface:4. Available: http://www.benton.org/Library/Kellogg/buildings.html (Accessed September 2, 1997).
11. Shavit, *Politics of Public Librarianship*, 1–5.
12. Ibid., 3.
13. Ibid, 7.
14. Charles R. McClure, John Carlo Bertot, and John C. Beachboard, "Enhancing the Role of Public Libraries in the National Information Infrastructure," *Public Libraries* 35, no. 4 (July/August 1996): 232.
15. Ibid.
16. Ibid., 233.

17.   George M. Eberhart, comp., *Whole Library Handbook 2: Current Data, Professional Advice, and Curiosa About Libraries and Library Services* (Chicago: American Library Association, 1995), 3–5.

18.   McClure, Bertot, and Beachboard, "Enhancing the Role of Public Libraries," 232.

19.   Ibid, 233.

20.   *Buildings, Books, and Bytes*, chapter 3: 2.

21.   Ibid., chapter 3: 3.

22.   Bill Crowley, "Library Lobbying As a Way of Life," *Public Libraries* 33, no. 2 (March/April, 1994): 96.

23.   Shavit, *Politics of Public Librarianship*, 23.

24.   Ibid.

25.   *Buildings, Books, and Bytes*, chapter 3: 3.

26.   Dennis P. Carrigan, "Public Library Fund-Raising: A Report Based on a Survey," *Public Libraries* 33, no. 1 (January/February 1994): 35.

27.   *Buildings, Books, and Bytes*, chapter 3: 4.

28.   Susan Goldberg Kent, "American Public Libraries: A Long Transformative Moment," *Daedalus* 125, no. 4 (Fall 1996): 218.

29.   Ellen Altman and Frank William Goudy, "Local Public Library Funding in the 1980s," *Public Libraries* 33, no. 1 (January/February 1994): 38.

30.   Ibid., 37.

31.   Kent, "American Public Libraries," 212.

32.   Ibid., 214.

33.   Preface, *Daedalus*, vii.

34.   Darlene E. Weingand, *Administration of the Small Public Library*, 3d ed., developed from previous editions by Dorothy Sinclair (Chicago: American Library Association, 1992), 34.

35.   Ibid., 35.

36.   *Buildings, Books, and Bytes*, summary: 2.

37.   Kenneth E. Dowlin and Eleanor Shapiro, "The Future of Major Public Libraries," *Daedalus* 125, no. 4 (Fall 1996): 182.

38.   *Buildings, Books, and Bytes*, summary: 1–2.

39.   Ibid., summary: 2.

40.   George D'Elia and Eleanor Jo Rodger, "Public Library Roles and Patron Use: Why Patrons Use the Library," *Public Libraries* 33, no. 3 (May/June 1994): 23. See also George M. Eberhart, comp. *Whole Library Handbook 2*, 4–5, 25–26.

41.   *Buildings, Books, and Bytes*, chapter 1: 3–4.

42.   Brian Lang, "Bricks and Bytes: Libraries in Flux" *Daedalus* 125, no. 4 (Fall 1996): 221.

43.   *Buildings, Books, and Bytes*, chapter 2: 9–10.

44.   Berry, "Just Take a Closer Look," 6.

45. Borgman and Gross, "Incredible Vanishing Library," 900.

46. Michael Gorman, "Foreword" in Michael Buckland, *Redesigning Library Systems: A Manifesto* (Chicago: American Library Association, 1992), v.

47. Cisler, "Weatherproofing a Great, Good Place," 42.

48. Ibid., 45.

49. Affonso Romano de Sant'Anna, "The Challenge of the Twenty-First Century," *Daedalus* 125, no. 4 (Fall 1996): 281.

50. Leah K. Starr, "The Future of Public Libraries: Divided They Serve," *Public Libraries* 34, no. 2 (March/April 1995): 102.

51. Ibid.

52. Ibid.

53. Ibid., 104.

54. Deanna B. Marcum, "Redefining Community Through the Public Library," *Daedalus* 125, no. 4 (Fall 1996): 201–202.

55. McClure, Bertot, and Beachboard, "Enhancing the Role of Public Libraries," 234.

56. *Buildings, Books, and Bytes*, chapter 4: 3.

57. Charles R. McClure at cmcclure@mailbox.syr.edu (Accessed March, 1997).

THE LIBRARY ENVIRONMENT

4

Lisa S. Payne

The public library does not exist in a world all its own. There are several other types of libraries that coexist along with the public library. Often these libraries work with and support public libraries and vice versa. The other libraries include academic libraries, school libraries, and special libraries. Special libraries can include medical libraries, government libraries, corporate libraries, research libraries, law libraries, and many others.

All of these libraries share a common denominator with the public library: These libraries exist to serve people. Many times these libraries share patrons. In today's world, people often cannot get all the information that they need from one source or place. Most people must patronize more than one library to acquire all needed materials and information. Some people might argue that the point of having specialized libraries is to have specialized information. In most cases, all libraries cannot be all things to all people; it is not physically or monetarily possible. The public library comes closest to providing the most services to the most people. Oftentimes, the public library cannot meet all of the needs and demands of its patrons, but this will soon be changing.

School Libraries

The school library probably comes closest to matching the services of the public library. Both school and public libraries have much to offer each other. The school library is often the introduction to a library for most children. "The school library media program is an integral part of the school curriculum and provides a wide range of resources and information that satisfies the educational needs and interests of students."[1] A positive, fostering school librarian can promote the use of the public library for students long after they have left school. A public library can benefit from the school library's early instruction to young patrons. The school library's limited budget and collection can be enhanced by borrowing materials from the public library.

Both the public library and the school library can share resources and money to offer joint programs to the community. One example of this is found in Texas, between the Austin Public Library and the Austin Independent School District.[2] These two organizations have come together to offer a summertime reading program to at-risk youth. The school system provides the facility, and the public library provides the staff. Everyone benefits.

Technology provides another way for the public library and the school systems to cooperate and benefit both organizations. Combining budgets allows for the purchase of more advanced computers and software that might not have been cost-effective and, in the process, reaches more people. In North Carolina, the Public Library of Charlotte & Mecklenburg County, in conjunction with the Charlotte and Mecklenburg public schools, Johnson C. Smith University, Central Piedmont Community College, and WTYI Channel 42, has developed a regional "free net" dubbed Charlotte's Web. This "free net" offers seven-days-a-week, 24-hours-a-day access to a wide range of information and communication services. Public access terminals are available at library branches, in classrooms, at school libraries, and through home PCs.

The Atlanta-Fulton Public Library system in Georgia also has a technological cooperative between the public library and the public school. The Atlanta-Fulton Public Library/High School Partnership for the Internet offers computer access and e-mail for more than 23,000 students in 21 schools.[3] Computer terminals are also available at the library branches. The web server allows access to the NII, the PASSPORT

System (Atlanta-Fulton's Library Information system), and databases that provide interactive learning. The AFPL provides technical support, Internet instruction to teachers, and incentives to students. This partnership is so successful that plans are under way to incorporate middle and elementary school students. In addition, this partnership has enabled the AFPL to fulfill its mission to promote independent learning for adults and provide educational support for K–12 students.

Academic Libraries

The public library often forms its most beneficial partnerships with academic libraries. The academic library plays a central role in the scholarly life of the college or university. Academic libraries are integral because these institutions design their collections and services to meet the specific needs of the instructional programs offered by their schools. The main goal of the academic library is to offer to the faculty and students of the university a collection that is broad and yet in-depth for the various schools of study. The academic library must be able to access and acquire information and resources from other libraries and information centers. The academic library strives to maintain a collection that includes standard works and classics for students as well as up-to-date research tools to help keep the faculty abreast of the latest advances in their fields.

Since academic libraries contain more research materials than a normal public library does, the academic institutions offer access to many scholarly publications that the public library would not usually acquire for its collection. "The number of volumes held at all academic libraries at the end of the fiscal year 1990 totaled about 717 million."[4] A public library can almost double its access to research materials by participating in cooperative agreements with academic institutions. The public library is not the only one to benefit; sometimes an academic institution can also benefit from the services of a public library. For example, the Broward County (Florida) Library has just such a relationship with its academic institutions.[5] The BCL operates a branch at the Broward County Community College that fills a need of the college and also offers the public library an opportunity for community outreach. The BCL's main branch provides the research library and other services for the downtown campus of Florida Atlantic University. In addition, the

Broward County Public Library works with other academic institutions in a program called SEFLIN (Southeast Florida Information Network), a consortium of 13 institutions made up of public libraries and public and private universities. The main purpose of this network is to provide information on local groups and activities, city and county governments, resource sharing, and Internet e-mail for the surrounding three-county community.

Special Libraries

Special libraries are those created and funded to fill specific needs and used by a specific patron group. Elizabeth Ferguson, former librarian of the Institute of Life Insurance, believes that there are three basic functions of an outstanding special library: 1) the library provides the material for essential research in the conduct of a business; 2) the library provides reference services; and 3) the library promotes its services so that employees and target groups look to it for assistance.[6] Special libraries at some point have either a direct or indirect effect on every person. It is surprising to discover the many types of special libraries available and the diverse and extensive materials that they offer. Special libraries include government libraries (like the Library of Congress), library research information centers of industrial companies, law libraries, art libraries, science libraries, medical libraries, and music libraries, to name just a few. Many books have been written on each specific type of special library, so the following paragraphs provide only an introduction to the other types of special resources available.

Law Libraries

The law library is one of the oldest and most diverse of the special libraries. The first law library, formed in 1802 by a group of attorneys, was named the Law Library Company of Philadelphia.[7] The traditional law library's function is to select, acquire, catalog, and classify legal materials for its users. Law libraries maintain the current laws and court opinions for their states as well as for the federal government. There are many types of law libraries. The following is a brief synopsis.

- *The Bar Association Library* serves practicing lawyers, and its focus is to provide for the research demands of litigation and client counseling. The Association of the Bar of the City of New York has one of the leading law libraries in the country.

- *The Company Library* is maintained by the legal departments of corporations and large businesses. The focus of this type of law library is to maintain a collection of law and related materials that deals with a specific type of industry. Some examples of this type of library include the Prudential Insurance Company Library, the Library of the American Telephone and Telegraph Company, and General Motors Corporate Library.

- *The County Law Library's* function is to serve the courts, public officials, and the bar. This type of library is usually funded publicly. One of the largest county law libraries is the Los Angeles County Law Library in California.

- *The Court Library* is a small library whose focus is to provide reference and law materials to the judge, jury, and court staff. New York City has the largest number of court libraries in the country.

- *The Government Library* consists of local, state, and federal agency law libraries. Washington, D.C., is the home of most of the federal law libraries. Some of these libraries are the United States Supreme Court Library, the Department of Justice Library, the Treasury Library, the Federal Trade Commission Library, and the Library of Congress. The Library of Congress is the largest law library in the world.

- *The Law Office Library* can have a collection ranging from 10 books to 50,000 or more. Law office libraries usually serve as an archives for the office by collecting records, briefs, and documents.

- *The Law School Library* is generally used exclusively by law students and faculty. However, if the school is publicly funded, the library may also be used by the local bar and bench. Law school libraries employ more librarians than any other type of law library.[8] An example of an outstanding law school library is the Harvard Law School Library.

■ *The State Law Library's* primary function is to serve state officials in all levels of state government. These libraries provide legislative reference services, case reports, statutes, and legal materials.

Medical Libraries

The medical library has three purposes: 1) education, 2) research, and 3) patient care.[9] The medical library, much like the law library, has a collection that can range from the very large—for example, the National Library of Medicine—to the small, working library in a local hospital. Medical libraries provide a higher level of service and research for their patrons than other libraries, as it is important to provide in-depth and timely medical information for the health care professional. Many medical libraries have outreach programs to enable health care professionals to access and use information as quickly as possible. The Medical Library Association, which is the second oldest U.S. library association, provides guidelines for medical libraries, continuing education, and certification for medical librarians.

There are different types of medical libraries. A hospital medical library often parallels a public library. A portion of the collection contains materials to provide recreational reading for patients. Some of the collection can be broad and include topics such as music, art, photography, and anything else that a health professional might use for patient therapy and rehabilitation. A large part of the collection supports the continuing education of doctors, nurses, and other medical staff members through texts, journals, and other research materials.

Research libraries in a university setting, such as the library of the Medical College of Virginia, have a more narrow focus but still provide a broad range of interdisciplinary research materials. A medical research library in a corporate or scientific setting, such as the Pfizer Pharmaceuticals Library, has a collection that focuses in-depth on the specific product or products of the company.

State Libraries

The state library acts as a facilitator for library services in each state. Some state libraries collect state documents and serve as an archives. This type of library also provides library and information service to state agencies and to the state government. In addition, some state libraries, or a state commission designed to encourage development of public libraries, administer state and federal grants to public libraries, develop reference and research networks, and provide additional training and support for public, academic, school, and special libraries. The state library also develops or outsources statewide electronic networks. Many of these activities are performed in collaboration with other state agencies, for example, the department of education, which normally oversees the public school library programs. Thus the state library plays an important role in the cooperative opportunities between public libraries and other types of libraries.

Because of the varying missions of individual state libraries, state library agencies or commissions, one should be aware of a publication in progress in early 1998. It is *The Functions and Roles of State Library Agencies* prepared for The Association of Specialized and Cooperative Library Services and the Chief Officers of State Library Agencies by Himmel & Wilson, Library Consultants.

Art Libraries

Art libraries can be found mostly in museums and art schools and institutes. Art librarianship is a specialized field developed because of the growth in the numbers of art connoisseurs, collectors, curators, students, and historians. There are four types of art libraries: 1) academic, 2) museum, 3) public, and 4) business.[10] Each of these libraries shares a commonality of reference tools and subject-related materials. The academic art library must meet the needs of its students, and therefore, its collection will reflect the various art disciplines taught at the institution. This collection will also reflect the research needs of the faculty. The art school library's main function is to provide visual resources for students and faculty. The scope of this collection depends on the type of medium studied. These collections usually contain an extensive collection of art slides, picture files, art periodicals, and exhibition catalogs. An art museum library contains materials focused on the museum's art collection. The primary patrons of this type of library are the museum's staff of curators, administrators, educators, and conservators. Usually area art students are also patrons. This library collection will contain reference materials supporting historical documentation of the museum's collection, auction catalogs, and works that detail conservation and museum management. The Metropolitan Museum of Art was one the first museums in the United States to develop a library. The art library is usually a department in a public library. The public library has the widest audience for these materials. Often the art library is combined with music and dance or theater arts.

Special libraries could benefit greatly from collaborations with public libraries. Many special libraries are small and could use the monetary and public relations benefits that come with a relationship with a larger public library. The public library would of course benefit from the specialized materials accessible in the special library's collection. For example, the Virginia Historical Society could give Richmond Public Library patrons access to its library for genealogical research. In return, the public library could display items from the museum to offer free publicity to the historical society. There are many different ways for the public library to cooperate with all types of libraries. It just takes initiative and creativity.

Technology

As the twenty-first century approaches and technology accelerates, the main word for the future will be access. Decreased budgets will continue to make the question of ownership versus access a major issue. Public libraries will need to develop open relationships and cooperative partnerships with other types of libraries to achieve maximum access for their patrons. The Benton Foundation reported in 1996 that a myriad of library leaders believed that "with some communities already experimenting with collaborations and cyberspace creating myriad cyber-communities for information exchange of all kinds, libraries should create broad-based, real-time networks with public service partners that can facilitate this exchange of information."[11] The most recent national survey found that approximately 760 library networks and cooperatives existed in the United States. This number is low compared with the vast number of libraries and the quantity of people needing information. The twenty-first century will definitely see an increase in the number of existing cooperatives. All libraries can benefit from exchanging and sharing information.

Interlibrary loan has been and is currently one of the major ways that libraries share resources. Interlibrary loan is the process by which a library requests or supplies materials to another library. "Interlibrary loan is essential to the vitality of libraries of all types and sizes and is a means by which a wider range of materials can be made available to users. In the interests of providing quality service, libraries have an obligation to obtain materials to meet the informational needs of users when local resources do not meet those needs."[12]

The National Interlibrary Loan Code is designed to provide general guidelines and to help regulate borrowing and lending between libraries. The guidelines established are as follows.[13]

The requesting library:

- should establish and maintain an interlibrary loan policy for its borrowers and make it available;

- should process requests in a timely fashion;

- should identify libraries that own and might provide the requested materials;

- should check the policies of potential suppliers for special instructions, restrictions, and information on charges prior to sending a request;

- is responsible for all authorized charges imposed by the supplying library;

- should send requests for materials for which locations cannot be identified to libraries that might provide the requested materials and be accompanied by the statement "cannot locate";

- should avoid sending the burden of its requests to a few libraries;

- should transmit all interlibrary loan requests in standard bibliographic format in accordance with the protocols of the electronic network or transmission system used;

- must ensure compliance with U.S. copyright law and its accompanying guidelines; copyright compliance must be determined for each copy request before it is transmitted, and a copyright compliance statement must be included on each copy request;

- is responsible for borrowed materials from the time they leave the supplying library until they have been returned and received by the supplying library; if damage or loss occurs, the requesting library is responsible for compensation or replacement, in accordance with the preference of the supplying library;

- should request a renewal before the item is due; if the supplying library does not respond, the requesting library may assume that the renewal has been granted for the same length of time as the original loan;

- should return materials by the due date and respond immediately if the item has been recalled by the supplying library;

- is responsible for following the provisions of this code; continued disregard for any provision may be reason for suspension of borrowing privileges by a supplying library.

The responsibilities of the supplying library include the following.[14] The supplying library:

- should establish and maintain an interlibrary loan policy, make it available in paper and/or electronic format, and provide it upon request;

- should process requests within the time frame established by the electronic network; requests not transmitted electronically should be handled in a similar time frame;

- should include a copy of the original request, or information sufficient to identify the request, with each item;

- should state any conditions and/or restrictions on use of the materials lent and specify any special packaging or shipping requirements;

- should state the due date or duration of the loan on the request form or on the material;

- should package the items so as to prevent damage in shipping;

- should notify the requesting library promptly when unable to fill a request, and if possible, state the reason the request cannot be filled;

- should respond promptly to requests for renewals; if supplying library does not respond, the borrowing library may assume that the renewal has been granted for the same length of time as the original loan period;

- may recall materials at any time;

- may suspend service to any requesting library that fails to comply with the provisions of this code.

One of the downsides of interlibrary loan is that it requires a lot of staff time. More than half of interlibrary loan transactions are requests for nonreturnable copies of materials, which requires extra time on the part of the staff to make copies of this information. According to the 1993 study of interlibrary loan costs done by the Association of Research Libraries, the average cost for an interlibrary transaction was approximately $19 for the borrower and $11 for the lender.[15] Public libraries, which historically have faced budget restrictions, may not be able to meet the demand of increased interlibrary loans of photocopied material. Public libraries may have to increase the cost of copied materials or only provide original copies.

The onslaught of the Internet brings new avenues into shared resources. The Internet may be the solution to the high cost of interlibrary loan. The twenty-first century will most likely see the interlibrary loan process become a process of downloading. This will shorten the often lengthy interlibrary loan process and reduce costs. However, it may increase copyright problems, and cost will still be a factor for some. Many special and academic libraries already have Internet access, while public libraries are slowly jumping on board. Will public libraries be able to catch up with the other libraries in the access game? Or will the haves and the have-nots become an issue for public libraries as it has already become for their patrons?

Discussion Questions

1. How will information brokers play a part in the cooperative efforts of the libraries?
2. In the future, if we have to face a society of have and have-nots with access, who will decide who gets the information and what kind of information will be supplied? Will it be the job of the public library?
3. What are some other relationships that a public library could pursue with nonlibrary organizations? Name some of these organizations.
4. Which would be the most beneficial relationship for the public library—public, academic, or special? Why?

Notes

1. National Center for Education Statistics, *Schools and Staffing in the United States: A Statistical Profile, 1990–91* (Washington, D.C.: U.S. Government Printing Office, July 1993), 204.

2. John N. Berry, "Library of the Year 1993: Austin Public Library," *Library Journal* 118, no. 11 (June 15, 1993): 30–33.

3. "Atlanta-Fulton Public Library/High School Partnership for the Internet," available: telnet://afplpac.as.public.lib.ga.us and URL: http://co.fulton.ga.us/library.htm (Accessed September 24, 1997).

4. National Center for Education Statistics, *Academic Libraries: 1990* (Washington, D.C: U.S. Government Printing Office, December 1992), 57.

5. John N. Berry, "Library of the Year 1996: Broward County Library," *Library Journal* 121, no. 11 (June 15, 1996): 28–31.

6. Elizabeth Ferguson, "Creation and Development of an Insurance Library" in *Public Relations for Libraries* (Westport, Conn.: Greenwood Press, 1973), 188.

7. Robert Wedgeworth, ed., *ALA World Encyclopedia of Library and Information Services* (Chicago: American Library Association, 1980), 300.

8. Ibid., 298.

9. Ibid., 348.

10. Lois Swan Jones and Sarah Scott Gibson, *Art Libraries and Information Services: Development, Organization, and Management* (Orlando, Fla.: Academic Press, 1986), 7.

11.   Benton Foundation, *Buildings, Books, and Bytes: Libraries and Communities in the Digital Age* (Washington, D.C.: Published by the Benton Foundation, November 1996), 39.

12.   Mary Jo Lynch, "Some Basic Figures," in *Whole Library Handbook 2: Current Data, Professional Advice, and Curiosa About Libraries and Library Services*, comp. George M. Eberhart (Chicago: American Library Association, 1995), 3.

13.   Ibid., 6.

14.   "National Interlibrary Loan Code for the United States," *RQ* 33, no. 4 (Summer 1994): 477–479.

15.   Marilyn M. Roche, *ARL/RLG Interlibrary Loan Cost Study: A Joint Effort by the Association of Research Libraries and the Research Libraries Group* (Washington, D.C.: Association of Research Libraries, 1993), 199.

PEOPLE AND LIBRARIES

5

Diane Wagner

Librarians

All library directors, according to Harold Billings, "value the quality of mind, communication skills, flexibility, character, and acquired knowledge base of a new professional colleague far more than the minimal level of application expertise one would expect a recent graduate to bring to the job."[1] Library and information workers who organize information in a timely, complete, and accurate way and make it accessible will be valued as their expertise and services meet the challenges of the information age. Professionals most in demand will possess knowledge and skills in traditional and nontraditional fields of technology to assist in the business of linking the most effective information provider and the user.

The library director plays an important role in the library and is responsible for seeing that all operations run as smoothly and efficiently as possible while using his or her influence to shape library services in creative ways. In the Winter 1996 issue of *Library Administration & Management*, James Piccininni offered the following helpful suggestions for first-time library directors.[2]

- Make open communication with your staff a high priority and listen to what employees have to say. Maintain control, yet provide autonomy.

- Keep goals and objectives of the library clear.

- Direct your energy to positive and constructive projects.

- Learn from the successes and failures of others.

- Treat people fairly even though this results in treating them differently.

- Place some distance between yourself and your job when the stress of the job builds.

> Only the librarian has the ability to manage the traditional library system as well as the evolving bionic library in which the traditional organic enterprise is extended by and merged with the new. The librarian is educated and trained to deal with the selection, acquisition, organization, service, preservation, and training activities that are required in the print-on-paper information model as well as the digital one. Many librarians have become especially quick studies in the new technologies without losing their feel for the old.[3]

Duties

What are the duties of a librarian? According to Billings, they include the following items.

> Establish a rational, comprehensive information selection program? Order a book or journal? Catalog and classify it? Process, house, service, preserve it? Only the librarian. Select for users a new, valuable source from the host of data on the Internet, much of it only loosely describable as "information"? Attach descriptors and access and retrieval pointers? House the system, provide a menu and interface that information seekers will understand, train users in the skills required to make effective use of these new capabilities? Surely the librarian.[4]

Herbert S. White in the April 15, 1994, *Library Journal*, wrote, "Libraries do not start with books but with librarians, particularly in this electronic age in which you can run a very good library without an in-house collection."[5] Is it necessary for the smallest libraries to hire professional librarians educated in accredited graduate library schools? White believes that the smaller the library is, the more important it is to hire an excellent professional because, although mediocre professionals can hide in larger libraries, they cannot be overlooked in the smaller ones. He states that librarians who try to provide library service to communities without large collections must be better librarians and "more assertive, more innovative, more people oriented, more caring, and more dynamic."[6]

Hiring and Salary

The October 15, 1996, issue of *Library Journal* reported the results of its 45th annual placement and salaries survey, and according to the survey, women entering the profession in a nontraditional field, such as a web developer, are likely to earn 4.5 percent more than those in a traditional job, such as collection development or acquisitions. Men in their first job as a librarian are likely to earn an average of 5.3 percent more than female counterparts no matter what the job title. One concern some librarians have is that, although the technical side of the library must be stressed, the service tradition must be preserved.

The survey reported that in 1995 more than half of the 4,222 graduates of library and information science programs seemed to find professional positions, and both mean and median salaries for full-time professional positions rose slightly. However, more graduates were being hired in part-time or temporary positions (21.3 percent of those reporting positions in libraries). Although the 1993 and 1994 surveys showed a decline in traditional library jobs and dramatic increases in nontraditional areas, this trend seems to have reversed in 1995. According to that survey, 78.1 percent of the positions were in traditional fields.

> For the purpose of this study, any respondent was considered to be working in a "traditional" field who indicated that she/he works in acquisitions, cataloging, collection development, media, administration/supervision, adult services, reference, or youth services. If the respondent indicated

that she/he works in some other type of library, in an information industry, or any other type or organization, she/he was designated as "nontraditional." Respondents were also included in the nontraditional pool if they worked in a "traditional" library but did not work in a traditional area such as acquisitions, cataloging, and so forth. Titles such as Internet reference, web developer, web page designer, web master, systems manager, and World Wide Web consultant were used to describe some of the positions held by these respondents. Of this year's respondents 21.9 percent are in "nontraditional" positions.[7]

In October 1996, *American Libraries* reported the rank order of position titles by mean of salaries paid.[8]

Title	1996 Salary
Director	$58,297
Deputy/Associate/Assistant Director	$52,650
Department Head/Branch Head	$42,766
Reference/Information Librarian	$35,789
Cataloger and/or Classifier	$36,614
Children's and/or Young Adult Services Librarian	$34,572

Personality Traits

In order to support her assumption that the personality preferences of librarians correlate with job specialty, Mary Jane Scherdin designed and conducted a multipart study in 1992 under the aegis of the Association of College and Research Libraries. The people chosen to participate came from a random sample of members of the American Library Association and the Special Library Association. In addition to a demographic questionnaire, each participant completed the Myers Briggs Type Indicator (MBTI) and the Strong Interest Inventory. The answers from the 1,600 respondents reveal that the preferences of librarians as a group sharply contrast with those of the general population; responses show 66 percent Judging, 63 percent Introverted, 61 percent Thinking, and 60 percent Intuitive. The two most frequent types among librarians were Introverted/Sensing/Thinking/Judging (17 percent) and Introverted/Intuitive/Thinking/Judging (12 percent). This contrasts with the traditional preferences

(Introverted/Sensing/Feeling/Judging) assumed to be typical of librarians by career counselors. Compared to the general population, librarians show a preference for Introversion and Intuition, with female librarians twice as likely to have the Thinking preference as women in the general population. According to the designer of the study, librarianship depends on diversity. With an array of dynamic qualities, library and information professionals are ready for the information age.

> The field needs those who are accurate and detail-minded (Sensing preference), as well as those with vision (Intuitive), those who get things done on schedule (Judging), and those who are open to new possibilities (Perceiving), those who plunge quickly into new opportunities (Extrovert), and those with a more cautious and questioning approach (Introvert). All approaches are valuable and complement one another. Wise managers can use the MBTI profiles of their staff to create particularly strong project teams that mesh well together.[9]

Janette S. Caputo, author of *Stress and Burnout in Library Service,* lists the qualities needed by library employees. Most work in libraries involves social interaction demanding appropriate skills. Library employees are expected to be calm when dealing with angry or frustrated patrons who don't admit to owing fines or having overdue books. They must be patient when explaining how to use the equipment innumerable times and effective when answering complex information requests. Librarians must be gracious when expressing gratitude for yet another moldy book for the book sale and soothing while explaining acquisitions policies to angry parents who do not approve of the books their children found in the library. Librarians are required to be informative by answering questions comprehensively and efficiently. They are expected to be helpful and courteous to all patrons. Impatience, anger, and frustration must be suppressed. Without being tyrannical, librarians are supposed to uphold the policies.

Opportunities for Contact

There are many opportunities for contact beyond the individual's department within the organization as well as contact beyond the organization.

> Today, librarians perform significant numbers of interlibrary transactions and provide other document delivery services; use automated systems for acquisitions, cataloging, and documents and serials control; and engage in multiple library cooperative efforts. Thus, in addition to the need to deal directly with the nonlibrarian public in social interaction, librarians carry the additional burdens of frequent interaction with their library peers both near and far.[10]

Paraprofessionals

Also known as technicians, paralibrarians, and nonprofessionals, paraprofessionals represent 60 to 70 percent of library staffs in this country. Chief satisfactions of the job are serving the public, job diversity, belonging to a dedicated staff, using new technology, and working with books. Paraprofessionals generally are less qualified and lower paid than librarians and are assigned clerical tasks, although they sometimes do work that once was done by an MLS degree-holder.

Attitudes Toward Jobs

In its first paraprofessional survey, *Library Journal* sought the attitudes of paraprofessionals toward their jobs and their superiors, and the results were printed in the November 1, 1995, issue. The survey was sent to 1,300 paraprofessionals throughout the country and received a 34 percent response rate with 442 returned. The responses showed that, although nearly 40 percent of the employees working in public libraries without an MLS do not feel that they get the recognition they deserve, they hope to build a more constructive relationship with librarians for the betterment of the profession. "More than 30% said they had attended college, 26% said they earned a college degree, while another 14% said they had undertaken some graduate study, and 13% had earned a graduate degree."[11] Paraprofessionals feel that their special skills, training, and experience are not respected by their directors. Although paraprofessionals are close to librarians in age and tenure, they make about one-third less in salary.

Organizations

As automation has emerged, more paraprofessionals see their work as a career, and they are attending conferences and organizing and participating in professional groups. There are paraprofessional offshoots of state library associations or separate paraprofessional associations in 38 states, and the Southeastern Library Association (SELA) is actively soliciting their participation. The American Library Association's Support Staff Interests Round Table (SSIRT) was designed to bring professional librarians and library support staff closer together. COLT, the Council on Library Media/Technicians, is close to being a national group for library support staffers.

For a comprehensive list of all the paraprofessional organizations in the United States, consult the Library Support Staff Resource Center home page on the World Wide Web. The address is: http://rodent.lib.rochester.edu./ssp/.

Challenges and Concerns

After attending a meeting of the New Jersey Library Assistants Association in 1989 and speaking at conference sessions sponsored by library technicians at state library association meetings, in 1992 John N. Berry wrote an editorial in support of their movement. Berry reported that paraprofessionals want compensation and recognition when they are assigned professional duties. They also want easy access to graduate library education with distance education for remote locations, programs brought to locations close to their jobs, or other ways to seek an MLS. Also important to paraprofessionals are growth in their jobs with compensation for the growth and alternative career ladders. With the same dedication to effective library service shown by professionals, they also are interested in providing information so that the public can be well informed.[12]

Despite their differences, support staff and librarians share the same challenges and concerns for the field. *Library Journal*'s November 1994 Job Satisfaction Survey revealed that librarians considered technology their most critical challenge, followed by budgetary constraints and redefining their roles/image. Budgetary constraints and technology also ranked one and two among support staffers' paramount concerns, except they ranked funding first and technology second. Sufficient training opportunities ranked third. Library support staffers—like librarians—are committed to libraries.[13]

Library Volunteers

Unpaid staff members, also known as volunteers, are of great importance to small libraries as well as to other institutions lacking adequate staff. Working within the same parameters as paid staff and with appropriate measures such as job descriptions and performance evaluations in place, unpaid staff members can make valuable contributions. Although they form an auxiliary labor force, they can do meaningful work by supplementing paid staff members, not replacing them. Mutual benefits can be received by the library and volunteer if attitudes are positive.[14] Volunteers must be managed and directed in ways that will assist the library. Although volunteers do work without pay, they need to receive training and supervision by paid staff members. Since volunteers usually work only a few hours a week, this can increase the likelihood for errors.

Volunteers are an especially valuable resource because they have chosen to give the library a gift of their time and talents. They deserve due recognition and thanks. The Austin Public Library, winner of the Gale Research/*Library Journal* "Library of the Year" award in 1993, has an amazing volunteer program enlisting 200 active volunteers per month. The volunteers contribute 24,000 hours of work annually that would otherwise cost the library $260,000.

Volunteers who like children tell stories, or staff the homework centers. Those willing and able to spend a bit of "quality" time with their elders work on the Walking Books

> Program. Believe it or not, some volunteers like to process materials, input data, and help with the paperwork in personnel. Most important, volunteers are used and treated as part of the library staff.[15]

Recruiting and Training

Recruiting and training volunteers is a task of the librarian, who must master the art of matching people to their volunteer jobs. The librarian can avoid future problems by interviewing potential volunteers before they are placed in the library. To determine suitability for various tasks, special volunteer application/aptitude forms are available. Although it may be difficult to turn down an applicant who wants to help out, placing volunteers in a mutually beneficial position will aid the library and not interfere with serving the public. To keep operations running smoothly, the volunteer must adhere to an agreed-upon schedule and follow the same rules as everyone else; they must meet acceptable work performance standards. Positive reinforcement and plenty of feedback will help volunteers develop into real assets of the library.[16] Some volunteers will quickly master several tasks, and some will require constant retraining. The talents of the volunteer must be directed where they will be most useful, and the ability of the worker must match the task. The manual person will be good at jobs requiring physical dexterity such as shelving materials, and the cerebral person will enjoy thought-provoking jobs such as reading the shelves and keeping records; the person with both skills will be good at a variety of jobs. A worker should not be forced to do a job he or she is afraid of or does not want to do.

The key to the success of a volunteer program is the training. Not all volunteers are adults, and in some cases, volunteers do not have the necessary skills. The training program helps volunteers understand their responsibilities. Students sometimes volunteer to work in the library for the experience or as part of a work/study program, and they can be screened according to how well they maintain their schoolwork and their performance. Although student mistakes should be treated as learning experiences, the work should be done completely and well. If students are paid employees, they are treated as staff members and work regular schedules.[17]

At times, the library may be contacted by a social services agency to supply a work site providing job experience for a client or to place an offender needing to complete community service hours assigned by the court. Applicants should be screened to make sure the offense is non-violent and not of a sexual nature. As with all volunteers, timesheets and performance evaluations ensure best results. The caseworker should be contacted immediately if a problem develops concerning attendance, attitude, behavior, or performance.

Problem Volunteers

Problem volunteers are difficult to deal with and can be the cause of bad publicity. What kind of problem volunteers are there? The social butterfly likes to visit and talk. If the butterfly is good at tasks and establishes rapport with patrons, this may not be a problem. However, if the chatter bothers patrons, all employees should be encouraged to talk more quietly. If the worker is inefficient, assign tasks that are simple and use the volunteer where positive public relations skills will do the most good. The grouch who does not get along well with patrons should be assigned tasks that are away from the public. An inefficient grouch may be good at clerical tasks that are time-consuming but not difficult. Occasionally a volunteer will be totally incompetent. Try to find a task for this person that does not require a lot of ability, such as stuffing overdue notices in envelopes, stamping books and magazines with the name of the library, counting out flyers, and so forth.[18]

Role of the Volunteer

Although Herbert S. White, writing in the April 15, 1993, *Library Journal*, admits that the role of the volunteer deserves respect, he emphasizes the need for a clear understanding of what volunteers can and cannot do. In public libraries, it is difficult for patrons to tell who is doing what, and they assume that anyone who works there must be a librarian. White is distressed about value systems that eliminate librarians, assuming that they are not as important as other things in the budget. He is concerned that librarians will be eliminated in many institutions if "buying and mending books and staffing the checkout desk is what defines a library."[19]

> Yet, all of the goodwill we have presumably generated by scrimping and saving, by doing backflips to be cooperative, and by not just permitting but often encouraging the use of volunteers to help hide the lack of regular staff have gained us very little. Where we seem to differ from those who manage hospitals and museums is in our failure to delineate quite clearly what volunteers do, and what volunteers never do.[20]

Although all work is important, there are certain tasks that only qualified librarians should accomplish. The appropriate role for all the people who work in libraries must be defined.

Library Board of Directors

The library board's basis of power comes from local ordinances and state codes and varies from state to state and locality to locality. Gordon S. Wade states in *Working with Library Boards*:

> Library boards for public libraries are established according to the laws of the people. In order to function properly they need to have a framework within which to operate. State and local laws and ordinances provide the basic structure, and bylaws created by each library board allow it to function effectively.[21]

Library trustees probably have been in existence for as long as libraries have, serving in Greece and Rome as early as 175 B.C. During the Middle Ages, monks supervised the development of the monastery libraries and established policies concerning hours, care of materials, and security. American social libraries in the eighteenth century elected permanent boards of trustees to appoint, dismiss, and pay employees, as well as to purchase books, supplies, and equipment. The first tax-supported libraries in Massachusetts were given the option to be controlled by their city council or to establish their own board of trustees.

Authority of the Board

The authority of the library board was maintained into the twentieth century with the librarian remaining merely the custodian of the books. Eventually, the board's absolute control of the library was ceded to the professional librarian as operations and tasks of administration became more complex. Even today in smaller towns with no professional librarian, library boards select materials and employ all staff members as well as formulate policies.[22]

In an effort to regain authority, some cities and towns are eliminating the autonomous board controlled by citizens and placing the library under the direct control of the local government. In this case, the library board becomes an advisory board with little power or authority. Although members are unable to better the library by taking constructive action or making real improvements, some library directors prefer working with an advisory board because it does not have any power. In 1991 only 23 percent of the public libraries studied in a survey by Wade were advisory. Another 10 percent were controlled by municipal authority with no library board at all, and the remaining 67 percent retained the traditional, fully empowered board.[23]

Wade endorses the board of citizens independent of municipal control as the best way to support and promote the public library. He states, "The people perceive the appointed or elected citizen library board as accountable to the taxpayers, and in this way the community feels more in control of its public library."[24] Also, the library board serves as a buffer between citizens and the elective body in deciding what materials are appropriate for purchase and what should and should not be removed because of patron complaint.

Board Relationships

According to John N. Berry, editor-in-chief of *Library Journal*, "Truly great public libraries nearly always display a very healthy, well-functioning relationship between their Boards of Trustees and their library directors."[25] Trustees in a great library represent as many facets of the community as possible and are proactive for the library, making the librarian more effective in the community. Although the board-librarian relationship sometimes is not easy for either side, the board of trustees serves as a vital link between the library and the general population. Members of the board participate in policy development, budget considerations, and long-range planning to represent the needs of the public. Although there are many areas where the duties of the trustees and the director overlap, it is up to the director to execute the policies enacted by the board. However, the border—"trustees make policy, librarians recommend and execute it"—sometimes is crossed from both sides with a strong, activist board. The relationship works best when it is a team effort and both parties trust each other. A wise director draws on the expertise of the board and encourages trustees to become proactive agents for the library in the community. Although the responsibilities of trustees in larger institutions differ from those of trustees in a small library (50,000 or less annual circulation), the director and the board must agree on what duties are shared and how they should be shared.

Effective librarians are great listeners and find ways to give the ideas from the trustees viability while using the talents of the board to build a better library. Trustees volunteer because they want to contribute to the community and improve the library. "The key element in a healthy relationship is to make sure that they feel they are making that contribution while they are on your board."[26]

Duties of the Board

Conducted in Pennsylvania in 1994, the Library Trustee and Director Survey was mailed to a cross section of 60 libraries based on circulation. The purpose of the study was to consider the differences between what the directors see as the duties of the board and what trustees see as their major duties. The goal was to clarify expectations and lessen dissension between directors and their boards. Disparity in the perception of their individual roles in the day-to-day operation of the library and in the evaluation and hiring of staff proved to be the greatest difference in opinion between the director and the trustees. The survey revealed that directors and trustees need to decide what trustees are to do and what their appropriate roles should be. Most trustees receive no training and do not know how they fit into the picture.

According to the survey printed in the November 15, 1995, issue of *Library Journal*, these are the top 15 duties of trustees from the trustee and librarian standpoint.[27]

Top 15 Duties of Trustees
(from Trustee and Librarian Standpoint)

Trustees		Librarians
Determine Goals & Objectives	1	Hire Library Director
Hire Library Director	2	Determine Mission
Determine Mission	3	Determine Goals & Objectives
Determine Policies	4	Approve Policies
Approve Final Budget	5	Lobby Locally
Approve Policies	6	Approve Final Budget
Prepare Budget	7	Run Fund Drive
Evaluate Director	8	Determine Policies
Run Fund Drive	9	Present Budget
Lobby Locally	10	Evaluate Director
Seek Grants & Donations	11	Prepare Budget
Evaluate Policies	12	Donate to Library
Lobby on State Level	13	Know Laws & Regulations
Know Laws & Regulations	14	Seek Grants & Donations
Set Director's Salary*	15	Analyze/Survey Community*
Learn Trends & Issues*		Hire Other Library Staff*
Approve Purchases over $1000*		
*tied for 15th place		*tied for 15th place

If library directors and boards are to maintain a balance between the professional skills of the director and the community representation of the board, both groups need to understand and appreciate what the other contributes. When the director and board are at odds, both the staff and the community suffer. Neither a board that micromanages, nor a director who circumvents a board, is acceptable.[28]

Managers

As the world becomes more information-dependent, the demands placed on libraries are changing, and libraries' goals and objectives are becoming increasingly complex. Dana C. Rooks, author of *Motivating Today's Library Staff: A Management Guide*, believes that to survive as viable organizations, libraries must adapt effectively and efficiently to these demands by establishing an organizational climate featuring cost-effectiveness, an atmosphere of trust, and the attainment of common goals.[29]

Motivation is "a technique or concept which influences the actions of an individual by integrating personal goals with the organization's work goals in an environment which can provide a common ground for these competing needs."[30] Because the ability to foster employee motivation is considered a trait of all good managers, most library managers are anxious to create an atmosphere conducive to achieving this goal. This complex process should pervade all aspects of management and supervision. To be an effective motivator, a manager must understand staff needs in addition to the factors contributing to the attitudes and behavior of employees. If there is a problem of morale, can the job be changed to allow for greater esteem? Can small work groups be organized to decrease the sense of isolation? Can more responsibility be delegated to staff members so that employees can use their special talents? Can initiative be encouraged?

Methods of Adding Job Value

Motivating Today's Library Staff: A Management Guide offers these methods to add value to a job:

1. Assign work allowing the employee to achieve personal goals.

2. Help the employee achieve a sense of accomplishment and an increase in self-esteem.

3. Reinforce the employee's successful achievement by providing rewards such as promotions, merit pay increases, or a valued assignment.[31]

Stress and Burnout in Library Service by Janette S. Caputo includes ways for managers to make jobs more enjoyable and worthwhile. Employees must know what is expected of them, the goals of their position, and the expectations of management. Employee individuality should be taken into consideration whenever possible as long as the goals of the organization are being met. Managers should assign tasks to employees that suit their needs and remember that sincere and timely praise is a strong motivator.

Organizational Climate

For library managers, organizational climate is an important consideration influencing the behavior and motivation of employees. This climate includes policies and procedures as well as the way employees interact. To be effective, managerial leadership must provide open information, administrative structure, and emotional support. Also necessary are opportunities for staff members to participate in decision making, an emphasis on innovation and creativity, and explicit policies and rules. A positive environment meets the needs of the organization as well as those of the employee. "Mutual goal setting, negotiation, clearly communicated needs, effectively assertive interpersonal skills, and a willingness to compromise at times are required for a win-win environment."[32]

Hierarchical Organization

To avoid ambiguity, defining the hierarchical organization of a library is important. The relationship between library managers and other staff members is one of the most important aspects of the hierarchical organization, with mutual trust being the most important factor for an effective supervisory relationship. To solve problems, librarians and their managers must be able to express feelings and identify problems without incurring sanctions.

High-quality supervision entails precision-tuned social skills and the ability to communicate clearly and directly in a nonthreatening manner providing effective, positive feedback; to notice potential for accomplishment and potential for discouragement; and to troubleshoot performance problems before they arise.[33]

Job Enrichment/Modification

Although job enrichment (recognition, growth, responsibility, and advancement) for personal achievement is the ideal for increasing job satisfaction, not all jobs are so designed. A more realistic goal might be job modification so that preferences can be considered when specialization is possible. People feel greater satisfaction and do a better job when they do what they enjoy. As long as the needs of the organization are met, job modification can include redesigning responsibilities, tasks, or functions to meet the individual's needs.

Autonomy

Autonomy should be exercised whenever possible to motivate professionals and other employees. Examples of putting this concept into practice include the scheduling of work hours not dictated by public service needs, the use of flextime, increasing control of resources, and expanded personal accountability for goal setting and measurement. To avoid the chaos that would result if every professional acted autonomously all the time, staff meetings could function to unite staff members in solving problems by making them group issues. Managers might want to consider having regularly scheduled meetings with professionals and other staff members (depending on the size of the library) where the opportunity to discuss activities, problems, and needs would be given. Developing shared goals by promoting open communication among staff members can contribute to organizational decision making.

Recognition

Everyone craves individual recognition. The library manager may not be able to provide all of the positive feedback that is necessary, but peer recognition can be encouraged. Through a rotation of recognition periods, appreciation programs increase peer support. Appreciation weeks recognize staff in different departments, encourage employees to demonstrate new technology or innovations to others, and provide opportunities for positive feedback. Recognition for work-efficient or cost-effective suggestions provides the basis for other appreciation programs.

Professional Growth

Opportunities for professional growth promote lifelong learning while increasing competence and enhancing self-esteem. The goals of employee development are the improvement of employee performance through the application of new skills, the assumption of a new assignment, or promotion to a position with increased responsibilities. Also helpful for all staff members is continuing library education opportunities because training and development provide motivational benefits. To be effective, staff development must involve meaningful changes to fulfill personal expectations and yield benefits to the organization as well as to the employee.[34]

In reality, professional growth is not promoted as it should be. A survey conducted in May 1993 of the members of the Urban Libraries Council found that because of a lack of training money, staff development consisted of less than one percent of personnel budgets in six out of ten libraries reporting. Two-thirds of responding libraries include a staff of 30 percent or less with the MLS degree, and there are few programs to upgrade skills of everyone else to equip them to meet the demands of a workplace with higher expectations. Results of the study were published in *Library Journal* (September 1, 1993). The study was mailed to 85 ULC members, of whom 68 responded.[35]

Mentoring

Mentoring, a process whereby a less-established person learns through work opportunities and experiences from an established employee, also provides professional growth. The new employee gains broader career opportunities, mentors are recognized as leaders, and the organization develops capable managers for the future. Good mentors continue to provide support until the student reaches the mentor's own level of skill. To offer opportunity to younger and less-experienced people, all committed employees should be included in the process. However, in an article printed in *Library Journal* (October 15, 1993), Roma M. Harris warns:

> One of the purported benefits of mentoring is that it allows the mentor to leave a job while ensuring that such departure will not result in a hole or void in the operation. This smacks of succession planning and may serve to encourage inequities in an organization: only those who have been groomed or preselected by the outgoing managers are prepared to take on their former roles. If this is the accepted method of operating in libraries, it is small wonder that we have ended up perpetuating a culture in which a disproportionate number of men have been promoted into the highest positions in the field where there are very few people of color at the top of the profession.[36]

To keep this from happening, Harris suggests that professionals interested in helping entry-level librarians should not develop special relationships with just a few inexperienced staff members but should take on broader advocacy roles to benefit all motivated employees.

Other Suggestions

It is important to have both follow-up systems to check that tasks have been completed correctly and in a timely manner and backup systems to keep primary services operating despite difficulties. Progress sheets listing goals and accomplishments-to-date help keep projects on track.

Another suggestion offered by Caputo in *Stress and Burnout in Library Service* is management-by-walking-around, a style allowing the manager to respond to needs when they occur by keeping an eye on what is happening. Good service demands that another librarian is asked to help at the public service desk during peak times and when several patrons are waiting in line. Managers who are aware of needs are better able to provide solutions to problems.

A variety of employee health and fitness programs are available to decrease absenteeism, help employees cope with workplace stress, develop positive workplace attitudes, and reduce work-related accidents. To keep employees coming back, these programs must be fun, accessible, and safe.

> Establishing and maintaining realistic goals and expectations is one way managers can help reduce chronic work-related stressors. An emphasis on providing opportunities for professional autonomy and giving positive feedback within a framework of clearly identified lines of authority and responsibility also helps the manager create a less stressful work environment for the staff. Perhaps most important, the manager can help provide and maintain an organizational climate that promotes win-win interactions rather than win-lose conflicts or no-win traps.[37]

In *Motivating Today's Library Staff: A Management Guide*, Rooks writes that the success of managers at all levels depends on the performance of subordinates, and that the manager's motivational efforts influence the quality of that performance. Managers who are aware of the needs of their employees and attempt to establish an environment to satisfy those needs will benefit from highly motivated and productive employees.[38]

Performance-appraisal systems have many uses and benefits and provide feedback to employees on their performance. For best results, performance should be related to organizational goals. Excellent performers can be rewarded and unsatisfactory performers can be removed. By identifying strengths and weaknesses, a plan can be formulated to contribute to the development of the employee's skills. Also, solutions can be sought to problems that prevent the employee from working effectively.[39]

Another View

Herbert S. White, columnist for *Library Journal* and professor at the School of Library and Information Science, Indiana University, offers a different view of library management. He believes that librarians must not crush the spirit of productive and innovative employees by demanding that they be "collegial." According to White, team building is a search for conformity that results in mediocrity, and he includes AACR2 when he states that committees never accomplish anything worthwhile. He is dismayed by the concept of being a team player and staying out of trouble by never calling attention to oneself. He states that it is a waste of the human mind to "first find out what everyone else thinks and then agree."[40] Part of diversity should be based on values, not just political definitions, because change usually comes from annoying individuals who see what others do not and insist that unpleasant facts be dealt with. Although managers are supposed to select the best qualified people and not necessarily the most congenial, White states that managers are unwilling to get rid of pleasant incompetents but prefer letting the unpleasant competents go. Studies indicate that women especially tend to prefer meek subordinates over confident and articulate ones.

New theories of management stress a different type of team. White writes, "It begins with the process of selecting and hiring the best possible people, as few of them as possible, paying them well, giving them the understanding of what needs to be done, and the tools with which to do it, and then walking away and leaving them alone."[41]

To develop the best possible organization with limited resources, managers should encourage diversity. Two people who are different can contribute more than two people who are exactly the same. It is not essential that they like each other, but they must work together in a professional manner. According to White, writing in the October 15, 1995, *Library Journal*, it is unfair to treat everyone exactly the same with promotion ladders and salary increases because there are people who deserve no such rewards. Good people will stay if treated fairly and incompetents might leave.

> What people "want" has not changed at all for a long time. They want to be treated as individuals and with fairness. They want to be properly paid, properly evaluated, and properly rewarded and recognized when they do something commendable. They want to be given assignments that can be accomplished within the prescribed time frame, with the tools and resources to make success at least possible. They want to be protected against insult and indignity from fellow workers, from outsiders, and from patrons. The development of a sense of self-worth is not a group exercise, it is an individual exercise.[42]

Characteristics of Bad Managers

In another *Library Journal* article of February 15, 1994, White gives the characteristics of bad managers as described by the psychologist Harry Levinson:

1. The narcissistic manager usurps praise while seeking self-promotion.

2. The sadistic manager overcontrols in a hostile and mean way in the classic sense of the bully.

3. The perfectionist never is satisfied and exerts inordinate pressure on subordinates for better performance and more time on the job, although this may not have anything to do with the needs of the organization.

4. Managers who are fixated on how a job is done rather than results do not delegate, and workers never develop a sense of participation.[43]

A fifth category of bad managers not included by Levinson is the too-nice boss who will not take charge and use authority for the good of the staff and the organization. The "wimp" boss may be taking the place of the "petty tyrant" in this era of participative management and empowered employees. Decision-avoiding managers stay away from face-to-face meetings, do not return phone calls, and do not read what is sent to them. If these bosses are not willing to act or take risks when representing the library to outside decision makers, nothing good will happen. In dealing with patrons, these same bosses refuse to protect other employees, although sometimes customers are wrong and the manager must be willing to stand up for the employee.[44]

Although individual values and expectations affect job satisfaction, library employees are motivated to do well when they feel a sense of achievement, gain recognition, and do work that is intrinsically satisfying. Most library employees feel an adequate level of job satisfaction, although this level could be raised significantly by managers who cultivate dedicated and productive employees. The skill, creativity, and knowledge of each employee must be nurtured for the betterment of the organization.[45]

Connecting with People

Because patterns of library use reflect how well the library promotes itself, effective library marketing techniques are vital to libraries. The library of tomorrow may be providing different services to meet the needs of its users. Effective marketing will explain the changes in a clear way so that the public knows why such changes are needed. "The primary pressures on librarians now are to quickly read the needs of the clientele and respond to them, understand the nature of the information sector competition, and clearly communicate the library's message to staff and clientele."[46] Good public relations is based on good public service. There is a PR effect from every contact the staff makes and every function that is performed.

For public relations to be most effective, employees must love the library and be eager to tell people about it. Effective promotion of excellent programs reaps benefits for the library. In larger libraries, a staff member may be responsible for all public relations. That person develops contacts with the local media and is familiar with deadlines as well as preferences for the content and format of news releases. He or she may be capable of designing posters, flyers, and bookmarks to advertise library events. On the other hand, smaller libraries may hold each department responsible for its own media releases.

Select the most effective contacts for the target audience. Publicity about programs for young children (10 and under) should be aimed at the parents as well as the children, while publicity for older children should be aimed directly at the child. Summer reading programs should be promoted at school and through PTA meetings and school newsletters. Although promotion through the media is good public relations for the library, it is not the best way to reach the audience for all programs.

When promoting a single event, send at least three press releases. The first informs the public about the program; the second reminds the public about the upcoming event; and the third shows how effective it was. The use of black-and-white pictures helps draw attention to the article and should be used whenever possible. Always include the who, what, when, where, and why information in a news release using simple and clear English. The first sentence should provoke interest in the article, and the name of the library and the program should be included next. Tell something about the program, and list the time, place, date, cost, and age limitations.[47]

Contact Groups

The public library must maintain contact with many groups. A list of these groups is given in *Improving Communication in the Library* by Barbara Conroy and Barbara Schindler Jones, and includes the following:

- Library users and potential users
- The community at large
- Other units of the library's organization (such as public library branches)
- Other libraries
- Library networks
- Charitable groups and individual donors
- Government bodies (such as city council and board of supervisors)

- Civic groups (such as the Chamber of Commerce)
- Educational institutions
- Professional associations
- Staff associations and unions
- Consultants
- Providers of service and supplies (vendors)[48]

Purposes of Communication

Also listed in the same book are the many purposes for external communication. They include:

- To communicate: establish and maintain effective, open, two-way communication channels between library personnel and the groups listed above.

- To become visible: project an image to the public of what the library is like and what services it offers.

- To promote: attract new users rather than passively waiting for new users to appear.

- To provide leadership: serve as a positive influence in the community and to make the library a focal point for community concerns, activities, and support.

- To create connections: ensure that the library is in touch with other libraries, library associations, and allied professional organizations for mutual problem solving and to keep up with developments in the field.

- To negotiate: work with library boards and governmental (or institutional) organizations in order to maintain or improve the library's financial and other support.[49]

Types of Media

There are many types of external media available. Advertisements in newspapers and magazines can be used to make announcements and to gain support. Although it is difficult to gauge their impact, they reach a wide audience and are relatively inexpensive. News releases and articles require careful preparation and can announce special events at little cost. Billboards allow the repetition of a short and simple message at a low cost, although some may criticize their use as not being aesthetic. When professionally done, brochures, pamphlets, flyers, and tote bags provide attractive items that are convenient to distribute, although they may have a short life. Printing and staff time are required for form letters and direct mail pieces to provide information and documentation. With form letters, the same message can reach many people, although personal letters may have a more positive impact. At meetings of outside groups, library staff members can communicate about the library if they do so with sensitivity. A quick method of dispensing information is the public presentation for clubs and associations. For a dynamic presentation, skill and effective audiovisuals are required. Many radio and television stations, as well as newspapers, offer free time for public service announcements, an often-overlooked opportunity. To inform and persuade, the telephone offers fast and direct feedback, and for best results, written confirmation should follow the conversation.[50]

Special Events

Special events to celebrate occasions such as National Library Week and Children's Book Week can be used to keep the library in the public eye. During these weeks, plan increased programming, host an open house with refreshments, or dress up the library. Hand out buttons, balloons, bookmarks, or other treats to the patrons.

When community groups organize a fair or bazaar, have a booth for the library. Brochures and flyers, pencils, bookmarks, balloons, and buttons that advertise the library can be distributed. Feature storytellers, puppet shows, and book readings, or sell old books, T-shirts, calendars, or candy. These activities may provide an opportunity to register people for library cards or to sign up children for reading programs or story times.[51]

Public Library of Charlotte & Mecklenburg County

The Public Library of Charlotte & Mecklenburg County (PLCMC) is an example of a foundering institution that had no political clout for funding in 1982. Since then, it has regained its position as a visible and innovative leader in the Carolinas. Chosen as *Library Journal*'s

Library of the Year in 1995, it owes its success to a marketing plan that fosters relationships with the community. Before winning the award, Helen Ruth Fleming reported on the library in the September 15, 1993, issue of *Library Journal*.

> Libraries, vital components in this new age of information delivery and technology, are part of the cultural fabric of every community. Librarians should investigate how they can position their institution to be a major community asset. The possibilities are endless, because access to good information is at the core of every business's strategic plan, every child's education, every banker's prospectus, every writer's story, every composer's music, and every journalist's article.[52]

To make sure that its budget is approved, PLCMC has developed relationships in the political and business communities, and with organizations, local colleges, and universities. In 1983, the Friends of the Public Library was started to develop a foundation of community support that still exists. Proactive library leadership was sought in board members, and, to strengthen its community support, aggressive marketing resulted in daily media coverage.

In 1991, the NOVELLO Festival of Reading was born to motivate more people to read and "celebrate the joy of reading." With broad-based support from literary, political, and business communities, the festival has become a major cultural event featuring well-known authors and a program of events for businesses, children, schools, the literary community, and the at-risk population. It also has been an excellent public relations tool for the library.

Tips for Marketing Programs

All libraries can afford marketing programs. In a September 15, 1993, *Library Journal* article, Helen Ruth Fleming included the following marketing tips for small libraries:

1. In your first-year plan target no more than five major categories.

2. Market your collection through programs and publicity. Booklists are helpful to accompany each program.

3. Contact the local paper to suggest features on library programs or a regular column.

4. Consult with local school officials to determine needs of students before developing programs.

5. Schedule local speakers from colleges or universities to speak on popular topics.

6. Attract local workers through brown-bag lunch series with films or booktalks.

7. Acquaint businesspeople with your resources at "Business Breakfasts" (coffee and doughnuts).

8. Contact financial institutions to present a series on financial planning. (No soliciting clients, please.)

9. Ask local genealogists to help patrons research family trees.

10. Promote reading through public service announcements.

11. Have a local marketing firm develop a brochure for you as a community service.

12. Fill a marketing position (modify an existing position) with someone from a private sector background.

13. Improve the appearance of your facility by reducing clutter.

14. Form a Friends of the Library volunteer group for fund-raising and as community advocates.[53]

The purpose of public relations for the library is to let the public know what is offered and to enrich the quality of service. It helps inform the people about how the library can fully serve them by inviting them to use the services and materials and enjoy the available programs. Because every library is financed by the people, they certainly should know what they are paying for through their taxes. "As far as libraries are concerned, effectively promoting the use of libraries *is* good service. And good service is good public relations."[54]

Conclusion

For the public library to be a significant institution in the future, there must be active community support, and the staff must believe in and be dedicated to the service ethic. The needs of the community served must be considered in the development of the three main products the library has to offer: programs, services, and collections. Good marketing techniques by the library are important to inform the people how the public funds are being spent for the betterment of the community.

To help solve the problems librarians encounter while meeting the requirements of users, Allie Beth Martin, former president of the American Library Association, emphasized a critical need for librarians to know:

> How to determine the library and information needs of each community
>
> How to develop plans—set goals—*with* not *for* users
>
> How to communicate what the library is doing so that it becomes truly visible
>
> How to manage libraries so effectively that they will receive needed support
>
> How to perform actively, not passively
>
> How to change and help others to change[55]

Libraries that are able to do these things well should not have to worry about their place in the future. Organizations that are needed because they provide valuable services always will be supported by the community.

> Since man first collected, passed on, and remembered his experience, some member of the community was made responsible for enlarging and using the precious body of knowledge. Librarianship is both old and new, but its expectations are unlimited.[56]

Discussion Questions

1. What do you think the role of the volunteer should be in the public library? Is a library staffed only with volunteers better than a library that is not open at all? Why or why not?

2. Is it vital for a public library to have a successful marketing plan? What are the components of a successful strategy?

3. Why is it necessary for board members to feel that they are making a contribution to the community as well as to the library when they serve as trustees? Why is it important for the board and the director to have a good working relationship based on trust? How important is it for the community to trust the library board? Why?

4. Is it just as important for small libraries to have a qualified librarian as it is for larger ones? Why or why not? How can small libraries cooperate to make available a qualified librarian?

5. What is a librarian? What skills do librarians possess that will meet the challenges of the information age? Is there a difference between a librarian and a cybrarian?

6. Why do you suppose many paraprofessionals feel that their skills, training, and experience are not respected by their directors? What could be done to remedy the situation?

7. What is motivation, and what can librarians and managers do to promote employee motivation?

8. Comment on Herbert White's opinion that managers are unwilling to get rid of pleasant incompetents but prefer letting the unpleasant competents go. Is this a good practice? Why or why not?

9. Of the five categories of bad managers, which type do you feel is most detrimental to the public library. Why?

10. Describe the ideal library manager.

11. List the pros and cons of a professional manager versus a librarian as manager in the public library.

Notes

1. Harold Billings, "The Tomorrow Librarian," *Wilson Library Bulletin* 69, no.1 (January 1995): 34.

2.   James Piccininni, "Advice for First-Time Library Directors on Managing a Library," *Library Administration & Management* 10, no. 1 (Winter 1996): 41–43.

3.   Billings, "Tomorrow Librarian," 36.

4.   Ibid.

5.   Herbert S. White, "Small Public Libraries—Challenges, Opportunities, and Irrelevancies," *Library Journal* 119, no. 7 (April 15, 1994): 54.

6.   Ibid., 53.

7.   C. Herbert Carson, "Beginner's Luck: A Growing Job Market," *Library Journal* 121, no. 17 (October 15, 1996): 34.

8.   Mary Jo Lynch, "Librarians' Salaries: Barely Any Increase This Year," *American Libraries* 27, no. 9 (October 1996): 59.

9.   Mary Jane Scherdin and Anne K. Beaubien, "Shattering Our Stereotype: Librarians' New Image," *Library Journal* 120, no. 12 (July 1995): 38.

10.   Janette S. Caputo, *Stress and Burnout in Library Service* (Phoenix, Ariz.: Oryx Press, 1991), 14.

11.   Evan St. Lifer, " 'We Are the Library!' Support Staff Speaks Out," *Library Journal* 120, no. 18 (November 1, 1995): 31.

12.   John N. Berry, "The 'Other Librarians' Organize," *Library Journal* 117, no. 18 (November 1, 1992): 8.

13.   St. Lifer, " 'We Are the Library!,' " 34.

14.   Darlene E. Weingand, *Administration of the Small Public Library*, 3d ed. (Chicago: American Library Association, 1992), 112.

15.   John N. Berry, "Austin Public Library," *Library Journal* 118, no. 11 (June 15, 1993): 33.

16.   Sally Gardner Reed, *Small Libraries: A Handbook for Successful Management* (Jefferson, N.C.: McFarland, 1991), 30–36.

17.   Beverly A. Rawles, *Human Resource Management in Small Libraries* (Hamden, Conn.: Library Professional Publications, 1982), 112–113.

18.   Ibid., 146–148.

19.   Herbert S. White, "The Double-Edged Sword of Library Volunteerism," *Library Journal* 118, no. 7 (April 15, 1993): 66.

20.   Ibid., 67.

21.   Gordon S. Wade, *Working with Library Boards: A How-to-Do-It Manual for Librarians* (New York: Neal-Schuman, 1991), 1.

22.   Ibid., 11–12.

23.   Ibid., 13.

24.   Ibid., 14.

25.   John N. Berry, "Great Libraries Have Great Boards," *Library Journal* 120, no. 6 (April 1, 1995): 6.

26.   Ibid.

27.   David Belanger, "Board Games: Examining the Trustee/Director Conflict," *Library Journal* 120, no. 19 (November 15, 1995): 41.

28. Ibid.

29. Dana C. Rooks, *Motivating Today's Library Staff: A Management Guide* (Phoeniz, Ariz.: Oryx Press, 1988), 81–82.

30. Ibid., 1.

31. Ibid., 22.

32. Caputo, *Stress and Burnout*, 143.

33. Ibid., 136.

34. Ibid., 136–144.

35. Evan St. Lifer and Michael Rogers, "ULC Study Finds Libraries Invest Little in Staff Development," *Library Journal* 118, no. 14 (September 1, 1993): 112.

36. Roma M. Harris, "The Mentoring Trap," *Library Journal* 118, no. 17 (October 15, 1993): 39.

37. Caputo, *Stress and Burnout*, 149.

38. Rooks, *Motivating Today's Library Staff*, 63.

39. Ibid., 97.

40. Herbert S. White, "Never Mind Being Innovative and Effective—Just Be Nice," *Library Journal* 120, no. 15 (September 15, 1995): 47.

41. Ibid., 48.

42. Herbert S. White, "Smearing with a Broad Brush," *Library Journal* 120, no. 17 (October 15, 1995): 42.

43. Herbert S. White, "Tough Times Make Bad Managers Worse," *Library Journal* 119, no. 3 (February 15, 1994): 132.

44. Ibid., 132–134.

45. Rooks, *Motivating Today's Library Staff*, 144.

46. Barbara Conroy and Barbara Schindler Jones, *Improving Communication in the Library* (Phoenix, Ariz.: Oryx Press, 1986), 160.

47. Mae Benne, *Principles of Children's Services in Public Libraries* (Chicago: American Library Association, 1991), 95–96.

48. Conroy and Jones, *Improving Communication*, 50.

49. Ibid., 51.

50. Ibid., 52–54.

51. Anne Gjervasi and Betty Kay Seibt, *Handbook for Small, Rural, and Emerging Public Libraries* (Phoeniz, Ariz.: Oryx Press, 1988), 155–156.

52. Helen Ruth Fleming, "Library CPR: Savvy Marketing Can Save Your Library," *Library Journal* 118, no. 15 (September 15, 1993): 32.

53. Ibid., 35.

54. Steve Sherman, *ABC's of Library Promotion*, 3d ed. (Metuchen, N.J.: Scarecrow Press, 1992), 5.

55. Virginia H. Mathews, *Libraries for Today and Tomorrow* (New York: Octagon Books, 1976), 137–138.

56. Ibid., 164.

PUBLIC LIBRARY SUPPORT GROUPS AND USERS

6

Lisa S. Payne

People make up a library, and people are the library's reason for being. A public library is for the people and by the people. Even with today's technology changing the world of the public library, the bottom line is still people. It is people interacting with people that gives the public library its unique ability to bring people into the world of books and information. It takes two main forces to keep a public library in existence: a force of people to staff the library and a force of people to patronize it. There would be no library without both of these forces.

The first force consists of all library staff both professional and paraprofessional. Most people assume that librarians are the most important figures in a library; however, it is a team effort! It takes librarians, technical staff, clerical aides, circulation staff, catalogers, administrative staff, custodians, volunteers, Friends groups, the library board, and many others to keep a public library running. Librarians, as well as other library staff members, are professionals, but they are also people—people who need support. Librarians are trained to be people helpers, and sometimes librarians need help themselves. There are several groups that provide support for librarians and library staff.

ALA

The most influential of these groups is the American Library Association. The ALA is the largest nongovernmental library organization in the world. Its purpose is to promote libraries and librarianship through education and advocacy. Several smaller groups within the ALA offer specialized guidance and support; these include the Public Library Association (PLA) and the Association for Library Service to Children (ALSC).

A major role of the ALA is to set the standards of the library profession. The ALA provides guidance to librarians in the form of a code of ethics. The ALA also provides optimal goals for operating a public library at its highest standard of access and service. These goals are established by the ALA's Intellectual Freedom Committee. The goals and guidelines are intended to help public libraries develop policies, procedures, and regulations that resist denying, restricting, or creating barriers to access. Here are the guidelines for formulating policies.

1. Policies should be developed and implemented within the legal framework that applies to libraries.

2. Policies should cite statutes or ordinances on which the authority to make that policy is based.

3. Policies should be developed and implemented within the framework of the Library Bill of Rights and its interpretations.

4. Policies should be based on the library's mission and objectives.

5. Policies should only impose restrictions on the access to, or use of library resources, services, or facilities when those restrictions are necessary to achieve the library's mission and objectives.

6. Policies should narrowly tailor prohibitions or restrictions, in the rare instances when they are required, so they are not more restrictive than needed to serve their objectives.

7. Policies should attempt to balance competing interests and avoid favoring majority at the expense of individual rights, or allowing individual user's rights to interfere materially

with the majority's rights to free and equal access to library resources, services, and facilities.

8. Policies should avoid arbitrary distinctions between individuals or classes of users, and should not have the effect of denying or abridging a person's right to use library resources, services, or facilities based on arbitrary distinctions such as origin, age, background, or views.

9. Policies should not target specific users or groups of users based on an assumption or expectation that such users might engage in behavior that will materially interfere with the achievement of substantial library objectives.

10. Policies must be clearly stated so that a reasonably intelligent person will have fair warning of what is expected.

11. Policies must provide a means of appeal.

12. Policies must be reviewed regularly by the library's governing authority and by its legal counsel.

13. Policies must be communicated clearly and made available in an effective manner to all library users.

14. Policies must be enforced evenhandedly and not in a manner intended to benefit or disfavor any person or group in an arbitrary or capricious manner.

15. Policies should, if reasonably possible, provide adequate alternative means of access to information for those whose behavior results in the denial or restriction of access to any library resource, service, or facility.[1]

When exercised, these guidelines ensure library policies that give all people, including special populations, fair and equitable access to the public library.

Along with the ALA, each state and/or region has a localized library support network, such as the Virginia Library Association (VLA). Within the library, there is usually a staff organization to promote good working conditions and cohesiveness among the staff and the branches.

Friends of the Library

One group that can be an excellent source of support is the Friends group. The Friends group consists of citizens who are associated on behalf of the library. Betty Rice defines a Friends group as a specific group of people who have paid to join a formal organization, "whose purpose is to support the public library financially and morally."[2] Some of these Friends groups can be purely social, and some may be more politically inclined; most fall somewhere in between. Friends groups have many functions that differ from library to library. Some of these functions can and do include the following activities. Friends help to raise money for services and materials that may be outside a library's normal budget. In some cases, the Friends enhance an existing budget. For example, a Friends group could buy several copies of a bestseller to offer patrons more access. Another function of the Friends group is to offer service by helping with special library programs and events. Friends can be a powerful source of public relations in the community. Advocacy goes along with public relations. For example, some members of the Friends may be prominent in the community or local government and can often activate a citizens' lobby effort. Last but not least, "an organized Friends group is living proof of the library's value to the community."

The Friends of Libraries U.S.A. (FOLUSA) put together guidelines for establishing a successful Friends group.[3]

1. The library director must want a Friends group.

2. The library staff must be willing to work with the Friends.

3. All parties involved must realize that a time commitment is involved.

4. The library must agree which of its resources will be used by the Friends.

5. A committed core group must exist.

6. The authority to which the library director reports must be aware of the Friends group.

7. Communication must be open to all groups involved in the use of the library.

8. All those involved in the Friends must realize that the Friends group does not make library policy, which is the function of the trustees.

9. The library must decide, in discussion with the Friends, the roles it wishes the group to play: advocates, social, fund-raising, volunteers, or a combination thereof.

10. All those involved must understand that trustees and Friends have separate functions, and liaisons should be developed between the two groups.

Patrons

Inside the public library, the force of people called the staff makes it possible to serve the force of people called patrons. The library should have a pulse on its surrounding community and its patrons' needs, but it should be aware of the people who are not being served by the library and why they are not. The public library should provide a wide variety of books and materials for all persons regardless of age, race, religion, intellect, and income. In today's politically correct world, the public library has to be more aware than ever of offering materials that are of relevance (to someone) and are accessible to everyone. The Freedom to Read Statement notes: "It is in the public interest for publishers and librarians to make available the widest diversity of views and expressions, including those which are unorthodox or unpopular with the majority."[4] So it is the public library's duty to provide the "freedom to read" to all people.

Many different types of people with many different needs make up a public library's patron base. The broadest division is the distinction between male and female users. According to a 1996 Gallup Poll, a higher percentage of library users were women. Of women polled, 69% were library users, compared to 65% of the men polled.[5] Some other interesting results of this poll showed that more than 77 percent of people surveyed had a yearly income of more than $50,000.[6] The poll also stated that "80% of those surveyed reported going to the library to take out books." This poll shows whose needs are being met: educated, affluent women and men, but what about the more diversified segments of the population? "While the doors of the public library, like the park's gates, are not closed in the face of any citizen seeking entrance, certain segments of the population have traditionally found the library unwelcoming and indifferent to their needs."[7] It is important to look at these patrons and potential users to see if the public library is providing for the needs and wants of all its patrons. The following segments of the population also make up the public library's patron base: senior citizens; children and youth; and minorities, non-English-speaking patrons, and the poor. Each group has special needs that, when identified, can give insight into providing the best service and access to materials and information possible.

Senior Citizens

Senior citizens make up a large portion of a library's patronage, and this portion is continually growing. By the year 2020, it is projected that the senior adult population will consist of more than 54 million people.[8] This means that, for the majority of public libraries, the largest patron group will consist of people aged 65 and over. Public libraries need to be prepared. Many libraries today offer inadequate programming and limited resources for seniors. "Aging will represent the major social challenge for the remainder of the twentieth century when vast resources will need to be directed towards support, care, and treatment of the old."[9]

In the past, the public library has concentrated on children's and youth services while ignoring the special needs of senior adult patrons. Some reasons for this neglect are based in demographics. It has only been in the past two decades that the senior population has swelled and become the majority. In the early years of public libraries, the senior population was much smaller. Also, it can be argued that in the early 1900s the older generation did not require library services to fulfill their recreational and psychological needs because their families fulfilled these roles. Older adults now have to rely on themselves to fulfill their needs. Today there are two types of senior patrons. One type is independent, well educated, and affluent. The other type is often dependent because of a disability, poor education, and limited income. "Poor eyesight, poor hearing, limited physical ability and educational handicaps often impede an older adult's ability to obtain information, which is why information and reference services can be invaluable to seniors."[10] Both types require access to recreational needs and information services, but their leisure time activities and information needs will be different. For example, while both groups might benefit from large-print books, both groups would probably not benefit from a travel seminar on cruises. In addition, providing a seminar on investments might benefit the affluent group more than would a tax preparation seminar. This is not to say that these programs should be offered only to one group or the other; it is only to point out that differences do exist among segments. It would be unfair to lump all seniors into the same category and only provide one type of access or information. Public libraries should be aware of all areas of diversity and make provisions for each.

Here are some guidelines, developed by the ALA, for the public library to consider when focusing on the senior population.

1. Exhibit and promote a positive attitude toward the aging process and older adults.

2. Promote information and resources on aging and its implications.

3. Assure services for older adults that reflect cultural, ethnic, and economic differences.

4. Provide library service to the special needs of all older adults, including the minority who are geographically isolated, homebound, institutionalized, or disabled.

5. Utilize the potential of older adults (paid or volunteer) as liaisons to reach their peers and as a resource in intergenerational programming.

6. Employ older adults at both professional and support levels for either general library work or for programs specifically targeted to older adults.

7. Involve older adults in the planning and design of library services and programs for the entire community and for older adults in particular.

8. Promote and develop working relationships with other agencies and groups connected with the needs of older adults.

9. Provide programs, services, and information for those preparing for retirement or later-life career alternatives.

10. Facilitate library use by older persons through improved library design and access to transportation.

11. Incorporate as part of the library's planning and evaluation process the changing needs of an aging population.

12. Aggressively seek sources of funding, and commit a portion of the library budget to programs and services for older adults.[11]

The Brooklyn (New York) Public library is a perfect example of a public library that is successfully following these guidelines. This public library operates a program called SAGE (Services to the Aging) that "balances the needs of the healthy, mobile elderly with those who are disabled."[12] More than one-third of the library's volunteer tutors are over age 60.[13] Senior staff members and volunteers also plan book discussions, films, musical performances, and seminars on age-relevant topics such as health and nutrition, money matters, and leisure interests. The programs are brought into local-area nursing homes, hospitals, and retirement centers.

The Plainedge (New York) Public Library publishes a newsletter called *Discovery* for its senior patrons. This newsletter not only gives information on library programs but also provides information on area programs and items of particular interest to older patrons. The Tulsa City-County Public Library maintains an information and referral service exclusively for senior patrons. Both the Los Angeles Public Library and the Cleveland Public Library have "grandparent" programs that use seniors as storytellers in the children's reading programs. In Milwaukee, the "Over 60" bookmobile makes stops at nursing homes and residential areas where the majority of seniors live.

These examples show the type of programming and services that can and should be offered to the senior population through the public library. It is up to the public library to reach out to, plan for, and provide services to this valuable special population.

Children and Youth

The next force to be reckoned with is the child and youth population. "Young people of all ages account for most of the circulation of books in most of our public libraries—as much as 50 to 70 percent. Once introduced to the library, they are likely to become eager, avid readers for life."[14]

The public library should draw young people in at an early age. "There are precious few environments where a youngster is encouraged to pursue his own interests unencumbered by directives from adults."[15] Mary Chelton advocates a public library's "promot[ing] knowledge that allows individuals to grow up as healthy, functioning, moral, productive, and socially competent individuals."[16] She believes that children should be taught the following fundamentals:

1. That one is valued

2. How to communicate

3. How to be a part of a community

4. How to learn

5. How to work

6. How to make choices

7. How to protect oneself

8. How to be a moral person

Chelton also believes that a public library can and should help impart all of this knowledge to children and youth. There are many special programs that can be offered to encourage children to read and to use the library. "The public library offers an atmosphere that encourages the mind to explore, to stretch out, to extend the perimeters of a child's capacity."[17] These programs include summer reading programs, bookmobiles, special events, homework helplines, and toddler story times. All of these programs reach out to children and encourage them to read and search for knowledge. Unfortunately, these vital programs are often the first to be cut because of budget restrictions. Such losses are especially felt by children who are economically deprived.

Minorities, Non-English-Speaking Patrons, and the Poor

Library services to minorities and the poor are often the most neglected by public libraries. Ironically, these are the very segments of the population that are most in need of the services a public library has to offer. The public library must provide equal access to materials and information to these people. With society moving toward the information highway, these populations are going to be left by the side of the road. The public library should be one source where the poor, illiterate, and non-English-speaking citizens of this country find help and access to information. If the public library does not help them, then who will? Minorities and the poor make up at least a portion of every public library's patron base. These patrons deserve just as much service from the public library as anyone else in that library's community. In order for a library to reinvent itself for the future, the library has to reevaluate its role in the community. This reevaluation should pinpoint any discrepancies in service and rectify them, and this often means implementing special programming.

In Ohio, both the Cuyahoga County Public Library and the Lorain County Public Library offer workshops on job-finding skills, résumé writing, and career decision making. The Hennepin County (Minnesota) Public Library has offered seminars on living within a budget. In Saint Louis, the public library system offers a computer-based Guidance Information System. This system offers information on occupations and how to train for them. Broward County Library in Florida has participated in a federally funded program (LSCA) to bring library services to migrant workers.[18] Although the poor are often members of a minority group, members of minority groups are not necessarily economically disadvantaged. Also, in some cases, these groups have a large base of non-English-speaking members. Minority groups form different cultures that also have special needs. If the public library is to survive, then, it has to start meeting the needs of all its diverse clientele, not just a select few.

Diversity in cultures is what makes our country unique. The public library should celebrate this diversity and use it to educate, enlighten, and inform. The Atlanta-Fulton Public Library is celebrating its African American community by opening the Auburn Avenue Research Library on African-American Culture and History. This is the second public library in the nation to open with a mission to serve as a repository for literature and materials on African American culture. Emma Darnell, a Fulton County commissioner, stated, "This library is not just for African Americans; it's for everyone to come and feel what it is like to be black in America."[19] The Redwood Public Library offers English classes, translators, and a job service for its non-English-speaking patrons.

Each of the special populations discussed has a right to public library services. In most situations, however, traditional public library services have failed to meet the needs of these patrons and potential patrons. In order to draw these populations into the library and provide for their needs, special services must be offered. Claire K. Lipsman defines special services as "activities or programs undertaken in addition to, or in place of, ordinary library services, with the intention of reaching or serving a disadvantaged population."[20]

Unfortunately, in today's public library, it is a "catch-22" situation. In order to provide for these populations, special programming must be available and accessible. With decreased budgets and fewer staff members, however, these special services often are the first to be cut. If the programs cannot be offered, then these special populations cannot be served adequately or, in many cases, cannot be served at all. It is therefore imperative to make the local government and administration aware of the importance of these groups and their needs and the ways in which the public library can benefit them. For example, if importance is placed on economically deprived children and the necessity for early reading, then perhaps a bookmobile program might not be cut. The public library cannot reinvent itself and prepare for the future if it has left its people in the past.

Discussion Questions

1. Many "special" programs are eliminated because of budgetary cuts. What are some ways to raise additional funds to support these programs?

2. Is it possible for a public library to attract and provide for special populations without offering special programming? If so, what are some of the ways in which to accomplish this?

3. What is the difference between the Friends of the Library and library foundation? Do their functions overlap? Should their functions overlap?

4. What are some strategies that public librarians could use to convince the administration that children's outreach programming—i.e., bookmobiles and homework helplines—are vital to the public library's mission to provide high-quality educational and leisure service to children?

5. One of the guidelines developed by the American Library Association for service to senior citizens states that senior adults should be involved in the planning and design of library services. What are some areas of the public library that might benefit from input by senior adults?

Notes

1. American Library Association, Intellectual Freedom Committee, "Guidelines for the Development and Implementation of Policies, Regulations and Procedures Affecting Access to Library Materials, Services and Facilities" (Chicago: American Library Association, June 28, 1994).

2. Betty Rice, *Public Relations for Public Libraries* (New York: H. W. Wilson, Co., 1972), 114.

3. Sandy Dolnick, *Friends of Libraries Sourcebook* (Chicago: American Library Association, 1990), 3.

4. American Library Association Office of Intellectual Freedom, *Freedom Manual* (Chicago: American Library Association, 1992), 283.

5. "LJ News: Library Use Up, Says Magazine Poll," *Library Journal* 121, no. 2 (February 1, 1996): 18.

6. Ibid., 20.

7. Marcia J. Nauratil, *Public Libraries and Nontraditional Clienteles* (Westport, Conn.: Greenwood Press, 1985), 52.

8. Allan M. Kleiman, "The Aging Agenda: Redefining Library Services for a Graying Population," *Library Journal* 121, no. 5 (April 15, 1995): 32.

9. Nauratil, *Public Libraries*, 52.

10. Whitney North Seymour Jr. and Elizabeth N. Layne, *For the People: Fighting for Public Libraries* (Garden City, N.Y.: Doubleday, 1979), 137.

11. American Library Association, Adult Services Division, *Guidelines for Library Service to Older Adults* (Chicago: American Library Association, 1987), 4.

12. Kleiman, "Aging Agenda," 33.

13. Seymour and Layne, *For the People*, 142.

14. Ibid., 17.

15. Ibid., 19.

16. Mary Chelton, "Your Right to Know" *Libraries Make It Happen* (Chicago, ALA, June, 1992) 35–44.

17. Ibid.

18. John N. Berry, "Library of the Year 1996: Broward County Library" *Library Journal* 118, no. 11 (June 15, 1996) 28.

19. Ron Chepesiuk, "Schomburg of the South: The Auburn Avenue Research Library," *American Libraries* 27, no. 2 (February 1996): 38–40.

20. Claire K. Lipsman, *The Disadvantaged and Library Effectiveness* (Chicago: American Library Association, 1972), 141–142.

PRESERVATION IN PUBLIC LIBRARIES

7

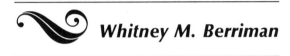

Whitney M. Berriman

Preservation is an important function within the public library. It is essential that librarians recognize the necessity of preserving library materials for future generations. Librarians should understand the history of preservation in public libraries and the importance of future preservation for public libraries in the twenty-first century.

Overview

Within most libraries, preservation usually falls under the domain of the technical services operation. Librarian of Congress Ainsworth Rand Spofford, circa 1876, "characterized the importance of preservation, within the larger field of public library administration as second only to the selection and utilization of books."[1] It should be noted that preservation is not a new issue for libraries. Great emphasis was placed on preservation during the second half of the nineteenth century due to the acidity of the paper manufactured during that period. Librarian Duane A. Watson has the following explanation.

> The preservation of library materials has been a concern of librarians for centuries, but it wasn't until a highly acidic process of chemically breaking down pulp for paper making was introduced in the 1850s that brittle paper became the foremost concern. Books printed on highly acidic paper began to crumble in twenty to fifty years, whereas the paper in most books printed before the early nineteenth century remained supple and strong.[2]

According to Barbara Buckner Higginbotham, a noted scholar on the subject of library preservation, nineteenth-century librarians had a "solid sense of preservation mission."[3] Higginbotham also noted that "in developing their collections, public librarians were sensitive to the need to balance the resources devoted to popular and permanent acquisitions."[4] However, regarding preservation sensitivity, conservator Nancy Carlson Schrock believes that "public libraries have been slow to see its relevance for high-use circulating collections that are weeded heavily."[5] According to Anne L. Reynolds, coauthor of a public library preservation survey, "Except for some major urban libraries such as New York Public, the response from public libraries has been far less dramatic."[6] Reynolds believes that, in fact, some public librarians may believe that their collections are expendable.

A few libraries actively attempt to preserve materials. At the Boston Public Library, emphasis is placed on preserving "such local items as handbills, street ballads, and newspaper clippings as expressions of popular local opinion."[7] During the latter part of the nineteenth century, one of the first large-scale attempts at preservation was undertaken by the Department of State's Bureau of Rolls and Library.[8]

In 1898, a conference on the preservation of library and archival materials was held in Saint Gall, Switzerland. This conference is notable because it was the first of its kind; however, no American librarians were invited to attend.[9]

Some of the pressing preservation concerns during the late nineteenth century involved the threat of fire, decay of leather, flimsy bindings, light damage, and paper deterioration, as well as building design. These concerns would continue in the twentieth century. Inferior book construction was the preservation hot topic during the early years of the twentieth century. In response to these issues, the American Library Association (ALA) formed the Committee on Bookbinding and Book Papers.[10]

Key Figures in Library Preservation

Throughout the latter part of the nineteenth century and into the early part of the twentieth, British library preservation research greatly influenced American librarians. According to Higginbotham, "well-developed public library systems and substantial academic and research libraries existed in both the United States and England."[11] In 1851, British chemist Calvert had discovered that the sulfuric acid used to tan leather was the major cause of decay in leather bindings.[12]

Other European librarians contributed to American knowledge of preservation. Italian librarians developed document repair techniques. Their focus on document repair was a direct result of the 1904 fire at the Turin Library. Photoreproduction of manuscripts was a Belgian librarian's special focus.[13]

In 1876, a noteworthy report was published by the United States Bureau of Education. The report, titled *Public Libraries in the United States of America: Their History, Condition, and Management*, was the first of its kind.[14] Clearly the preservation of materials had begun to concern public libraries during this period.

After World War I, there was a notable increase in preservation research. Librarian Harry Lydenberg established a paper treatment laboratory at the New York Public Library. It was also during this time that film became a viable preservation option.[15]

During the latter portion of the 1930s, William J. Barrow, a document restorer at the Virginia State Library, developed the cellulose and tissue lamination method.[16] This method bears his name. Barrow focused on the problem of paper deterioration. On June 1, 1957, Barrow began the first of his many studies on the physical strength of paper used for non-fiction book publishing from 1900 to 1949.[17] The results of his study revealed that "only 3 percent of the volumes studied had paper which could be expected to last more that fifty years." Barrow's Research Laboratory was a major preservation center for at least a decade.[18]

In November 1996, an event occurred that brought preservation issues to the forefront. The flooding of the Arno River in Florence, Italy, illustrated the need for disaster planning. This was a new issue to be addressed by all preservation librarians.

Organizations, Associations, and Programs

Various organizations have been instrumental in the development of preservation knowledge, goals, objectives, and solutions. Scholarly journals also provide information on the subject. The January 1956 issue of *Library Trends*, for example, was devoted to preservation topics. Edited by Maurice Tauber, it was the first of its kind.[19]

One of the first organizations to affect preservation activities within librarianship was the Council on Library Resources (CLR). CLR was founded in 1956 and headed during the first 15 years by Verner Clapp. CLR funded William J. Barrow's research for approximately 20 years.[20]

Another organization, the Association of Research Libraries (ARL), established its own Standing Committee on the Preservation of Research Library Materials in 1960. A work prepared by Gordon Williams for this committee was considered a "preservation landmark."[21] The report was titled *The Preservation of Deteriorating Books: An Examination of the Problem with Recommendations for a Solution.*[22] In it, Williams called for the establishment of a central federal agency to address preservation issues. The agency would

> preserve a physical copy of every "significant written record" and provide copies to other libraries as needed. Microfilming was endorsed as an important element of a program to preserve text and reduce wear on original copies.[23]

As stated earlier, professional organizations and associations play an extremely important role in preservation. Professional associations include the ALA's ALCTS Preservation and Reformatting Section (PARS) and the American Association for Image and Information Management (AIIM). Organizations include the Commission on Preservation and Access (CPA) and the Library of Congress Preservation Section. Links to these and other professional organizations and associations can be found on the Internet. Internet addresses are listed at the end of this chapter.

Possible Solutions to Preservation Issues Faced by Public Libraries

Educating users on preservation issues is certainly important for public libraries as they face the twenty-first century. Users must be taught that their treatment of library materials has a direct bearing on the materials' future. Librarians also need to educate paraprofessional and clerical staff regarding the care and handling of library materials. The Southeastern Library Network (SOLINET) has a web site listing guidelines for handling books in general collections. The Preservation Directorate at the Library of Congress web site contains a similar list of guidelines. In addition, technical leaflets pertaining to this issue may be obtained from the Northeast Document Conservation Center (NEDCC). (The citations for the web sites and these leaflets appear at the end of this chapter.)

The National Information Standards Organization (NISO) has a Z39 committee, NISO-Z39, which is devoted to "developing standards for book production, paper, and for the wide variety of information media available today."[24] According to preservation authority Susan G. Swartzburg, "standards, especially those for electronic media, will have a strong bearing on issues of preservation and access in the future."[25]

Digital imaging is a controversial preservation method at this time. Digital imaging involves the acquisition and storing of images via image scanning. This method is comparable to microfilming; however, it has definite shortcomings that must be addressed before it can be used as a viable preservation method. Storage capacity and the ability to retrieve stored data are two drawbacks to this technology.[26] According to the technical leaflet provided by the Northeast Document Conservation Center,

> digital imaging for long-term preservation should be undertaken only with extreme caution and should include concurrent production of an archival microfilm or an archival paper copy.[27]

In a survey of the Wellesley Library, Anne L. Reynolds noted that the "public library response needs to take place on several levels."[28] She suggests the following levels.

> First, communities must realize that library collections are capital assets. Second, libraries need to understand the books as a physical object whose frailties must be acknowledged at every step of the progression through our collections. Third, it is very clear that a library's goals of service, level of use, and collection development policies have a major bearing on the condition of each collection.[29]

Although Reynolds has enumerated the public libraries' responsibilities for preservation, there are still many unanswered questions pertaining to preservation issues faced by public libraries.

Discussion Questions

1. Do public libraries have a responsibility to preserve materials or should preservation matters be the responsibility only of academic and/or research libraries?
2. Describe some methods that may be used by public libraries in order to educate users about the importance of preservation of library materials.
3. What are some of the ways access may be affected in public libraries if preservation needs are not addressed?
4. Digital imaging appears to be the latest trend in preservation advances; however, it has notable drawbacks. Can its obstacles and drawbacks be overcome? Why or why not?

Additional Readings and Internet Addresses

Association for Library Collections and Technical Services Historical Information Available: gopher://ala1.ala.org:70/00/alagophxiii/alagophphxiiialcts/alagophxiiialctshistory/50714046.document (Accessed Jan.-Apr., 1997).

Guthrie, Kevin M., and Wendy P. Lougee. "The JSTOR Solution: Accessing and Preserving the Past." *Library Journal* 122, no. 2 (February 1, 1997): 42–44.

Lesk, Michael. *Image Formats for Preservation and Access: A Report of the Technology Assessment Advisory Committee to the Committee on*

Preservation and Access. Available: http:www.nlc-bnc.ca/documents/libraries/net/lesk.txt (Accessed April 9, 1998).

Preservation Directorate: Library of Congress. *Mission of the Preservation Directorate*. Available: http://lcweb.loc.gov/preserv/mission.html (Accessed Jan.-Apr., 1997).

Report on the Implementation of the ALA Preservation Policy. Available: http://www.well.com/user/bronxbob/pars/policy.html (Accessed Jan.-Apr., 1997).

Shaughnessy, Thomas. "Public Libraries and the Challenge of Preservation." In *The Library Trustee: A Practical Guidebook*, edited by Virginia G. Young. Chicago: American Library Association, 1988.

SOLINET. *Handling Books in General Collections*. Available: http://www.solinet.net/presvtn/leaf/hndlbook.html (Accessed Jan.-Apr., 1997).

———. *Preservation Planning: A Basic Bibliography*. Available: http://palimpsest.stanford.edu/solinet/planbib.htm (Accessed Jan.-Apr., 1997).

———. *Readings in Preservation*. Available: http://palimpsest.stanford.edu/solinet/presbib.htm (Accessed Jan.-Apr., 1997).

———. *Related Internet Resources*. Available: http://www.solinet/presvtn/links/org.htm (Accessed Jan.-Apr., 1997).

Stevens, Norman D. "Editorial: Preservation—A Concern of Every Library and Every Librarian." *Library Administration and Management* 4 no. 3 (Summer 1990): 123–126.

Stitt, Maxine K. *A Practical Guide to Preservation in School and Public Libraries*. Syracuse, N.Y.: Syracuse University Press, 1990.

USMARC 583 Field and Its Use in Preservation. Available: http://karamelik.eastlib.ufl.edu/automate/583/intro.html (Accessed April 9, 1998).

Notes

1. Barbara Buckner Higginbotham, *Our Past Preserved: A History of American Library Preservation, 1876–1910* (Boston: G. K. Hall, 1990), 7.

2. Duane A. Watson, "The Divine Library Function: Preservation," *School Library Journal* 33, no. 9 (November 1986): 41.

3. Higginbotham, *Our Past Preserved*, 9.

4. Ibid., 10.

5. Nancy Carlson Schrock, "A Collection Condition Survey Model for Public Libraries" in *Advances in Preservation and Access,* ed. Barbara Buckner Higginbotham and Mary E. Jackson (Westport, Conn.: Meckler, 1992), 2: 210.

6. Anne L. Reynolds et al., "Preservation: The Public Library Response," *Library Journal* 114, no. 3 (February 15, 1989): 128.

7. Barbara Buckner Higginbotham, "To Preserve the Best and Noblest Thoughts of Man: American Beginnings," in *Advances in Preservation and Access,* ed. Barbara Buckner Higginbotham and Mary E. Jackson (Westport, Conn.: Meckler, 1992), 1: 3.

8. Ibid., 7.

9. Ibid., 8.

10. Higginbotham, *Our Past Preserved,* 179–180.

11. Ibid., 184.

12. Ibid., 195.

13. Ibid., 184.

14. Ibid., 195.

15. Ibid., 187.

16. Pamela W. Darling and Sherelyn Ogden, "From Problems Perceived to Programs in Practice: The Preservation of Library Resources in the U.S.A., 1956–1980," *Library Resources and Technical Services* 25, no. 1 (January/March 1981): 10.

17. Ibid., 11.

18. Ibid., 17.

19. Jan Merrill-Oldham and Merrily Smith, eds., *The Library Preservation Program: Models, Priorities, Possibilities* (Chicago: American Library Association, 1985), 9.

20. Darling and Ogden, "From Problems Perceived to Programs in Practice," 10.

21. Merrill-Oldham and Smith, *Library Preservation Program,* 9.

22. Ibid.

23. Ibid.

24. Susan G. Swartzburg, *Preserving Library Materials: A Manual* (Metuchen, N.J.: Scarecrow Press, 1995), 246.

25. Ibid.

26. Northeast Document Conservation Center, *Digital Imaging Basics,* technical leaflet (Andover, Mass.: NEDCC, 1994), 1.

27. Ibid.

28. Reynolds, "Preservation: The Public Library Response," 131.

29. Ibid.

8 | TECHNOLOGY AND LIBRARIES

 **Fran White**

Overview

Technology is defined as:

1. The application of science, especially to industrial or commercial objectives.

2. The body of knowledge available to a civilization that is of use in fashioning implements, practicing manual arts and skills, and extracting or collecting materials.[1]

Technology, as defined above, can be applied to libraries, historically and developmentally. The cave paintings at Lascoux, considered to be among the first records kept in civilization, still exist because the creators used the "latest" technology when producing them. Throughout history, from Babylon to Greece to Rome to the monastic scribes of the Middle Ages, the forms of the records of civilization changed as technology changed. In the fifteenth century, a major development took place — Gutenberg's introduction of the movable type printing press, "perhaps the single most important precursor of the information age."

> Gutenberg developed his press by combining features of existing technologies: textile, papermaking and wine presses.

> Perhaps his most significant innovation, however, was the efficient molding and casting of movable metal type. . . . Gutenberg foresaw enormous profit-making potential for a printing press that used movable metal type. Despite their rapid growth in numbers, secular scribes simply could not keep up with the commercial demand for books.[2]

In the sixteenth century, libraries began to emerge throughout Europe, not only as repositories of records, but also as gathering places where patrons could read newspapers, books, and political treatises. Traveling and private libraries were formed as the technologies of transportation and printing became more "user-friendly."

Printers joined the pioneers traveling to the New World and brought with them the power of the written word and the impetus for establishing libraries in America. Benjamin Franklin is credited with the idea of the "Public Library," but it was in Peterborough, New Hampshire, that the first tax-supported public library was founded in 1833. Technology continued to affect public library growth and development as transportation, communications, printing, binding, photography, and papermaking became simpler and more cost effective. Libraries were able to obtain and manage more resources and provide them to more patrons.

Not every new development was of benefit to libraries, however. Acidic paper and the ensuing problem of brittle books have had a tremendously negative effect on library preservation. (See chapter 7.)

> As the demand for paper rose, the supply of rags and linen used in papermaking could not keep up with the demand for more and more pulp. In the mid-nineteenth century, wood replaced these materials as the major cellulose feedstock. Wood pulp contains lignin and hemicellulose that easily break down in air, causing discoloration and forming acidic compounds. Acidic processes were developed to remove the lignin because it discolored paper.[3]

In the twentieth century, political forces, especially the world wars and the Cold War, quickly and dramatically advanced technical research. Computers entered the scene as did improved telecommunications. Academic libraries in Ohio implemented these new technologies as a means to share resources and reduce costs by founding the Ohio College Library Center (OCLC).

> But the beginning of bibliographic networks based on MARC not only changed the availability of cards but also introduced the truly cooperative availability of cataloging data. The first network was OCLC—at first the Ohio College Library Center, but now the Online Computer Library Center. Libraries can become member libraries and then contribute original cataloging to the system. Any member library can use records found in the system contributed by the Library of Congress, several other national libraries, or any other member library.[4]

Ensuing technological developments had a profound effect on public libraries as they became part of the OCLC network and had access to standardized authority files, information, and eventually the Machine Readable Cataloging (MARC) record. The information age began when computers became readily available to individual users and organizations. This accessibility of information technology affected public libraries in several ways:

- The number of documents increased as the price of producing them decreased.

- Library operations became automated.

- There were fewer distinctions between library departments causing more cross-training and reeducation.

- Libraries and librarians worldwide shared and accessed data seamlessly across computer platforms.

- Patrons obtained more equitable access to information.

In the 1990s "technology" has become synonymous with computer-information science. The explosion in popularity of the Internet combined with concepts such as the digital and virtual libraries has brought public libraries to the fore in implementing new systems. As libraries begin to determine the direction they will take in the twenty-first century, they must remember that all decisions ultimately are based on the mission statement of the library.

> Certainly technology means new tools, new skills, new job descriptions and more carpal tunnel surgeries. But I'm not sure that we've changed what we do, except that we've become more formal educators. Who's teaching people how to use the new information resources and tools? For many, the answer is "the public library."[5]

Every aspect of library operations has been affected by automation. Although each department of a public library has specific needs, one formula can be used to evaluate potential system implementation.

- Determine the purpose of the library: This should come from the vision and mission statements, and proposed goals and objectives.

- Decide if the purpose of the automation system meets the purpose of the library: What are the objectives of the system?

- Evaluate the details of the system: Can the system requirements be met? Consult with several vendors. Look at the systems in use in other public libraries.

- Draw your conclusions. Select a new system.

- Evaluate: Once the system is implemented, do an analysis to determine if it truly is meeting the needs of the library—reevaluate as needs change.

The Public Catalog

The purpose of automating systems is to make traditional operations more effective. To the patron, perhaps the most noticeable change in libraries has been in the public catalog. What was once universally the card catalog is now most frequently found in an online version. The OPAC (online public access catalog) has been developed as a means to automate and integrate patron access to the library's information database and the circulation system. The "Circulation Flow Chart" (figure 8.1) illustrates the basic functioning of an automated circulation system. The differences in OPACs derive from the user interface employed. Many public libraries are using graphical user interfaces (GUIs) and mounting their systems on World Wide Web servers. It is important to

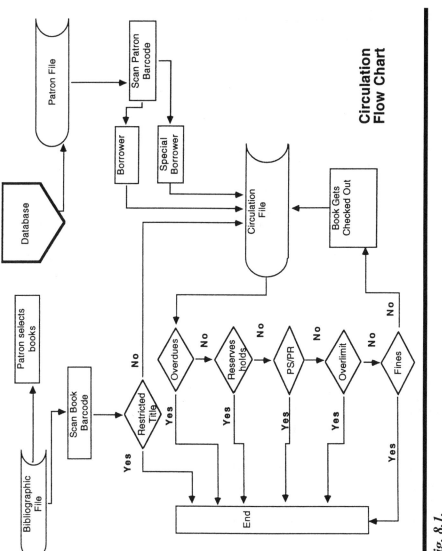

**Circulation
Flow Chart**

Fig. 8.1.

be aware of problems in human interactions with computers when selecting such a system. Vendors will be able to explain their specific interfaces and should be able to provide a list of other libraries using them. Other considerations are primarily related to compatibility. If the library is part of a consortium, should the OPACs be uniform? Does the new system make use of existing equipment?

The Cataloging Department

Technology has invaded the cataloging department. The task of original hand-cataloging of every item in the library was forever changed with the establishment of OCLC and the MARC record in the 1960s. The use of authority files in the OCLC Online Union Catalog and the uniformity of information fields in the MARC record have allowed catalogers to use copy cataloging techniques. Cataloging skills can be better used when more complicated items have to be entered into the library's system. Catalogers can use online tools in their work. The Catalogers Toolbox is one such site (URL). Rather than having shelves full of reference works, virtually everything the cataloger needs is available at his or her workstation, either from web sites or in answer to questions posed to listservs. Jobbers and publishers also provide a wide variety of catalog files. This broad availability of cataloging resources has made this department a prime target for outsourcing—hiring outside professionals to do the cataloging of the library rather than maintaining in-house staff. This decision can be a cost-cutting venture, or it can sacrifice the quality of the cataloging. Each library has to look at its own situation before making determination about outsourcing.

> The trend toward outsourcing library services has even spread to public libraries. A classified advertisement in *Library Hotline*, June 17, 1996, p. 10, indicates that the Public Library of Charlotte & Mecklenburg County, North Carolina, was looking for a database manager who would manage the outsourcing contract and database that would be the result of outsourcing their Technical Services Department.

Hawaii State Librarian Bart Kane told the library community in May 1996 that "the organization that can shave delivery and turnaround time, provide better quality, and tailor its products and services to a customer's precise needs is an organization that will succeed in the 21st century." He made this statement when discussing the five year contract that the Hawaii State Library has signed with Baker & Taylor for choosing the books to be cataloged, labeled, and delivered to the 49 public libraries in Hawaii. "Under the new agreement, Baker & Taylor will provide new books in ten days, compared to the 47 it takes the Hawaii State Library under previous ordering and processing arrangements. Customer service has driven the entire re-engineering process for Hawaii this past year. In the public library world, without customer service and without lower cost, half of the public libraries in the United States will be out of business in ten years," Kane declared. "Staff should be on the floor 90 percent of the time, not the 40 to 50 percent average in American libraries," in Kane's view.[6]

The Acquisitions Department

The effect of technology on acquisitions and collection development (CD) has been rapid and profound. Libraries no longer have to own everything. What they do have to provide is the access to the information that their patrons need.

I do not mean to imply that our mission has changed; we still are responsible for surveying the universe of information resources, now in both print and electronic form, and selecting, organizing, and preserving those resources that constitute the record of knowledge.[7]

Library consortiums (often consisting of academic, special, school, and public libraries) may affect collection development policies. Advanced telecommunications and the Internet allow for easy communication with and access to the consortium collections.

Interlibrary Loan (ILL) departments, while possibly operating independently of acquisitions, are being used to increase access to information. Delivery systems make it possible to allow digital transfer from one library to another and from the library to the patron.

OPACs aid the acquisition department in checking what the library owns and the circulation records for many items. Some have the capability of reporting meaningful statistics that would be helpful in the development of CD policies. For example, since collection development consists not only of selection, but also of weeding, a quick look at the circulation history of a particular item can give the CD office the information needed to make that weeding decision. Acquisitions personnel must stay current with changing formats for information delivery and work closely with systems administrators in an effort to make optimum use of emerging technologies.

The Serials Department

Access to remote databases and to electronic journals has changed the way serials are handled in public libraries. There are tools online specifically designed for serials acquisitions and many expanded databases with full text and images. ILL departments open avenues for access to many serials not housed in the library. OCLC provides the database CONSER, which contains the records of more than 500,000 serials.

The Preservation Department

As mentioned previously, technology has had some negative effects on preservation. When technology is used with commercial objectives in mind, there is a tendency to overlook potential side effects. Cheaper paper made books more accessible but also caused their earlier deterioration. As with most cycles, however, the downside of the brittle book crisis has allowed for development of different technologies, such as the deacidification process developed by William J. Barrow of the Virginia State Library. His process is used in several forms in programs aimed at saving books. Additional beneficial technologies deriving from the preservation crisis include digitization and microfilming of records.

While the books may be disintegrating, the intellectual content will be preserved.

Other technologies affecting preservation issues include the development of highly sensitive hygrometers that measure relative humidity; the measurements enable technicians to provide the optimum environment for libraries. Highly sensitive light meters and new techniques in light control strike a balance between what is best for the book and what is best for the patron searching the stacks. Computerized heating and air conditioning systems, often manufactured with alarm systems, maintain the environment and keep minor crises from becoming devastating to the collection. There are book repair manuals, as well as preservation listservs and professional groups accessible online to assist this crucial department.

Programs

Traditional public library programming brings to mind summer reading programs, children's story times, and book groups for adults. Technology has not made these programs obsolete, but it has augmented them and created avenues for new programs. Many libraries have instituted programs aimed at computer instruction for young and old alike. Children's story times are being invigorated with multimedia presentations. Patrons with special needs are receiving special programs (see chapter 10 "Technology and Services for the Special Population").

Office Automation

An area frequently overlooked in a discussion of technology is the effect it has had on office and administrative procedures. Word processing and desktop publishing decrease the time necessary for completing correspondence and writing policies and procedures. Computerized accounting software makes budgeting more efficient. Fax machines and networkable copiers make transmission and duplication faster. E-mail accounts and listservs benefit both professional and paraprofessional staff members who can communicate quickly with colleagues around the world. Sites of library-related listservs and discussion groups can be found on the World Wide Web.

Information Retrieval

Technology has influenced the way in which librarians and patrons interact when searching for and retrieving information. Before online searching became available, the relationship was very straightforward. The patron made a request and then the librarian performed the search and presented the findings to the patron. Using online databases allows the patron to perform his or her own searches, often with the assistance of a librarian. The relationship of the librarian to the patron is more instructional. Reference departments provide a wide variety of databases in the forms of CD-ROMs, networked CD-ROMs, online catalogs, and Internet accessible online databases. As with traditional reference tools, librarians must assist the patron in determining the need (in a reference interview); represent the need in a searchable form; match the need to the database; and have a way to display the results. E-mail has also affected reference service as many public libraries now accept reference questions in person, over the phone, and by e-mail. Often questions that are difficult to answer are posted to listservs such as Libref-L or PubLib in the hope that another librarian will have completed a search on the subject and will be able to help the patron.

Patron Services

In addition to changing traditional patron services, technology has created new opportunities to serve patrons. The use of local area networks (LANs) in public libraries not only connects patrons to OPACs and databases and library branches to each other, but they also allow for the installation of computer terminals capable of running local software programs. From the terminals, patrons have the ability to use word-processing programs and résumé makers, along with other popular packages.

> When the Liverpool (New York) Public Library was offered free computer training from the Liverpool Central School District way back in 1980, library director Fay Golden suspected that computing might be a passing fad, as she will tell you with a laugh. Fortunately for her and the library,

she didn't rely on those suspicions. Instead she sent assistant directors Jean Armour Polly and Peggy Fulton for the training. Her foresight in doing so, combined with the initiative of those two computer neophytes, set Liverpool Public Library on a path that has earned it the reputation of being on the cutting edge of library computer service to patrons. Along the way, the library has defined for itself a new and obviously needed role in the community by offering computer access, training, and information services to the public. And it has discovered in its computer users a group of staunch and powerful supporters.[8]

Allowing patrons to use software has created difficult issues for librarians. Are these services "value added," and can fees be charged for computer usage? Do librarians have to be trained in the use of these programs, and will they be relied on to teach the patrons? If the library assumes the cost, which line in the budget do these expenses come from? Again, an evaluation of library services must follow, with each library reviewing its mission statement and patron base. Large urban libraries may find that their patrons have a much greater need for technology hardware and software than their suburban counterparts, whose patrons often have home computers. The words of the director of the Detroit Public Library, stated in 1973, hold true today:

The welfare of the public library is inextricably interwoven with the destiny of the city, the financial dilemma of libraries being one manifestation of characteristic urban ills. Although we are a predominantly urban nation, there is widespread indifference or resignation to the desperate plight of cities. . . . It seems increasingly evident that we can no longer depend solely on the traditional cornerstone of public library service to adults—reference work, reading guidance, and programming—to stimulate sufficient interest and satisfy a broad enough range of needs.[9]

Internet Access

The ethical issues revolving around needs and access are nowhere more debated than in public libraries' deciding whether to provide Internet access. It is clear that the Internet has established itself firmly in American culture and operates without constraints, with the exception of needing a server, a computer, and an Internet browser. Anyone can access information on the Internet. The information obtained is not necessarily reliable or within copyright laws, but it is accessible. Public libraries have a responsibility to provide equal access to information (ALA Code of Ethics). President Bill Clinton has called on libraries to be part of the National Information Infrastructure. Does this mean that public libraries are mandated to provide free unlimited Internet access to their patrons? Perhaps that can be argued in theory, but the reality of the situation makes it much more complex. There are many people who see the Internet as a wilderness, as unnavigable as the "Wild West," and librarians as the trailblazers. But if these people do not sit on library boards and city councils, where will the funding come from? Censorship also becomes an issue when access is granted. Does the library allow patrons to go anywhere on the web without restrictions? How will this be viewed when people begin to access pornography?

The positive influences of the Internet include increased access to information and increasingly creative formats for presenting the information. As more and more patrons ask for Internet access, libraries are developing new and creative ways to provide the services for their user communities. Here are four projects from libraries around the country.

Fee-Based Internet Service Profitable at Cedar Rapids

The Cedar Rapids Public Library (CRPL) has been providing individual access to all Internet services through its Personal Internet Connection program since December 1993. This fee-based program has been a revenue generator for the library for over two years. The income supports the service and will make technology enhancements possible, according to Bryan Davis, assistant director. The library has 275 users signed up for its program, which operates through 21 phone lines. Of the 275 users, 105 have signed up for the new PPP access. "We are currently generating about $5,000 to $6,000 per month in revenues," said Davis. "However, the picture is changing as more dial-up Internet providers are entering the market locally. Depending on how they fare, our earnings may grow or suffer as customers look for the best deals." CRPL was able to offer the services with no upgrades to its equipment beyond those need for dial-up access, although it is looking to add a Web server in the near future. "Many people think this is a great service," said Davis. "We see messages from people complimenting us on the service. I believe that some of our users sign up and stay with us because they see it as helping the library." Davis warned that offering this kind of service is not for the technologically faint-hearted. "However, it is getting much easier to do than when we first began," he said. "Packages are now available that have the software and hardware rolled into one. . . . A library may also find a commercial provider that would work with it in providing this kind of service with the library getting some of the income. There are many creative ways libraries could get into this business, and I encourage those who are interested in this kind of service to investigate the possibilities in their areas."

For more information on the Cedar Rapids Public Library's fee-based Internet access, contact Bryan Davis at davis@crpl.cedar-rapids.lib.ia.us or at 319-398-5145, ext. 223.

Washoe County Library Opens Its "Internet Branch"

Public library World Wide Web sites are not a new idea, but the Washoe County Library in Reno, Nevada, had a new idea: It designed and promoted its new Web site as a "branch library on the Internet." The site has two goals, according to John Kupersmith, Internet services librarian. The first is to provide information about the Washoe County Library, its branch hours, locations, programs, and policies. The second is to provide links to other Internet resources.

Designed along the lines of a traditional library branch, the Washoe Web site offers information about the library system. It has a catalog area, a reference desk, and book stacks, as well as rooms for news and periodicals, government documents, maps, and children's materials. Users can click on any of the options with a Netscape browser and connect to information on such things as the Friends of the Washoe County Library, government resources, currency rates, and the current Reno City Council agenda. "I don't try to gather every resource on the Net," said Kupersmith, "but enough to provide a useful starting point and a user-friendly experience." The Net resources Washoe offers include sources that mirror the traditional reference works, such as Bartlett's and the Thomas Register, as well as those that represent unique Internet capabilities, such as CNN Interactive and Carlos' Coloring Book. Each week the library offers a "featured link" to demonstrate the types of things available. The Washoe Internet Branch also provides a gateway to other libraries and a way for users to pose questions and make suggestions. In the first 12 days of operation, the Internet Branch had 124 accesses. Users offered comments like these: "This Internet branch is the best thing going. Thank you for providing such wonderful services to our community." "Congratulations to whoever thought of taking the library onto the Web." The service is provided through the facilities of Powernet, a Reno-based Internet access company.

For more information, contact John Kupersmith at jkup@washoe.lib.nv.us or 702-785-4742. To access the Washoe County Library Internet Branch, visit http://www.washoe.lib.nv.us.

Equal Access for Children

Using a separate workstation and a Netscape browser, the Rolling Meadows Library in Rolling Meadows, Illinois, began offering Internet access and formal training to youth last September. Each young person going through the one-hour training class gets hands-on instruction on how to navigate the Net. Students in grades 5 through 8 learn how to locate the information they need as well as tips on Internet "safety." "We've had no complaints about Internet access for kids," said Lucia M. Khipple, assistant director, youth services. "I've seen kids show parents how to use it." Twelve youngsters took the training class in the fall, and more were expected to register in the winter. Interest picked up when a local junior high school teacher offered extra credit for those who attended the class. The teaching workstation is located near the reference desk, and a copy of the library's Internet policy is posted on all of its terminals. "Most of our kids seem to be interested in computer gaming tips," said Khipple.

For more information on the Rolling Meadows Library's Internet for Kids project, contact Lucia M. Khipple at lkhipple@nslsilus.org or 708-259-6050.

Multiple Internet Services

The State Library of Ohio is running an Internet project with several components. The library has developed a home page with sources of interest to state government and public libraries, an Internet Access program that sells accounts to public libraries and state agencies for $85 per year, and a home page service for its participants. The Internet accounts offer full functionality including ftp, electronic mail, telnet capability, and access to Usenet news groups. Each participant's annual fee buys up to 5 megabytes of storage as well as preferential long-distance rates through Litel Communications International. The State Library of Ohio's home page is called WINSLO and contains links to information about Ohio and its state government, the HANNAH Online full-text database of Ohio legislation, federal and international government info, and other Internet resources. Access climbed from about 5,000 users initially to over 30,000 per month in the first six months of operation, according to Georgiana Van Syckle, networking services consultant.

For more information about Internet access at the State Library of Ohio, contact Georgiana Van Syckle at gvansyck@ winslo.ohio.gov or access WINSLO at http://winslo.ohio.gov.[10]

(See also chapters 9 and 12 for further Internet information.)

Staff Training and Reeducation

Changes in technology always require the upgrading of skills, but changes in library operations have had more far-reaching ramifications. Schools of library science have made curriculum changes—adding more technical courses. The traditional library background in the liberal arts is often a second choice to a computer science degree. Public libraries are hiring systems administrators to manage the automation.

Over the last decade the demand for networks and Internet access has transformed the roles of computing services staff and librarians. While computing grew increasingly more decentralized and libraries were busy with automation projects, librarians became more knowledgeable about hardware, network configurations, software applications, and troubleshooting. Having focused primarily on information access and organization, librarians became the champions of Internet access in many organizations and viewed the Internet as the vehicle for expanding access to information beyond the library's walls. The lines between computing professionals, often called information technologists, and librarians continue to blur. The specialties of systems librarian and electronic resources librarian are examples of an increasing emphasis on technology and networking in the library environment. Although information technologists and librarians have different academic preparation and credentials, they have overlapping functions in meeting users' needs. With lean budgets and growing needs in all organizations, the two groups share expertise and collaborate on joint projects.[11]

Discussion Questions

1. As technology continues to change, what archival role will libraries serve? Does information have to be preserved in the form in which it was created, or can it be updated? If it is preserved, how can libraries maintain the equipment needed to display it (e.g., 5-1/4" diskettes)? If it is updated, how does a library select what and how that is to be done?
2. Society is becoming more and more dependent on Internet resources. Is the provision of these resources the responsibility of libraries, government agencies, or individuals? Why?
3. Copyright issues have become complicated with the advent of on-line databases, the Internet, and digitalization of both images and words. How should librarians confront these issues? Are the ALA codes of ethics comprehensive enough?
4. Technical training has become important in libraries. When a library director is planning for future technology changes or additions, should he or she search for staff with strict technology backgrounds or would a person with a library background who shows the ability to learn technology be preferred? What would be the benefits of either selection? What would be the cost to the library for retraining from technology to library science vs. library science to technology?
5. Are library education programs currently meeting the need for training in information and technology science? What types of graduate level courses should be offered to library science students? How is the profession encouraging additional education for those already in the field?

Additional Readings

Abrams, Stanley E. "Developing Partnerships Through Public Library Automation." *Illinois Libraries* 74, no. 1 (January 1992): 22–24.

Barnes, Susan J. "The Electronic Library and Public Services." *Library Hi Tech* 12, no. 3 (1994): 44–62.

Batt, Chris. "The Cutting Edge: Buddy, Can You Spare £4,750,000?" *Public Library Journal* 9 (November/December 1994): 167–169.

————. "The Cutting Edge: The Last Migration." *Public Library Journal* 10 (November/December 1995): 159–161.

————. *Information Technology in Public Libraries*. 5th ed. United Kingdom: Library Association, 1994.

Berda, Kathleen. "Lake County Public Library Keeps in Step with Technology." *Indiana Libraries* 14, no. 2 (1995): 33–35.

Bodle, Philisann. "The Role of Automation in the Future of Public Library Service." *Public Libraries* 35, no. 1 (January/February 1996): 27–28.

Canepi, Kitti. "Information Access Through Electronic Databases for Rural Public Libraries." Master's thesis, University of Arizona, 1995. MAI, vol. 34-04, 1323–1369.

————. "Center for Technology Staff Trade Places." *Library Journal* 121, no. 17 (October 15, 1996): 12–13.

Clark, David R. *Pikes Peak Library District's MAGGnet*. Chicago: American Library Association, 1995.

Commings, Karen. "Skokie Public Library Expands Electronic Resources." *Computers in Libraries* 16 (February 1996): 24–25.

Crawford, W., and M. Gorman. *Future Libraries: Dreams, Madness & Reality*. Chicago: American Library Association, 1995.

DiMattia, Susan Smith. "Largest PL Online System Launched." *Library Journal* 120, no. 20 (December 1995): 19.

Drake, Karen, and Rene Jordan. "Sidebar 5: UNICORN in the Public Library." *Library Hi Tech* 12, no. 4 (1994): 43.

Fender, Kimber L. "Patron Initiated Interlibrary Loan Through FirstSearch: The Experience of the Public Library of Cincinnati and Hamilton County." *Journal of Interlibrary Loan, Document Delivery and Information Supply* 6, no. 1 (1995): 45–48.

Files, Kathy. "D.O.A. (Dysfunctional Orders in Acquisitions)." *Library Mosaics* 6 (March/April 1995): 11.

Gee, Pam. "Automation in the Warren County–Vicksburg Public Library." *Mississippi Libraries* 59 (Spring 1995): 6–7.

Graham, Bob. "Librarian Hopes Song Index Evens the Score for Musicians." *American Libraries* 27, no. 9 (October 1996): 55–56.

Grosch, A. *Library Information Technology and Networks*. New York: Marcel Dekker, 1995.

Gunter, Judith B. "Online Networking in Jefferson County, Washington." *Rural Libraries* 15, no. 1 (1995): 3–9.

Harris, Richard John. "The Effect of an Integrated Library Computer System on Job Characteristics in Public Libraries." Ph.D. diss., Old Dominion University, 1996. DAI, vol. 57-05A, 1893.

Hole, Carol Combs, and Russ Topping. "Parnassus on the Interstate: The Information Highway Hits the Road; An Administrative Perspective." *Public Libraries* 34, no.5 (September/October 1995): 272.

Jackson, Mary E. "The Use of Technology in Public Libraries: A Brief Survey." *Public Library Quarterly* 14, no. 2–3 (1994): 39–47.

Jaquay, Sarah. "Avoiding Obsolescence." *Public Libraries* 35, no. 1 (January/February 1996): 29–30.

Kieran, Steven. "A Model Library for Technology: Updating the Old in Order to Respond to the New." *Public Library Quarterly* 14, no. 2–3 (1994): 29–38.

Lynch, Mary Jo. "How Wired Are We? New Data on Library Technology." *College and Research Libraries News*, no. 2 (February 1996): 97–100.

Maryland Public Libraries. 1994. Available: http://sailor.lib.md.us Sailor Web Site.

Mayer, Chris Marie. "Librarians and the Information Superhighway: A Multimedia Presentation." Master's thesis, San Jose State University, 1994. MAI, vol. 33–05, 1368–1384.

McCaffrey, Kate. "Technology Helper." *School Library Journal* 42, no. 1 (January 1996): 44.

Moore, Matthew S. "Results of a Query Concerning Florida Librarians' Use of Telecommunications." *Florida Libraries* 38 (March 1995): 44–45.

Neff, Paul. "Virtual Librarianship: Expanding Adult Services with the World Wide Web." *RQ* 35 (Winter 1995): 169–172.

Nelson, N. *Technology for the '90s*. Westport, Conn.: Meckler Corp., 1989.

Newell, Bruce. "Reference Point: Update." *PNLA Quarterly* 59 (Winter/Spring 1995): 24–25.

Olivares, Olivia. "Public Libraries and Homeless Problem Patrons in the Wake of *Kreimer* v. *Morristown*: Writing Patron Behavior Codes That Pass Constitutional Muster." Master's thesis, University of Arizona, 1995. MAI, vol. 34–04, 1323–1393.

Schuyler, Michael. "Libraries and Schools—The Technology of Coopera-tion; Plus, Whose Responsibility Is the Data?" *Computers in Libraries* 16 (January 1996): 43–45.

———. "Many Systems Make Up the Library Organism." *Computers in Li-braries* 16 (February 1996): 44–46.

———. "Seattle Public Library Establishes Center for Technology." *PNLA Quarterly* 59 (Summer 1995): 14.

Shera, Jessa. *Foundations of the Public Library*. Hamden, Conn.: Shoe String Press, 1949.

St. Lifer, Evan, and Michael Rogers. "PLs Play Big Role in High-Speed Local Online Service." *Library Journal* 121, no. 18 (October 1, 1996): 14.

Tope, Diana Ray. "A Little Bit of a Miracle." *Georgia Librarian* 31 (Fall 1994): 66–68.

Tucker, David C. "DeKalb County Public Library: The Use of Lottery Funds for Technology." *Georgia Librarian* 31 (Fall 1994): 69–70.

Walker, Robert, and Judy Fuller. "Technology and Training: Longview Public Library." *Alki* 10 (July 1994): 22–24.

Waters, Richard Lee. "A Global View of Technology: Implications for Public Libraries." *Public Library Quarterly* 14, no. 2–3 (1994): 49–59.

Williams, Lisa Powell. "Info 'Nots' vs. Info 'Nuts': Pondering How to Serve Both." *Library Mosaics* 6 (November/December 1995): 21.

———. "Zombie Mommy; or Further Adventures Along the Techno Trail (Technical Support Wish List for Electronic Products)." *Library Mosaics* 7 (September/October 1996): 25.

Wilson, William James. "Service Implications of 'Staying the Course.' "*Public Library Quarterly* 14, no. 2–3 (1994): 23–27.

Zemskov, Andrei I. "Access Versus Holdings: CD or Paper?" *IATUL Pro-ceedings* 4 (1995): 114–121.

Notes

1. *The American Heritage College Dictionary*, 3d ed. (Boston: Houghton Mifflin, 1993), 1393.
2. "Info-Tech Guide: Johannes Gutenberg & the Printing Press," Available: http://www.webcom.com /pcj/it-nf/itn-104.html (Accessed 1997).

3.   John N. DePew, *A Library, Media, and Archival Preservation Handbook* (Santa Barbara, Calif.: ABC-CLIO, 1991), 157.

4.   Bohdan S. Wynar, *Introduction to Cataloging and Classification*, 8th ed, ed. by Arlene G. Taylor (Englewood, Colo.: Libraries Unlimited, 1992), 20.

5.   Terry Dawson, director of the Appleton Public Library, Appleton, Wisconsin, e-mail received March 7, 1997.

6.   Betty Eddison and Susanne Bjorner, "Our Profession Is Changing: Whether We Like It or Not," *Online* 21, no. 1 (January/February 1997): 72.

7.   Joseph J. Branin, "Fighting Back Once Again: From Collection Management to Knowledge Management," in *Collection Management and Development Issues*, ed. Peggy Johnson and Bonnie MacEwan (Chicago: American Library Association, 1994), xiv.

8.   Karen S. Cullings, "The Public Library As Cornerstone of the Community," *Computers in Libraries* 16, no. 1 (January 1996): 30.

9.   "Public Library Community Information Activities." Available: http://www.si.umich.edu/Community/taospaper.html (Accessed April 8, 1998).

10.   Karen Commings, "Four Creative Internet Projects (Public Libraries Offer Access to Internet and World Wide Web)," *Computers in Libraries* 16, no. 3 (March 1996): 20.

11.   Laverna Saunders, "Changing Technology Transforms Library Roles (Internet Librarian)," *Computers in Libraries* 16, no. 5 (May 1996): 49.

Permission

9 THE TECHNOLOGY: WILL THE END JUSTIFY THE MEANS?

 *Lisa Crisman*

In the rush to adopt new and constantly changing technologies, public libraries and librarians will need to address a number of concerns. Careful review and evaluation of current and newly introduced electronic practices based on the library's mission and policies should be foremost in the decision-making process. The library's place within the community may be directly affected. Another factor to consider is the cost of electronic databases, including hardware and software. The storage and archival capabilities of these new technologies must be studied and considered before deleting current print sources. Most important, the equity of access for all people must remain in the forefront of the decision process when changing current library collection-and-distribution practices.

Acceptance of New Roles

"Planning for the implementation of technology will continue to be a challenge in places where people have really not thought much about the library and its community role."[1] The introduction of new technologies increases the roles the library plays. By adapting a new catalog, the library accepts the challenge of educating its patrons on the use of the catalog. Online databases and Internet access may be combined with the library's OPAC or they may be on separate terminals used for other activities, such as word processing or electronic mail. The library is faced with the need to adapt new policies to address the initiation of these new ideas. "Crucial to the future of small town America and its information services is the articulation of specific roles that are determined at the local level."[2] Many librarians and library planners may face communities that do not see the need for increased funding for computers and electronic information. It is the responsibility of the library to present the new technologies in a manner that is appealing and understandable to its patrons. Access to electronic information from home computers may remove the vision of the library as necessary to support a town's information needs.

"Technology may indeed be inevitable, but it is not neutral; it is demanding and creates an insatiable desire for more."[3] Libraries will continually have to rethink their position on the adoption of emerging technologies. "The dominant ethic of librarianship is service. Libraries exist to serve the individual, community, and society as a whole. . . . The question 'how will this change improve the service that this library gives?' is an analytical tool of great effectiveness."[4] This idea places great importance on the value of technology and cautions librarians and planners not to adopt new electronic resources for their novelty alone. The authors, Walt Crawford and Michael Gorman, encourage the combination of current resources with those most appropriate to the mission of the particular library. "The plain fact is that each new means of communication enhances and supplements the strengths of all previous means."[5] Technology is not a replacement for original sources and all reference works; it is a complement to those sources. It should be viewed in this context.

The Internet

The Internet has become one of the most pervasive influences affecting decisions and development of libraries today. Accuracy and relevance of information on the Internet and the inability to locate the correct information in a timely manner continue to be some of the main concerns for librarians and patrons alike. An interesting experiment was published in the April 1997 *PC Novice*. The author, Joel Strauch, compared the search results between his online access to the World Wide Web and his success in his local public library. He developed a list of questions, searched online and in the library, and tallied the results. This test uncovered "some of the infamous snags of the Web, such as misleading site names, bogus links among pages, and temperamental connections."[6] In the end, the public library actually averaged a shorter retrieval time for answers, if one did not factor in the drive to the library and parking. "Of course, the Web won't replace the library anytime soon, but as it becomes faster, more organized, and more accurate, it will solidify its reputation as an alternate resource for quick information."[7] Truly the idea of the Internet as an "alternate resource" is more realistic than the common assertion that the World Wide Web will replace the library as we know it. Biophysicist Richard Cone states, "I like to get out of my own lab and go to a public place and meet other people, surrounded by all those lovely books. Walking through the stacks or going through journals, I always seem to run across something I'm interested in, but wasn't looking for."[8] (See also chapters 8 and 12.)

Electronic Formats

An additional concern with the adoption of new electronic technologies is the idea of print sources versus electronic sources and the intrinsic differences in their storage, access, and use. "The store of knowledge in a library is the raw material for further progress as well as our assurance that progress to date has been reliable, that it can be depended upon."[9] The various formats for electronic storage are constantly changing. Word-processing programs and online search streams are written in different languages. Libraries will need to look closely at the format and the presentation to determine which is the most accessible by their patrons. "There are still discrepancies in standards and protocols, and the finite storage lifetimes of digital media continue to cause concern."[10]

Libraries will need to define their role as an archive in the community. "Libraries will consciously choose to archive in print because the longevity of current electronic formats precludes their use for archival functions. Electronic formats today are not sufficiently durable to serve as the medium for permanently preserved data."[11] For public libraries this concern addresses their role as a provider of information to the community. Public documents are one of the many parts of the library's collection that patrons expect. A combination of print and electronic sources best serves the largest number of patrons. "The need to serve a local constituency first in a timely manner will not change" and "collection development librarians will always be challenged to access and purchase, when needed, fitting sources for the primary users."[12]

In the February 1992 issue of *Johns Hopkins Magazine*, Aaron Levin's article, "The Log-On Library," addresses the issues of electronic storage:

> Archiving everything in the vast memory of computers sounds attractive, but it's not permanent. Not only does hardware change, but computer disks or tapes need to be copied frequently. A compact disk, often hailed as a mass storage medium, will probably last only eight to ten years, if that. Hard disks need not even deteriorate to give you trouble. And floppy disks—well, who knows? One business magazine has suggested that floppies be copied and replaced every three months. Public libraries will need to weigh the costs in time and money to complete this type of data storage. When viewed as an archive for the community's history, electronic storage does not necessarily represent the most practical alternative.[13]

Commercial industry remains the driving force behind new computer technologies. "CD-ROM products are being produced and marketed to maintain the overall profits of producers—not to maximize access."[14] The pervasive influence of the commercialization of information frames decisions that librarians will make when reviewing new technologies in the library and their influence on the general public. Again, the mission, and in turn, the policies of the library should govern collection and acquisitions. "In our moves toward electronic sources, are we forsaking a commitment to basic (book) literacy? How fundamental is this older kind of literacy to the new literacies—cultural, media, information? It is not the obvious effects of information technology that worry me, but rather the power of the machine to set the limits of what is valuable, informative, socially worthwhile, and logical."[15]

Need for User-Friendly Systems

In addition to the storage capabilities of the system, the computer system itself must be "user-friendly." "There are over 50 'significantly different OPAC systems in libraries' with little progress toward standardization."[16] Many patrons are still not comfortable with the new developments even as their introduction has increased. "The primary component is the dichotomy of sophisticated searching features vs. the user-friendliness of the system."[17] It will be many years before the entire library population will be familiar with the online catalog. Librarians at all levels will need to be aware of the inexperience of some users and be willing to instruct them in the new technologies. "How can we balance the needs of the few (librarians and sophisticated researchers) with the needs of the many (the typical patron who uses the library only intermittently)?"[18] OPAC designers are currently studying a variety of users and interfaces, but the technology has a long way to go to appeal to the majority of public library patrons. "What about the novice, low-use, less intelligent, or computer-illiterate patrons? Librarians often discover these people using inappropriate databases or caught hopelessly in some maze-like software loop. . . . As more features are added, the less friendly the system becomes for them."[19]

At this time, the software designers are designing for experienced users. This leaves the majority of patrons on the outside of the information loop. "We must also be conscious that the low-use or medium-use patrons may be much less vocal about their needs than the small percentage of high-profile, heavy-use patrons. . . . Despite our best intentions, designers and librarians are not, and can never, represent typical users."[20] This presents a definite challenge to librarians to review carefully new products and software with the patron in mind. An open dialogue should be established between librarians and designers to document and enhance current usage and plan for adaptations and changes in the future. In an article in the April 1994 issue of *Database*, Karen A. Becker addresses the idea of "creeping featurism" and gives the following suggestions to establish such a dialogue:

1. Target: Develop different systems targeted to different types or levels of patrons.

2. Modularize: When complex search options need to be added to an existing system, provide these options in a second, hidden tier of menus.

3. Bypass: Provide a command mode search option where complicated searches can be done directly, without having to go through numerous menus and screen displays.

4. Design: Librarians should support vendors and purchase products that follow these rules for good software design.

   a. Keep knowledge in the world; don't require it to be in the head. In other words, provide whatever guidance and information is needed within the system; don't require users to learn (and retain that learning) in order to use the system.

   b. Make functions visible to users.

   c. Be consistent between systems. Standardize!

   d. Be clear. Watch language, error messages, and acronyms.

   e. Prevent searchers from making dangerous or disastrous errors. Provide "recover" and "undo" functions.

   f. De-emphasize dependence on keyboards and move to graphical user interfaces.

   g. Invite exploration and experimentation.

   h. Simplify the structure of tasks.[21]

A real commitment by librarians is required to establish this type of relationship with the producers as well as the library patrons who use the resources.

Long-Range Costs

Investments in technology and telecommunications are not a one-time cost. They are ongoing, and that is a financial issue that is often unfamiliar to governing authorities. While most local governments understand the need to buy a computer, they have not yet come to terms with the continual need to purchase newer, faster computers so that new information software can work.[22] For many public libraries, cost is one of the most important factors in the decision to adapt new technologies and electronic resources to the collection. Fay Zipkowitz, associate professor, Graduate School of Library and Information Studies, University of Rhode Island, teaches "the importance of good stewardship of public funds."[23] She sees the need for a balance between what the libraries, librarians, and the public need and what is available with the resources at hand. When confronted with the idea that libraries are "stuck in the fifties," she replies, "their problem is not that they're stuck in the fifties, but that their budgets probably are. Where will they get the equipment? Who will pay their phone charges? What will they have to give up?"[24] These are just some of the challenges inherent in the cost of new technologies in libraries. "Many, perhaps most, of the nation's public libraries, though, can only dream of a digital future. The tremendous pressure on municipal and county budgets, which on average provide 79% of a community library's funds, makes it difficult for many of them to simply stay open. Washington contributes only [$.57] per citizen for library spending, and this year, the Commerce Dept.'s National Telecommunications & Information Administration grants, used by several libraries to fund technology projects, have been slashed from $64 million to $34 million."[25]

Libraries are increasingly faced with the decision of acquiring the print or the electronic version of certain resources. " 'The bottom line is that we will be spending more of our budget for access to information and less on ownership of information,' VPI librarian Paul M. Gherman wrote. 'This change strikes at the basic economic model of libraries, which traditionally have bought information once and shared it many times with their users.' "[26] Additional unsolved problems accompanying the new technology are:

- What about copyright issues?

- Who pays for the downloaded text from an online journal? Is the payment part of the acquisitions budget, part of the cost of acquiring materials for our clientele, or should the client pay? How much? And exactly what are we paying for online time, copyright, royalties?

- Does it ultimately mean that more, rather than less, paper will be consumed when everyone can print off a personal copy? At present, people aren't willing and don't have the time to read text on the screen. That's why we have printers on our OPAC terminals and CD-ROM workstations.

■ What becomes of the public service librarian in this environment?[27]

Access

Public service is the foundation of public libraries. What will happen to those thousands of individuals who have no access to the information highway and electronic resources if the technology itself makes the library obsolete? "The American public library system is a unique and uniquely effective part of society, representing a public sector service and a safety net that actually work. . . . Libraries should not be discussing access *vs.* collection, but determining the correct balance of access and collection; . . . no library is merely a place for obtaining up-to-the-minute facts."[28]

According to James H. Billington, Librarian of Congress, "the public library system in this country is unique among nations. Universal accessibility and openness to knowledge at the community level have been built in."[29] Public libraries need to remember their underlying principles, including the universal access to information for all people, which in turn can lead to the acquisition of knowledge. The view of technology experts that online access will undermine the importance of libraries is a threat to this principle and to the thousands of people who will never have computer access in their homes. "Open access is threatened by the fact that this flood of information has the unintended but inexorable effect of dividing us into information haves and have-nots. This is a real and increasing threat not because anyone is trying to monopolize access to information but simply because the costs and constraints faced by open, public institutions are such that more and more people will have to buy highly priced equipment and private services to get information."[30]

"A 1993 Census Bureau report found that nearly sixty-two percent of all families with incomes of seventy-five thousand dollars or more owned personal computers. Unsurprisingly, the percentage dropped with income, to just under seven percent for those with an annual income below ten thousand dollars. The census figures on minorities are equally striking: Twice as many whites as either blacks or Latinos have home computers."[31] When making decisions on the implementation of new technologies, true access for all will continue to be the most important issue facing public libraries today. "Changing demographics, continuing high levels of illiteracy, and the tremendous disparity in economic conditions all mean that public libraries should become even more relevant and more critically important than they have been during their two-hundred-plus-year history in this country. . . . Equity does not mean equal, and it does not mean that every public library in every community must have the same resources. It does mean, however, that at every entry point to the global information infrastructure (i.e., at every public library), people have the ability to access the entire world of information."[32]

Throughout the history of public libraries, there have been continuous challenges and changes to the various ways information has been accumulated, stored, accessed, and circulated. Technology is the challenge most affecting libraries today. Decisions on format and costs to the library as well as the patron will need to be resolved with strict attention to the mission and policies of the library. Most important, the library will need to structure its implementation of new technologies to meet the requirements of its users, the basis for the library's existence. "The challenge, therefore, for librarians is to insure that technological advances in libraries go hand-in-hand with a renewed commitment to serving people, that the commitment to online searching be matched by a commitment to reader's advisory services, that the dollars invested in systems research and development be matched by the dollars invested in staff development, and that the attention devoted to evaluating the effectiveness and response time of our computers be matched by the attention we devote to communicating with the people who pay the taxes to support our libraries."[33]

Discussion Questions

1. How does the inclusion of technology affect the public library's role in the community?
2. Who determines the limits to the acquisition of new technologies in the public library setting?
3. What role does the Internet play in meeting the information needs of a community?
4. What guidelines are used to determine print resources versus electronic resources?

5. Which reference sources are best stored in print form? Electronic form? Who decides?

6. How will resources be redistributed to cover the additional costs of maintaining an electronic archive within a public library?

7. Do computer interfaces' designs need to reflect the knowledge of the average user?

8. Where do online services fit in the world of the public service library?

9. Do taxpayers in lower-income areas deserve additional funding to provide additional access to the most current electronic resources? Who should provide the additional funds?

10. Can information equity truly be achieved in a culturally and economically diverse community?

Notes

1. Bernard Vavrek, "Rural Libraries and Community Development," *Wilson Library Bulletin* 69, no. 5 (January 1995): 42.

2. Ibid., 44.

3. Ibid.

4. Walt Crawford and Michael Gorman, *Future Libraries: Dreams, Madness, and Reality* (Chicago: American Library Association, 1995), 8.

5. Ibid., 9.

6. Joel Strauch, "The Web vs. the Library: An Information Showdown," *PC Novice* 8, no. 4 (April 1997): 80.

7. Ibid., 82.

8. Aaron Levin, "The Log-On Library," *Johns Hopkins Magazine* 44, no. 1 (February 1992): 12–19.

9. Brian Lang, "Bricks and Bytes: Libraries in Flux," *Daedalus* 125, no. 4 (Fall 1996): 221–234.

10. Ibid., 5.

11. Vicki Anders, Colleen Cook, and Roberta Pitts, "A Glimpse into a Crystal Ball: Academic Libraries in the Year 2000," *Wilson Library Bulletin* 67, no. 2 (October 1992): 37.

12. Ibid.

13. Levin, "Log-On Library," 3.

14. John Buschman, "Asking the Right Questions About Information Technology," *American Libraries* 21, no. 2 (December 1990): 1026, citing Gail

Perskey, "Freedom of Information: The Impact of Technology," *LITA Newsletter* (Spring 1989): 20.

15. Buschman, "Asking the Right Questions," 1029.

16. Ibid., citing Lawson Crowe and Susan Anthes, "The Academic Librarian and Information Technology: Ethical Issues," *College and Research Libraries* (March 1988): 128.

17. Karen A. Becker, "Corralling 'Creeping Featurism': Nurturing a More Human-Centered Technology," *Database* 17, no. 2 (April 1994): 8–9.

18. Ibid.

19. Ibid.

20. Ibid.

21. Ibid.

22. Susan Goldberg Kent, "American Public Libraries: A Long, Transformative Moment," *Daedalus* 125, no. 4 (Fall 1996): 6.

23. Fay Zipkowitz, "Let 'em Eat Megabytes," *Wilson Library Bulletin* 69, no. 7 (March 1995): 26.

24. Ibid.

25. John W. Verity, "Welcome to the Cy-brary," *Business Week* (May 29, 1995): 90–91.

26. "Hard Times for Libraries: The Issues," *CQ Researcher* 2, no. 24 (June 26, 1992): 556.

27. Anders, Cook, and Pitts, "A Glimpse into a Crystal Ball," 39.

28. Crawford and Gorman, *Future Libraries*, 133.

29. James H. Billington, "A Technological Flood Requires Human Navigators," *American Libraries* 27, no. 6 (June/July 1996): 39.

30. Ibid.

31. Sara Mosle, "The Wrong Box: Why Public-School Students Are Falling Through the 'Net," *New Yorker* 71, no. 19 (June 19, 1995): 6–7.

32. Kent, "American Public Libraries," 8.

33. Will Manley, "Facing the Public," *Wilson Library Bulletin* 59, no. 4 (December 1984): 271.

10 TECHNOLOGY AND SERVICES FOR THE SPECIAL POPULATION

 *Melanie Carlson*

The freedom to read and to learn is a fundamental right in our society. For people with physical disabilities, however, reading and using written materials has not always been a freedom they could enjoy. Their disabilities barred them from this fundamental right and limited the personal, educational, and vocational abilities of their lives. In 1829, this changed when Louis Braille, a Frenchman visually impaired since the age of three, invented the braille system of raised-point writing. Since then, those visually impaired, as well as other special-needs people, have taken great strides toward literacy.

Visually Impaired Patrons

History of Services

For the visually impaired in the United States, as well as in France, 1829 was a watershed year. Massachusetts became the first state to pass legislation to train and educate the visually impaired. By the end of the nineteenth century, most states had such laws. In 1879, Congress passed the "Act to Promote the Education of the Blind." In the meantime,

135

braille and different versions of raised writing swept across the country. In 1880, a particular type of braille, Moon, was created for older people who were less sensitive to touch than their younger counterparts. Outside of the special schools, however, reading materials for the visually impaired remained scarce.

Public libraries began to respond to the demand for books in braille. In the late 1800s, several public libraries tried to fill this need but found that once the book was "read" by a patron, there was no further need for it. At the 20th general meeting of the American Library Association (ALA) in 1898, H. M. Utley, librarian for the Detroit Public Library, suggested that perhaps one central library in each state should house and distribute books for visually impaired patrons.[1] The previous year, the Library of Congress had opened a special reading room for the visually impaired and asked patrons to suggest the types of books they preferred. Postal laws were changed in 1904 to allow free mailing of books, as postage costs dug deep into public libraries' budgets. Still, libraries lacked books for the visually impaired.

The ALA continued to discuss the concerns of librarians about inadequate materials for the visually impaired. In 1915, the ALA published *Library Work with the Blind*, the first book for library services for the visually impaired. This book was a guide to book selection, classification, circulation, and shelving of braille books.

After World War I, Congress gave more money to the Veterans Bureau to publish braille books for veterans. In 1924, the ALA's committee on Work with the Blind recommended libraries display an ALA-published list of books printed in type larger than normal—large-print books. The American Foundation for the Blind (AFB) conducted a study of library materials for visually impaired patrons in the United States and Canada and concluded that patrons were not receiving the best or equal service.[2] Based on the study, the ALA and the AFB recommended that the federal government supply the visually impaired with books from an approved list. This suggestion led to the Pratt-Smoot Act of 1931, which authorized the Library of Congress to purchase books in braille for adults. Thus began the Library of Congress's National Library Service for the Blind and Physically Handicapped (NLS). The program was expanded in 1952 to include children, and again in 1966 by Public Law 89-522 to include individuals with physical impairments that prevent the reading of standard print. President Lyndon B. Johnson signed Public Law 89-511, the Library Services and Construction Act (LSCA)

Amendments of 1966, which provided funding to state libraries to strengthen services to those with physical disabilities.

Talking Books

The Pratt-Smoot Act of 1931 was amended in 1932 to include books in record form. During the early 1900s, library services were being developed for people with other disabilities. After World War I, with the return of disabled veterans, this became even more necessary. Even before Congress passed this amendment, books were available on records to be played by talking-book machines. In 1877, Thomas Edison listed "recorded books for blind people" as a potential use of his phonograph, but it was not until 1932 that these machines came into use.[3] That same year, the AFB developed a laboratory for the further development of talking books.

The Talking-Book Service began in October 1934. Talking-book machines at the time included radios, as so few "books" were available. The first titles consisted of the four Gospels, the Declaration of Independence, the Constitution of the United States, Lincoln's Gettysburg Address, Shakespeare's *As You Like It*, and six works of fiction. These first records were heavy, easily broken, and only played for three to five minutes per side. Records had to stand up to the rigors of circulation and mailing, so new materials were constantly being sought. As the years progressed, new technology improved the quality and playing length of the records. The year the talking-book service began, the AFB raised enough money to purchase 1,200 talking machines while Congress provided the talking-book records. By June 1937, the Books for the Adult Blind project had distributed approximately 145 books (16,700 containers of talking books) and 16,200 machines.[4]

With the return of wounded servicemen after World War II, talking-book equipment underwent a major reevaluation, as the program had not changed since it began in 1934. This assessment resulted in up-to-date recordings and machines. In 1959, the NLS began circulating books recorded on open-reel magnetic tape. By July 1961, the collection had grown to 350 master tapes produced by volunteers using their own equipment and 1,200 tapes provided by the AFB. This proved to be an excellent way to distribute magazines as the tapes could be reused. Audio cassettes began to be tested in 1968, as visually impaired patrons were having trouble rewinding reel-to-reel books, and began circulation in 1969.[5] Today, books and reference materials are available on digital CDs and CD-ROM databases.

National Library Service for the Blind and Physically Handicapped (NLS)

The mission of NLS includes these two goals: "To develop and maintain a collection of braille and recorded materials which will meet the reading preferences and information needs of a highly diverse clientele, and to develop coordinated library service to all citizens eligible for this service."[6] As of 1981, the NLS network included 4 multistate centers, 56 regional, and 101 subregional libraries in the public library itself. Through this free reading program, physically disabled individuals across the United States and American citizens abroad can borrow recorded and braille books and magazines. Eligible patrons may also borrow special playback machines and other equipment. Among those eligible are persons who are completely visually impaired, who cannot see well enough to read standard print even with glasses, or who cannot hold or handle printed books because of a physical disability, even if temporary. People with physically based reading disabilities, such as dyslexia, may also be eligible. Recorded and embossed books are distributed from contracting producers directly to regional and subregional libraries.

Each regional library keeps at least one copy of every NLS title on its shelves or in circulation. A directory published by the NLS (*Library Resources for the Blind and Physically Handicapped, A Directory with FY 1994 Statistics on Readership, Circulation, Budget, Staff, and Collections*) lists all NLS network libraries and machine-lending agencies arranged alphabetically by state. It also includes regional and subregional libraries. This wonderful reference tool is available free of charge by writing to:

> Reference Section
> National Library Service for the Blind
> and Physically Handicapped
> Library of Congress
> Washington, DC 20542

The NLS provides an array of accessories to patrons with physical impairments. The following is a sample of those offered:

- solar-powered, battery-recharging units for patrons with no electricity

- earphones with individual volume control for each ear for the hard-of-hearing patron

- remote control devices to turn talking-book machines on and off or a breath switch for patrons with severe disabilities

New Technology

The conversion of text into synthesized speech by the NLS has improved the lives of the visually and physically impaired. This technology is relatively new. The Kurzweil Reading Machine, built in 1974 by Ray Kurzweil, for the first time allowed visually impaired patrons to read books and other printed materials without using braille by converting print into synthesized speech. The machine electronically scanned each page of text, then recognized characters and converted them to speech, and read them aloud synthetically, or printed them in braille. The first machine took up half a room, but today desktop versions are available and computer software may be used that allows for the navigation of Microsoft Windows and the reading of faxes.

No single reading aid can serve all purposes. Different aids are needed for home, school, and work. The following is a sample of other aids available through either the NLS or private purchase:

- Talking books.

- Large-print materials.

- Optical low-vision aids to enlarge print. They can be handheld or stand-mounted magnifiers, some filtered with batteries and a high-intensity bulb.

- Electric low-vision aids such as television magnifiers with a magnification range from six to forty-five times.

- Portable battery-operated electric scanner/magnifiers with display screens so patrons can explore library stacks on their own.

- Battery-powered page turners for motion-impaired patrons. Pages are turned by a puff of air, a pushbutton switch, or a radio frequency sender device.

- Mouth stick, head-mounted switches, voice recognition system, or eye-gazing detection devices are all accessories that can be used in place of a computer mouse.

Braille can now be encoded digitally on magnetic tapes or diskettes that are then recorded on small machines. This technology has become especially useful for word processing, personal filing, and storage and retrieval systems, as well as for the braille-reading user at computer read-out terminals. With the proper equipment, library terminals can display the text in large print on a television screen and generate synthetic speech.

Electronic text also offers the visually impaired computer user the opportunity to read many materials other than those in braille or in recorded form. This type of text is created by converting the text of the printed page from analog to digital form or by entering materials directly into the computer. This digital information is then stored in the computer or on a computer-readable medium and is later converted into visual, tactile, or audible outputs that a visually impaired patron can read. Optical Character Recognition (OCR) software converts the text in the image into digital form. Many publications already exist in this format, so computer files can easily be used to create electronic text. A text stored in digital form can be read using a braille display, magnification system, or speech-output machine. Electronic text is available in a variety of formats; the two most popular are online and CD-ROM. Books on computers are available to anyone with the right equipment.

Resources

The Montgomery County Public Library System in Maryland offers a variety of full- or partial-text resources over the telephone lines. Users dial in to access data such as full-text encyclopedias and several magazine indexes. Similar services are available in other parts of the United States. The University of Michigan School of Information and Library Studies has a program called the Internet Public Library. Many resources found in the traditional library are available at this site, which can be accessed at http://ips.sil.umich.edu/index.text.html.[7]

Two other Internet sites containing information about products and services for the visually impaired are:

- The Disability Page (http://www.disability.com/index/html) is maintained by Evan Kemp Association, Inc. (EKA).

- Disability Resources on the Internet (http://www.disability.com/cool.html) is maintained by DKA.

Library Journal, December 1995, pages S46 and S48, provides a long list of products for libraries for use by the physically challenged.

Hearing-Impaired Patrons

As with the visually impaired, advances in technology have enabled the hearing impaired to lead a more normal life. Two particular inventions specifically applicable to the public library are sign language and the TDD telephone device. American Sign Language (ASL), a language of gestures and hand symbols, was created by a Frenchman, Laurent Clerc, in 1816. He later came to America to set up the first American school for the hearing-impaired. ASL uses 26 hand symbols, one for each letter of the alphabet. The Internet has available a number of web sites for the hearing-impaired. One such site is the "Interactive ASL Guide"—http://www.disserv.stu.umn.edu/AltForm/guide.cgi—which contains an interactive finger spelling alphabet display on the computer screen. The user clicks on any letter from A to Z to see the finger spelling sign for that letter. This site would be useful in the public library setting. As mentioned earlier, the Disability Resources on the Internet home page also offers a site called the "Disabilities Mall"—http://disability.com/dismall.html—which offers descriptions of listening devices and the company from which the item can be purchased. Other excellent sites and resources can be found in the magazine article by Susan Gilbert Beck, "A Galaxy of Rustling Stars: Places on the Web and Other Library and Information Paths for the Deaf," *Library Hi Tech*, 52, no. 13 (1995): 4.

The Telecommunication Device for the Deaf (TDD/TTY) is another innovation useful in the public library. TDD is a small machine, hooked into a standard electrical outlet, that allows two people who each have a telephone and TDD machine, to type messages back and forth to each other. TT (text telephone) types messages across a small screen on the TDD machine. These messages can also be printed out.

One library that offers services to hearing-impaired patrons is the Public Library of Nashville and Davidson County in Tennessee. In 1978, the library established the Library Service for the Deaf, which operates a telephone line that prints out news, sports, and community information in the home of the hearing-impaired. The library service also offers signed or captioned videos and an extensive book collection on sign language.

Planning and Goals

The public library, with the above-mentioned tools and technology available, must create a needs assessment in its long-range planning goals to improve services to the physically disabled. These improvements should include the training of library staff, expansion of currently available materials, and upgrading of technology. Training should not only teach use of the new systems but should also teach appropriate communication and behavioral skills when helping a patron with a disability. Staff members should be taught to feel as comfortable helping that patron as they would any other.

The Americans with Disabilities Act (ADA) factors into these planning and assessment policies. Passed in July 1990, its intent is to provide equal treatment for all people regardless of disabilities. For the library, this means equal access to information, programs, and resources. However, with budget constraints, public libraries may not be able to acquire all the materials they need. In 1973, the Illinois Library System Directors Organization (LIST) created a Task Force on Library Services to the Blind and Physically Handicapped. In the Task Force report submitted to LIST in 1974, the following was stated in the introduction.

> It is recognized that smaller community libraries may be unable to provide the special resources required to provide the blind and physically handicapped with the same wide range of quality library and information services available to the non-handicapped. However, the library retains its basic responsibility of providing service to the total community and should provide that service to the handicapped

> which is within its capacity with strong support from the system. Responsibility for service which cannot be provided at one level should be shared with libraries at other levels.[8]

It is at this level that the NLS comes into the picture. Dr. Jean L. Preer, associate dean, School of Library and Information Science at The Catholic University of America, Washington, D.C., spoke about the NLS at a talk she delivered to the National Advisory Group on Collection Building Activities meeting on September 21, 1994. She stated that the "NLS seeks to provide its users with the same types of books and information available to the general public through public libraries."[9] The NLS networks aid public libraries by providing material, instruction, and information to eligible patrons. The public library must market the services and programs they do provide so the community is aware of them. They should also have available references to other resources, such as the NLS. Patrons may not be aware of the vast amount of materials available to them through the NLS or even at their local level. Public libraries and the NLS must work together to provide programs and services to meet the needs of the disabled as well as those who are not disabled, and, in doing so, provide equal access to all.

Older Patrons

Public libraries also need to take into consideration the library information needs of the growing number of Americans over the age of 65. According to the 1980 census, there were 25.5 million Americans over the age of 65, or 11.3 percent of the total population. This compares to 1970 with 20.5 million, or 9.9 percent.[10] In 1996, 33.8 million, or 13 percent, were 65 or older.[11] It is estimated that this number will increase by 100 percent by 2030.[12] This trend suggests that public libraries will need to change their priorities to provide more services for this aging population. (See chapter 6.)

History of Services

The 1970s began to see a major growth in the special needs of the elderly. Even before then, services for older patrons had been established. In the 1940s, the Cleveland Public Library opened the Adult

Education Department with a "Live Long and Like It Library Club" for patrons over 60.[13] By 1956, Congress had passed the first Library Services Act (LSA), which recognized the need for libraries to expand community involvement. At this same time, the American Library Association (ALA) expanded its Adult Education Board to include the Adult Services Division and appointed a permanent committee on Library Service to the Aging. In 1964, Congress passed the Library Service Act, later renamed the Library Services and Construction Act (LSCA), which provided construction funds for libraries to alter the physical structure of their buildings to meet the needs of the elderly and physically disabled. LSCA also helped increase the availability of large-print collections and services. In 1966, through a federal grant, the Donnell Library Center of the New York Public Library began a program to demonstrate the use of large-print titles to encourage their publication and collection.[14] Before this project began, large-print books were dated, bulky, and unattractive. This program created a catalog of more than 400 titles. In the 1980s, R. R. Bowker's *Large Type Books in Print 1982* listed more than 5,000 titles.

The Pratt-Smoot Act of 1931, mentioned earlier, was amended in 1966 to make more persons eligible for use of special book formats. Title III of the Older Americans Act also advanced library services to the aged. This included increasing large-print collections and providing specially equipped bookmobiles.

From 1961 to 1971, a study was conducted throughout the United States by the consultant firm of Booz, Allen, and Hamilton for the Cleveland Public Library, funded by the U.S. Office of Education. The purpose of the study was "to determine the scope of library services rendered to persons over 65 by public libraries and libraries at state and federal institutions." Public libraries in each state that were offering outstanding service to the aging were identified by questionnaires sent to state libraries, regional library services, and LSCA officers. Questionnaires were mailed to 390 public libraries. This national survey found that public library service to the aging was minimal, that it was given low priority by public libraries as well as by those state and federal agencies providing the funds, and that only a small minority, 4 percent, of those 65 or over were receiving special services. Other informal studies conducted in eight states confirmed this. As a result of this study, the 1970s was the turning point in library service for the patron over 65.[15]

The Office of Libraries and Learning Resources, United States Department of Education, administers the LSCA. According to a 1973 LSCA-supported national study, elderly patrons represent one of the largest user groups of public libraries. Throughout the 1970s, LSCA improved access to library services and materials for senior patrons. As of 1982, nearly 75 percent of public libraries in the United States were offering some specific program or service to older adults.[16] Services included large-print books, audiocassettes, and reading aids such as magnifiers and book holders, the same services available to the visually impaired and physically disabled. Services also included outreach programs in nursing homes, hospitals, housing projects, and inner-city neighborhoods. These programs encompassed anything from lectures on retirement to consumer education. (See chapter 11 for LSTA discussion.)

Services Today

Library services have continued to grow, and libraries are continuing to plan and implement new ways to improve access to services and materials with a focus on providing programs for the institutionalized and homebound as well as the mobile and healthy. Involving the older patron in the planning of these programs, in volunteering, and in participating on library boards actively uses their talents to improve service and allows the public libraries to receive valuable input as well.

Below is a sampling of services and programs offered by public libraries throughout the United States. As mentioned earlier, many of these services duplicate those used by physically disabled.

- Books-by-mail—offered through National Library Service for the Blind and Physically Handicapped (NLS).

- Bookmobiles—this service can be especially adapted to serve the elderly with custom-designed vehicles with hydraulic lifts to allow wheelchair-bound patrons access to bookmobiles and vans.

- Outreach programs—to the homebound or to those in nursing homes. Some libraries even provide transportation to the library.

The Boston Public Library was the first to implement such an outreach program in a nursing home. In 1939, the BPL set up a collection of materials at a local nursing home. In 1941, the Cleveland Public Library adopted a similar program, which began as a pilot but grew from there.[17] An outreach program can include concerts, hobbies, health issues, films, and booktalks.

An example of how these programs work together can be found in the SAGE Project (Service to the Aging). SAGE is an implementation of the Brooklyn Public Library, where in 1984, more than 10 percent of its approximately 2 million population was over 65. This program provides the following services: books and talking-books by mail to the homebound; bus transportation to museums, concerts, and special events; and a variety of reading aids. SAGE also employs seniors at 16 of its branches to help as library aides with these programs. This project is funded by a consortia of foundations, LSCA, state, New York City Department of Aging, and general library funds. SAGE is being implemented in a number of libraries throughout the United States.[18]

Planning and Goals

In order to plan and implement these programs, librarians will need further and special education to learn who the aged are, what special needs they have, and what other libraries are doing to meet these needs. This will be essential to serve the older patron just as special training is needed to serve the young and those with physical disabilities. In 1965, Title II of the Higher Education Act (Library Career Training and Library Research Demonstration) funded such educational programs for workshops and research. A number of library schools offer educational programs for the elderly. These classes include management skills and program design. The Catholic University of America, School of Library and Information Science, in Washington, D.C., began offering to students pursuing an MLS in the 1981–82 school year fellowships for those concentrating in service to the disabled. The fellowships provide tuition and allowances for participants.[19] Continuing education is also an excellent way to keep up with these needs. Forty-four library staff members working with the SAGE Project have done just that. Further education and public awareness will help continue growth of library services to the older patron.

Discussion Questions

1. What is the mission of the NLS (National Library Service for the Blind and Physically Handicapped), and how has it changed since it began in 1931?
2. Discuss types of training that would be helpful to librarians to better serve special populations.
3. Discuss ways the public library can better market services to special populations.
4. What is the ADA? Discuss ways it has changed services in the library.
5. Using the SAGE Project as a basis, create other programs that would be beneficial to the older patron.

Additional Readings

Beck, Susan Gilbert. "A Galaxy of Rustling Stars: Places on the WEB and Other Library and Information Paths for the Deaf." *Library Hi Tech* 13, no. 4 (1995): 93–100.

Casey, Genevieve M. *Library Services for the Aging*. Hamden, Conn.: Library Professional Publications, 1984.

Dorman, David. "Technically Speaking: Products for the Blind and Visually Impaired." *American Libraries* 26, no. 11 (December 1995): 1143–1144.

Hahn, Ellen Zabel. "Library Services to the Blind and Physically Handicapped-Local Commitment." In *Library Services for the Handicapped Adult*. edited by James L. Thomas and Carol H. Thomas. Phoenix, Ariz.: Oryx Press, 1982.

Holt, Cynthia, and Wanda Clements Hole. "Assessing Needs of Library Users with Disabilities." *Public Libraries* 34, no. 2 (March/April 1995): 90–93.

Library of Congress, *Library Resources for the Blind and Physically Handicapped: A Directory with FY 1994 Statistics on Readership, Circulation, Budget, Staff, and Collections*. Washington, D.C.: Library of Congress, 1995.

———. *NLS Policy on Copyright*. Washington, D.C.: Library of Congress, 1995.

Lovejoy, Eunice. "History and Standards." In *That All May Read*. Library of Congress, National Library Service for the Blind and Physically Handicapped. Washington, D.C.: Library of Congress, 1984.

———. "A History of the National Library Service for Blind and Handicapped Individuals, Library of Congress." In *That All May Read*. Library of Congress, National Library Service for the Blind and Physically Handicapped. Washington, D.C.: Library of Congress, 1984.

Majeska, Marilyn Lundell. *Talking Books: Pioneering and Beyond*. Washington, D.C.: Library of Congress, 1988.

Preer, Jean L. "Collection Building and the National Library Service for the Blind and Physically Handicapped." Paper Presented at the National Advisory Group on Collection Building Activities meeting, Washington, D.C. September 21, 1994.

"Physically Challenged," in *1996 Sourcebook: The Reference for Products and Services. Library Journal* 120, no. 20 (December 1995): S46, S48.

Projects & Experiments: Another Source for Books. The Library of Congress, Fall, 1995.

Turock, Betty J. *Serving the Older Adult: A Guide to Library Programs and Information Sources*. New York: R. R. Bowker, 1982.

"United States Population." *The World Almanac and Book of Facts, 1997*. Mahwah, N.J.: K-III Reference Corp., 1996.

Notes

1. Eunice Lovejoy, "History and Standards," in *That All May Read*, Library of Congress, National Library Service for the Blind and Physically Handicapped (Washington, D.C.: Library of Congress, 1984), 2.

2. Ibid., 6.

3. Eunice Lovejoy, "A History of the National Library Service for Blind and Handicapped Individuals, the Library of Congress," in *That All May Read*, 80.

4. Marilyn Lundell Majeska, *Talking Books: Pioneering and Beyond* (Washington, D.C.: Library of Congress, 1988), 4, 12.

5. Ibid., 46–49.

6. Library of Congress, National Library Service for the Blind and Physically Handicapped, *NLS Policy on Copyright* (Washington, D.C.: Library of Congress, 1995), 1.

7.   Library of Congress, National Library Service for the Blind and Physically Handicapped, *Projects and Experiments: Another Source for Books* (Washington, D.C.: Library of Congress, 1995), 9.

8.   Ellen Zabel Hahn, "Library Services to the Blind and Physically Handicapped-Local Commitment," in *Library Services for the Handicapped Adult*, ed. James L. Thomas and Carol H. Thomas (Phoenix, Ariz.: Oryx Press, 1982), 49–50.

9.   Jean L. Preer, "Collection Building and the National Library Service for the Blind and Physically Handicapped," (paper presented at the National Advisory Group on Collection Building Activities meeting, Washington, D.C. September 21, 1994).

10.   Genevieve M. Casey, *Library Services for the Aging* (Hamden, Conn.: Library Professional Publications, 1984), 1.

11.   "United States Population," *The World Almanac and Book of Facts, 1997* (Mahwah, N.J.: K-III Reference Corp., 1996), 377.

12.   Casey, *Library Services for the Aging*, 1.

13.   Betty J. Turock, *Serving the Older Adult: A Guide to Library Programs and Information Sources* (New York: R. R. Bowker, 1982), 6.

14.   Ibid., 7.

15.   Casey, *Library Services for the Aging*, 41–42.

16.   Ibid., 54.

17.   Turock, *Serving the Older Adult*, 8.

18.   Ibid., 113–114.

19.   Ibid., 88.

11 SOURCES OF FUNDING FOR PUBLIC LIBRARIES

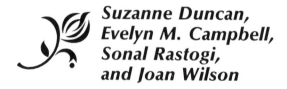

Suzanne Duncan,
Evelyn M. Campbell,
Sonal Rastogi,
and Joan Wilson

The 1970s marked the beginning of the first round of library budget cuts that would still be felt more than 20 years later. President Richard M. Nixon set the wheels in motion when he proposed a fiscal 1974 budget that would cut federal library funding from $140 million to zero.[1]

This was the beginning of the end for the boom in library funding that had begun in 1956 when Congress passed the Library Services Act to provide funds to encourage states to extend library services to rural areas. This favorable trend in library funding continued in 1964 when President Lyndon Johnson signed the Library Services and Construction Act, which gave state agencies authority to distribute federal money to local libraries for new buildings, services for the disabled, and interlibrary loan programs. Urban libraries saw their funds increase sevenfold.[2]

Although Congress restored much of the library funding that Nixon proposed cutting in 1974, the ensuing oil crisis, recession, and inflation resulted in many local libraries shutting their doors. Under the Carter administration, federal funding for libraries did not improve

150

much, but 2,000 library professionals and supporters did gather at the first White House Conference on Library and Information Services in 1979. Congress declined to follow up on the conference's recommendation for a large increase in federal aid, but many participants agreed that the meeting helped galvanize grassroots support for local libraries around the country.[3]

Federal funding for libraries continued to diminish in the 1980s under the Reagan administration, and federal funds, which represented 3.7 percent of public library moneys in 1982, fell to 1.4 percent by 1992 and have continued to fall to .68 percent in 1996. Decreased funding for libraries has meant the closing of library branches throughout the country, cutbacks in hours of operation, slashing of materials budgets and programs, cuts in staffs, and hiring freezes.

These cutbacks have been judged worse than those of the Great Depression. "In 1937, for example, all branches of the Queens Borough Public Library [in New York City] were open six days a week as long as 12 hours a day," recalled the borough's library director, Constance B. Cooke. "Compare that to the scenario of early this year [when] 30 percent of them were open only two or three days a week, six to seven hours a day."[4]

In response to the drastic decreases in funding for public libraries, however, a new attitude has evolved among librarians of the 1990s—a more militant one. Librarians are fighting back aggressively by seeking alternate sources to fund their decreased budgets. Fifty percent of public libraries now conduct fund-raising activities, compared with 42 percent in 1995.[5] More than one-third of all public libraries that do fund-raising have formed a special fund-raising arm in the last five years. And each library that had a fund-raising program raised 25 percent more money for FY96, with an average of $143,367 per library.[6]

It is obvious that fund-raising will continue to play a crucial role in how libraries make up for the decreases in their budgets. Libraries, therefore, should understand the ins and outs of fund-raising. The following discussion is intended to identify the primary public and private sources of funding for public libraries, highlight some of the main elements in fund-raising programs for libraries, look at examples of ways in which some libraries have successfully carried out their fund-raising programs, and lastly, study some of the factors that would affect the funding of public libraries.

Sources of Funds for Public Libraries—
Public Sector

Data from *Library Journal*'s "1997 Public Library Budget Report"[7] indicate that public library budgets remained relatively healthy across the board with total budgets rising by 6.3 percent, which was an improvement over the previous year's 5.6 percent growth. The *LJ* survey broke down public libraries' funding base into the following order:

Municipal funding	45.25 percent
County funding	32.06 percent
State funding	15.35 percent
Fund-raising	3.08 percent
Grants	1.81 percent
Federal funding	.68 percent

Although federal funding trails the other avenues for funding, it is still an important source that generates a number of different types of grants, and librarians should know how those federal funds are allocated. The recent reauthorization of federal funding for libraries under the Library Services and Technology Act (LSTA) has provided new hope for public libraries.

When President Bill Clinton signed the Library Services and Technology Act (LSTA) on September 30, 1996, he was giving approval to the major federal grant program designed specifically for libraries. The LSTA is a major revision, simplification, and updating of the Library Services and Construction Act (LSCA), which had expired.[8] It is worth noting the ways in which public libraries benefit from LSTA and what differences there are, if any, between LSTA and LSCA.

Library Services and Technology Act (P.L. 104-208)

LSTA, which was originally developed by the American Library Association, the Chief Officers of the State Library Agencies, and the Urban Libraries Council during 1993–94, was passed in 1995 in different forms by both the House and Senate within larger bills (H.R 1617 and S. 143).[9] The House and Senate worked out a compromise version of

LSTA, which did not incorporate all of the library community's recommendations, but which was still widely supported by the library organizations. The compromise version of LSTA was issued as part of the conference report (H. Rept. 104-707) on H.R. 1617 on July 25, 1996, and this was the version that was eventually enacted in September.

LSTA is administered by an independent, newly created Institute for Museum and Library Services (IMLS). The IMLS's purpose is to improve museum, library, and information services and consolidate federal programs of support for museums (which are currently administered by the Institute of Museum Services) and programs supporting libraries (which were previously administered by the Department of Education). Evan St. Lifer applauds this move and says that the shift in federal funding from the Department of Education to IMLS "provides it with a much brighter future in its new home under the Institute of Museum & Library Services, a relatively safe haven, according to Washington insiders."[10] Library funding was more precarious under the Department of Education, which, St. Lifer points out, many Republicans in Congress target for drastic cuts.

LSTA has been authorized for six years at a total of $150 million for fiscal year 1997, with most of the funds allocated to state library agencies for statewide services or to subgrants for technological innovation, electronic linkage purposes, or outreach services. Activities funded through the state-based program can involve public, school, academic, research, and special libraries.

Below is a summary of LSTA as provided by the American Library Association at its web site,[11] which is also used by the National Commission for Library and Information Sciences (NCLIS)[12]:

Museum and Library Services Act of 1996

- Subtitle—General Provisions
- Subtitle—Library Services and Technology Act
- Subtitle—Museum Services

Establishment of Library Services and Technology Act

- $150 million authorized for FY97, such sums each year through 2002.

- Funds go to the secretary of education, who transfers them to Institute of Museum and Library Services.

- Allotment of LSTA funds:

  91.5 percent or more allotted to states via state library agencies,

  4 percent for national leadership competitive grants/contracts,

  1½ percent for services for Indian tribes,

  3 percent limit allowed for federal level administration.

Purposes for which state-based LSTA funds could be used (in any proportion) by state library agencies directly or through subgrants or cooperative agreements:

- establishing or enhancing electronic linkages among or between libraries;

- electronically linking libraries with educational, social, or information services;

- assisting libraries in accessing information through electronic networks;

- encouraging libraries in different areas, and encouraging different types of libraries, to establish consortia and share resources;

- paying costs for libraries to acquire or share computer systems and telecommunications technologies;

- targeting library and information services to persons having difficulty using a library and to underserved urban and rural communities, including children (from birth through age seventeen) from families with incomes below the poverty line.

State-based LSTA program requirements:

- Minimum allotment of $340,000 with remainder on population basis;

- 4 percent limit on funds used for state-level administration;

- One-third matching required from nonfederal, state, or local sources;

- Maintenance of effort (MOE) on state-level expenditures for similar purposes;

- Allotment to state reduced by percent MOE less than average of last three years;

- Waiver of MOE for exceptional or uncontrollable circumstances;

- Five-year state plan; revisions allowed;

- Plan must be publicly available, developed with library/library user input;

- Broadly representative state advisory council permitted, not required;

- Independent evaluation/report required prior to end of five-year plan.

Services for American Indian Tribes:

From a 1½ percent LSTA set-aside, the Institute will make grants to organizations primarily serving and representing American Indian tribes for electronic linkages and targeted services (purposes similar to state-based uses of funds).

National Leadership Grants or Contracts:

From 4 percent LSTA set-aside, Institute to make competitive bids for:

- Education and training of persons in library and information science, particularly in areas of new technology and other critical needs, including graduate fellowships, traineeships, institutes, or other programs;

- Research and demonstration projects related to the improvement of libraries, education in library and information science, enhancement of library services through effective and efficient use of new technologies, and dissemination of information derived from such projects;

- Model programs demonstrating cooperative efforts between libraries and museums.

Establishment of Institute of Museum and Library Services:

- Amends Museum Services Act and adjusts Institute of Museum Services (IMS) to create an Institute of Museum and Library Services (IMLS).

- Director: to serve a four-year term, Ex. Schedule III level permitted, appointed by President, confirmed by Senate; first director is head of IMS at time of enactment, then alternates between individuals with special competence with regard to library and information services, and museum services.

- Office of Library Services created, headed by deputy director with graduate degree in library science and expertise in library and information services, appointed by the director.

- Office of Museum Services created, headed by deputy director with expertise in museum services, appointed by director.

- National Commission on Libraries and Information Science has responsibility for advising Institute director on general policies related to financial assistance for library services, and any joint library/museum projects, as well as coordination between the Institute and other activities of federal government.

- National Museum Services Board has responsibility for advising Institute director on general policies related to financial assistance for museum services and any joint library/museum projects.

- NCLIS is to meet jointly with museum board at least annually on general policy with respect to financial assistance for joint library/museum projects; two-thirds vote of total Commission/ Board members present required on such decisions.

Continuation/Revision of Museum Services:

- Authorizes $28.7 million for FY97, such sums through FY2002.

- Purposes: for grants, contracts, cooperative agreements for the federal share of increasing, improving, and strengthening museum services. Ten percent limit allowed for federal administration.

Transfer of functions and transition provisions:

- Transferred to the Institute director all functions of the director of the Institute of Museum Services and of the director of Library Programs in the Office of Educational Research and Improvement in the Department of Education (along with related functions of the Department of Education).

- Transferred government personnel are given certain protections; technical provisions ensure continued effect of legal documents, proceedings, and so forth.

- In appointing employees of the Office of Library Services, the director is to give strong consideration to individuals with experience in administering state-based and national library and information services programs.

- The Office of Management and Budget is to take appropriate measures to ensure an orderly transition from the Department of Education Library Programs to the Institute for Museum and Library Services; such measures may include transfer of funds.

- The secretary of education is to transfer at least $200,000 to the Institute director to ensure the orderly transition from Office of Library Programs to the Institute. Within six months, the Institute director is to submit to Congress any needed technical and conforming amendments as recommended legislation.

Federal Grants

Federal support for libraries usually comes in two forms—*direct funding* of the so-called national libraries (Library of Congress, National Archives, National Library of Medicine, and the others) and *grants-in-aid programs*.

The world of tax-supported grants has become very complex, and librarians must understand what these different types of grants are and become familiar with them. Below are brief descriptions of common types of grant programs.

Block Grants—Block grants are made by the federal government to states or localities that then award the money to eligible organizations to carry out activities that are specified by the authorizing legislation. The Library Services & Technology Act (LSTA) is a block-grant program.

Formula Grants—Formula grants are awarded based on a set of objective criteria, for example, census data, and usually on such factors as population characteristics, number of people served, income, and so forth. The legislature that authorizes the grants will set out the formula that is to be used. These grants are more a method for allocating funds than they are real grants.

Categorical Grants—Categorical grants are designed to meet a specific need or to serve a particular group, and examples of these types of grants are those under Subtitle B—Library Services and Technology, Chapter 3, Subchapter B, Section 261—Services for Indian Tribes.

Project Grants—Project grants are made on the basis of the merits of the proposal, which are judged in competition with other similar proposals. Experts from outside the agency are used to evaluate applications, but the agency still exercises broad discretion in selecting the projects to be funded and the amounts that are awarded. Most of the federal grant programs available to libraries through the National Endowment for the Humanities and others are project grants.

Demonstration Grants—Demonstration grants are those awarded to test new and unique approaches to solving problems. They generally benefit the target group being served, and their main purpose is to prove the effectiveness of the new methodology and to promote its wider use by other organizations.

Research Grants—Research grants are intended to support the gathering, interpretation, and analysis of information to find new solutions or understanding of fundamental issues and problems. Research grant projects, if successful, may lead to demonstration and project grants.

Matching Grants—In matching grants, the recipient uses some of its own resources to supporting the activity being underwritten by the grants. Most government grants have matching requirements.

Challenge Grants—Challenge grants are made contingent on the grantee's raising additional support from private nongovernmental sources. In the National Endowment for the Humanities (NEH) Challenge Grant Program, first-time recipients are required to raise three dollars in private contributions for every dollar in federal funds. Second-time recipients are asked to raise four dollars for each federal dollar awarded. The $500,000 challenge grant awarded by NEH to the Rosenbach Museum & Library in Philadelphia is a three-to-one match grant, which means that the Rosenbach will ultimately spend $2 million.[13]

Under the challenge grant program which began in 1977, NEH has distributed $340 million in federal funds as seed money to encourage the development of endowed sources of funding. These grants have generated more than $1.15 billion in nonfederal support for the nation's libraries, colleges, museums, and other organizations.

Federal Grant Programs

The most important federal grant-making agencies in terms of library support are:

- National Endowment for the Humanities
- Institute for Museum and Library Services (functions of the Library Programs of the Department of Education are in the process of being transferred to IMLS.
- National Historical Publications and Records Commission
- National Science Foundation
- National Library of Medicine
- Council on Library Resources

Hwa-Wei Lee and Gary A. Hunt, authors of *Fund-Raising for the 1990s: The Challenge Ahead,*[14] emphasize that it is important to work from current information, even in the earliest brainstorming phase of any fund-raising proposal or program, because there may be completely new funding initiatives or existing programs may be redirected, scaled back, combined with others, or eliminated. For the most up-to-date information on any grant program, librarians should contact the agency directly.

NATIONAL ENDOWMENT FOR THE HUMANITIES

The NEH was created by the National Foundation on the Arts and Humanities Act of 1965 (P.L. 89-209) and has three divisions—Education and Research, Preservation and Access, and Public Programs; it has two offices—Challenge Grants and Federal/State Partnership.[15]

The Endowment is directed by a chairman, who is appointed by the President and confirmed by the U.S. Senate for a term of four years. Advising the chairman is a National Council of 26 distinguished private citizens who serve staggered six-year terms and are also appointed by the President and confirmed by the U.S. Senate.

NEH grants are awarded on a competitive basis. In the last fiscal year, the Endowment funded about one out of every six applications it received. Funding decisions are made on the basis of the application's merit and the significance of the project.

From its creation in 1965 through the end of FY96, the Endowment has awarded nearly $3 billion for more than 54,000 fellowships and grants, which have been matched by more than $333 million in nonfederal contributions.

INSTITUTE FOR MUSEUM AND LIBRARY SERVICES

The IMLS was created when President Clinton signed LSTA into law on September 30, 1996, to reauthorize federal library and museums programs, and to move federal library programs from the Department of Education to the Institute.[16]

The library programs are primarily state block grants for technology and service to underserved communities. There is a small allotment for programs of national significance; these programs may include support for joint museum/library collaborations. The library program is authorized to receive $150 million in FY97. Congress appropriated $134 million for FY97.

The legislation for museum programs remains much the same as it has for the past 20 years. The new legislation authorizes the director, with the advice of the National Museum Services Board, to make annual National Award for Museum Service awards. The museum program is authorized to receive $28.7 million in FY97. Congress appropriated $22 million in FY97.

NATIONAL HISTORICAL PUBLICATIONS AND RECORDS COMMISSION (NHPRC)

The NHPRC is a federal agency that has focused its energy and resources on the documentary needs of the United States to save endangered historical documents and to make plans and set priorities for preserving archival materials.[17] Commission grantees have begun to study ways to deal with the mounting challenge of preserving electronic records, to save historical photograph, motion picture, television, and sound-recording collections, to encourage new archival programs in local governments and Native American communities, and to work with state leaders in locating, preserving, and publishing documents relating to many facets of American experience.

In 1992, the NHPRC completed a major new strategic plan for documentary progress in the 1990s and beyond—*To Protect a Priceless Legacy:*

The Preservation and Use of America's Historical Records, which sets out goals and objectives to which the Commission has made a commitment for the coming years. In November 1996, the Commission reviewed and revised that 1992 plan.

The 1992 plan contained 17 objectives at four levels of priority. To reduce confusion for grant applicants, the Commission consolidated those objectives into just four categories in which grants will be offered. The Commission also gave two of those categories priority.

In the revised plan, priority will go to grants for improvements in documentary fields (research and development, tools, training, publications), and grants for state collaborative efforts on documentary needs (state plans, state regrant programs, and work under collaborative agreements).

The other two categories are grants for documentary publications (currently supported ongoing editions, new projects, and publication subventions); and grants for documentary preservation, access, and use (archival, education, and promotional projects).

More than a year may be necessary to implement the revisions, which must go through an approval process within the government[18] and then be explained in new guidelines that will be issued in ample time for grant applicants to become aware of changes.

NATIONAL SCIENCE FOUNDATION

The National Science Foundation (NSF) is an independent U.S. government agency responsible for promoting science and engineering through programs that invest more than $3.3 billion per year in almost 20,000 research and education projects in science and engineering.[19] The NSF was established by the National Science Foundation Act of 1950, as amended, and related legislation, 42 U.S.C. 1861 et seq., and was given additional authority by the Science and Engineering Equal Opportunities Act (42 U.S.C. 1885), and Title I of the Education for Economic Security Act (20 U.S.C. 3911 to 3922).

The NSF consists of the National Science Board of 24 part-time members and a director (who also serves as ex officio National Science Board member), each appointed by the President with the advice and consent of the U.S. Senate. Other senior officials include a deputy director, who is also appointed by the President with the advice and consent of the U.S. Senate, and eight assistant directors.

For FY98, the NSF has requested $3.4 billion, 56 percent ($1,872 million) of which will be spent on research project support (an increase of 2.7 percent from FY97), 20 percent ($684 million) on research facilities (an increase of 3.5 percent), 20 percent ($669 million) on education and training (an increase of 3.5 percent), and 4 percent ($142 million) on administration and management.

NATIONAL LIBRARY OF MEDICINE

The National Library of Medicine (NLM) is the world's largest research library in a single scientific and professional field. It collects materials in all major areas of the health sciences and to a lesser degree in such areas as chemistry, physics, botany, and zoology.[20] NLM is a national resource for all U.S. health science libraries through a National Network of Libraries of Medicine, consisting of 4,500 "primary access" libraries (mostly in hospitals), 140 resource libraries (at medical schools), 8 regional libraries (covering all geographic regions of the U.S.), and the NLM itself is a national resource for the entire network.

The Extramural Programs Division of NLM provides a variety of grants to support research and development activities leading to the better management, dissemination, and use of biomedical knowledge. Grants are available to support research in medical informatics, health information science, and biotechnology information, as well as for research training in these areas. Network planning and development grants support computer and communication systems in medical centers and health institutions, and the study of new opportunities with high-speed computer networks in the health sciences. Health science library resource grants assist in improving information access and services for health professionals. Research and publications in the history of medicine and the life sciences are also supported. NLM's appropriation for FY97 was $141 million and $161 million for FY98.

COUNCIL ON LIBRARY RESOURCES

The Council on Library Resources, Inc., is a private, nonprofit 501(c)(3)-operating foundation established in 1956 to look toward the future on behalf of libraries, to address problems experienced by libraries in the aggregate, and to identity innovative solutions.[21]

It has helped libraries take advantage of emerging technologies to improve operating performance and expand services for an increasing number of users. CLR interests have evolved to include, along with advancing technologies, a wide range of topics such as the characteristics and use of information, the management of libraries and information systems, bibliographic systems, and equitable access to information. An area of special interest has been professional education.

CLR supports work by individuals and organizations on matters pertinent to libraries and information services, with a primary objective of improving their quality and performance. Individuals and organizations with specific interests and expertise are encouraged to take the initiative and propose for consideration projects within the following three areas of CLR's programs.

Leadership Development—to encourage innovative ideas for preparing future leaders who will manage new information technologies and systems.

Economics of Information Services—to promote research that analyzes the costs and benefits of traditional and evolving library services and to investigate the economic issues of the transition to electronic library systems.

Transition from the Traditional to the Electronic Library—to bring attention to the specific issues faced by libraries generally as they develop electronic services appropriate for their communities and to promote models of excellence in the transition to the electronic library.

Sources of Funds for Public Libraries— Private Sector

The beginning of private support for libraries began in 1638 when the Reverend John Harvard bequeathed some 300 volumes from his private collection to a struggling exclusive college in Cambridge, Massachusetts, that would later bear his name.[22] Other private and church libraries were established in the late seventeenth century, including a number of "revolving libraries" that were small private collections transported from town to town.

In 1731, Benjamin Franklin launched the Library Company of Philadelphia, the first subscription library in this country, which would serve as a model for libraries in Europe and North America. As books were so expensive, members banded together to share their copies, the effect of which some historians have called "a more even distribution of intellectual wealth, the establishment of an intellectual democracy."[23]

The distinction of being the first tax-supported library, however, goes to the Peterborough Town Library in New Hampshire, where in 1833 the Reverend Abiel Abbott persuaded other citizens to use state money to start the library. Nevertheless, the birth of the public library movement in this country really did not begin in earnest until the mid-nineteenth century.

Along with the growth in public libraries came an unprecedented growth in private support of these libraries. The late nineteenth century became known as the age of the robber barons, and it was also a time of celebrated philanthropy. Philanthropists, such as Jacob Astor in New York City, Joshua Bates in Boston, and Enoch Pratt in Baltimore, would give generously to libraries, but none would lend his name so synonymously to library philanthropy as Andrew Carnegie.

The multimillionaire steel magnate from Scotland donated more than $56 million to finance the construction of 1,679 libraries in 1,412 communities, and 830 more overseas.[24] Carnegie conditioned his generosity on a promise of future support from local governments, and after his death in 1919, the Carnegie Corporation continued his grants to libraries.

Since Carnegie's day, the way libraries operate has changed dramatically, but the traditional function of libraries has not changed. What has changed is that now libraries are faced not only with the rapid growth of information but also with continued increases in costs for materials and services that most often exceed the rate of inflation. These needs can no longer be met by traditional tax-supported dollars, and libraries have once again begun to look toward the private sector to help fund public libraries in this country.

Public librarians should know where to look for private sponsorship; a basic resource is *The National Guide to Funding for Libraries and Information Services,* 2d edition (1993). The *Guide* contains entries for 574 grant-making foundations and 28 direct corporate-giving programs that have shown a substantial interest in libraries (either by their stated purpose or through the actual grants of $10,000 or more). The grant makers listed in the *Guide* do not represent all the potential foundations or corporate funding sources, but the *Guide* does provide invaluable information that grant seekers need to know.

Grant seekers should read each foundation- and corporate-giving program description carefully to understand the different types of organizations and the types of grants they are offering.

Foundations

The National Guide to Funding for Libraries defines a foundation as a nongovernmental, nonprofit organization with its own funds (usually from a single source, either an individual, family, or corporation) and a program managed by its own trustees and directors, which was established to maintain or aid educational, social, charitable, religious, or other activities serving the common welfare.

All of the grant makers in the *Guide* fall into one of the following five categories.

Independent Foundation—A fund or endowment designated by the Internal Revenue Service as a private foundation under the law (Sec. 501[c][3]), the primary function of which is the making of grants. The assets of most independent foundations are derived from the gift of an individual or family. Some function under the direction of family members and are known as "family foundations." Depending on their range of giving, independent foundations may also be known as "general purpose" or "special purpose" foundations. Among the best-known of the "general purpose" foundations are the Ford Foundation, the Kellogg Foundation, the MacArthur Foundation, the Carnegie Foundation, and the Rockefeller Foundation. The American Heart Foundation, the Asia Foundation, and the Council on Library Resources are examples of "specialized" foundations that provide funding for particular areas of need.

Company-Sponsored Foundation—A private foundation under the tax law deriving its funds from a profit-making company or corporation, but independently constituted, a company-sponsored foundation functions for the purpose of making grants usually on a broad basis. Company-sponsored foundations are also known as "corporate" foundations and are legally distinct from programs administered within the corporation directly from corporate funds. Prominent corporate foundations include the Procter and Gamble Foundation, the Scripps-Howard Foundation, and the Exxon Foundation.

Direct Corporate Giving—Direct giving includes other contributions of a company that are not turned over to a foundation to administer. Direct-giving programs are unregulated and are restricted only by the limit of taxable earnings allowable as charitable deductions. In addition to cash contributions, corporate giving may also include noncash gifts of goods and services. Donation of company products, supplies, and equipment is the most common form of in-kind giving.

Operating Foundation—An operating foundation exists to support a specific nonprofit organization, whether it is a hospital, a college or university, a performing arts group, or a social service agency. In effect, it functions as the fund-raising arm of the parent organization and exists to serve its own programs. Its charter may also permit it to make outside grants.

Community Foundation—A community foundation is a publicly supported organization that makes grants in a specific community or region. In its general charitable purposes, a community foundation is much like a private foundation; however, its funds are derived from many donors rather than a single source. Examples of community foundations include the Cleveland Foundation, the San Francisco Foundation, and the Kanawha Valley Foundation in West Virginia.

Corporations—According to the *Guide*, the research process for corporate funding is similar to other institutional grant-seeking—identifying companies that might be interested in the organization's mission and program, learning as much as possible about those companies, determining the best method of approach, and articulating program objectives so as to conform to the company's giving rationale.

There is great diversity in methods and style of giving among corporations, but the single greatest determinant of corporate philanthropy is profitability. This often requires a shift in perspective from appealing to benevolence to promoting a company's self-interest. There are many competing demands on a company's net earnings—capital investment, product research and development, wage and benefit increases for employees, and dividend increases for shareholders. Any commitment the company makes will go first to those demands before it will support external causes, no matter how worthy. Careful and thorough research must always be done before any company is approached for funds.

Individuals

Individual donors account for the vast majority of the charitable dollars each year, and any fund-raising plan needs to emphasize them.[25] Hwa-Wei Lee and Gary A. Hunt find that some librarians seem to resist the logic of devoting more time to individuals than to other kinds of prospects because there is something impersonal about approaching governmental agencies, foundation staff, or corporate giving officers. The authors say that studies have shown that individuals in the long run will provide most of the dollars needed.

Individuals tend to make unrestricted gifts that can be applied to the library's greatest need. They can also help obtain gifts from their relatives, friends, or business contacts. Every personal contribution the library receives has a potential multiplying effect that can extend for a lifetime.

Lee and Hunt also point out that one must remember that some individual donors have a great deal more money than others, and a few will be capable of making that $1-million gift. The authors give the example of businessman W. T. Young who pledged $5 million to the University of Kentucky Library campaign.

Where can one start looking for those individual donors? Lee and Hunt recommend the following categories.

- Prior donors—those who have given to a cause are more likely to give again.

- Friends, members, and volunteers—a Friends group is a good place to start when it has reached a certain size and maturity with a pattern of year-to-year increases in annual giving. The University of Illinois Library has a Friends organization of 4,000 members who give $330,000 a year.

- Library users—even library users should be considered potential prospects, assuming they are satisfied with the service they have received. The *1985 ALA Yearbook* reported that the Virginia Beach Public Library in Virginia received the entire estate of a local couple who had been heavy library users and "wanted to give the city something for everyone."[26]

Elements of a Fund-Raising Campaign

Most libraries tend to supplement their budgets with book sales and small gifts from individuals, and while these sources are important, a more ambitious fund-raising campaign should be undertaken.[27] Working from the successes and mistakes of a North Carolina library fund-raising campaign, Steve Sumerford offers 12 steps for raising money from corporations, foundations, and individuals within one's community.

Step 1: All fund-raising methods must start with a statement of the need for funding. Sumerford says that the challenge is to identify and describe needs from the community perspective rather than from the library perspective. The needs statement should clearly document the effect that a particular problem has on the community and how the proposed project can solve the problem.

The mistake grant seekers make in writing most needs statements for their grant proposals is to base the need on circular logic—for example, suppose that the library needs a new bookmobile because the current one is old. Instead of emphasizing the age of the bookmobile, a good needs statement will answer the question of why a community needs a bookmobile in the first place, who will benefit from a new bookmobile, and how a new bookmobile will make the community better. The needs statement should also demonstrate that the community has had input into developing the statement, through focus groups, interviews with community leaders, and surveys.

Step 2: Get a good reading on the current fund-raising climate in the community before making any decisions about a fund-raising strategy. Talk to fund-raising mentors in organizations such as United Way agencies, college development offices, and others.

Locate people who will share information, then quiz them on the priorities and trends of local foundations, corporations, and other community donors. Timing is of critical importance in a fund-raising campaign, and the state of the local economy will clearly have a major effect on the availability of local dollars.

Step 3: Create a fund-raising advisory committee, made up of friends, community leaders, experienced fund-raisers, donors, and staff members. Sumerford advises that librarians should "remember people give money to people, not to institutions or agencies."[28] One essential aspect of the project's design is to involve representatives of the targeted population (e.g., teenage mothers, literacy students, and others) in the planning process—not only will they give good ideas, but they will also give the request more credibility.

Step 4: Develop a comprehensive, community-based fund-raising strategy based on diverse fund-raising methods, such as grant proposals, corporate solicitations, raffle sales, special events, and direct mail requests. To facilitate this diverse fund-raising strategy, the advisory committee must be organized into separate subcommittees for each of the groups of potential donors. Try to find people with appropriate experience and expertise to serve on these subcommittees. Usually the first step for the subcommittee is to set a goal of how much money will be raised and then determine its strategy for reaching that goal.

Step 5: Make arrangements for all donations to go into a fund that is tax-deductible. A Friends of the Library group can be an excellent tax-deductible conduit for donations and may in fact already have a nonprofit status.

Step 6: Frame the request in a project format with outcomes that match the priorities and "image" of the potential donor. A project format assures the donors that, if they award the grant, there can be measurable and recognizable outcomes.

Remember that the donors also have a reputation to maintain, and they want their list of funded projects to look impressive in their annual report. If the project is given a name that expresses its mission and gives the project its identity, the potential donor will look more favorably on the request.

Step 7: Research foundations to determine which ones might be more receptive to the project. Determine which foundations match the library's needs, then set up an appointment with the foundation director or a staff member, who is most often the proposal gatekeeper and will be the one who screens the proposals and decides which ones will go to the board. After the initial meeting, send a thank-you note and periodically send newspaper clippings, newsletters, or flyers about the project. Also, in preparing the formal proposal, be sure to follow the foundation's guidelines very closely.

Step 8: Research the giving patterns of local corporations. Corporations need to give away some money each year for both tax purposes and good public relations. The community relations officer can provide advice on how to submit a request. Personal contact is the key to corporate donations, and corporate leaders respond best to other corporate leaders, so the library's proposal should be made by one who is a peer of the corporate executive.

Even if a corporation does not give cash, it may be able to give thousands of dollars of in-kind services such as printing, used equipment, volunteer hours, and publicity. Remember, too, that corporations like lots of publicity when they make a donation—have the Friends group plan a community celebration and invite the press.

Step 9: Ask individuals to make donations and pledges through personal visits and direct mail fund appeals.

Step 10: Organize special events during the campaign and generate as many press releases as possible. According to Sumerford, nothing is sweeter than having an article about the library's project in the paper on the very day that a donor is making the decision about whether to fund the project. Develop a list of friendly reporters, feature writers, and editors, and send press releases directly to them.

Step 11: Find other organizations with which to collaborate. Almost every fund-raiser asks whether the library is working in partnership with other organizations. In addition to getting these organizations to become part of the project, look for organizations that will write letters of support and endorsement for the project.

Step 12: Stay in touch with the donors who give as well as those who do not. One must begin cultivating donors for the next request before one deposits the check from the last one. Communicate with the donors and supporters regularly, and let them know how their money is being used. Also, after receiving a gift, give the donor as much publicity as possible; this will tell potential donors that if they fund future projects, they will get just as much good publicity.

Sumerford notes that the last and happiest step in the process is to deposit all those fat checks from foundations, corporations, and other donors, and then continue providing the community with the library service it needs.

Factors That Affect Funding

Local Politics

Library advocates say that the surest way to maintain funding for public libraries is to build community political support,[29] and the best way to accomplish that is to have tax revenues and local bond issues that are specifically tied to libraries. Tax revenues that benefit libraries vary from state to state. In Kansas, for example, state law earmarks a percentage of every dollar of property taxes for libraries, and in Las Vegas, libraries get a percentage of the sales and motor vehicle taxes.

Experts have found that bond issues are most likely to be approved by voters when they deal with libraries separate from other public services.[30] *Library Journal*'s "1997 Budget Report" found that public libraries are holding their own, particularly in the area of library referenda.[31] Voters supported bond issues nearly 80 percent of the time, an improvement over the previous year's 72 percent.

The *LJ* report stated that perhaps the most direct evidence that public library services continue to garner enthusiastic support from local residents and officials comes in the form of another increase in per capita funding. Public libraries projected an average of $23.41 for FY97, a 5.1 percent increase over FY96's per capita funding average of $22.23. This does seem to lend support to what many library advocates believe—that political support of libraries appears closely related to the state of an area's economy.

Examples of Success Stories in Elections

On March 6, 1995, the Kalamazoo Public Library won an election that increased library support from $2.8 million annually to $4 million. Before the election the library had worked with a variety of consultants, architects, and volunteers to identify needs and to determine the level of community support for a positive vote.[32] The Library Board decided in October 1994 to seek additional millage support to institute changes identified by the community as necessary to make a good library better, including paying for the renovation of two branches, the replacement of two branches, the complete renovation and expansion of the central library, and funding for a bookmobile.

More recent examples are cited in a January 1996 *American Libraries* article[33] that found that libraries fared better than Democrats and incumbents in the November 8, 1995, elections around the country. Although some of the largest funding issues went down in defeat, libraries batted somewhat better than .500—not a bad average, given the antigovernment, antitax sentiment reflected in other election results.

In California, only one library-funding measure succeeded—Santa Clara County and the city of San Jose voted on advisory measures to create new assessment districts for libraries. Elected officials who backed the measures have promised to assess taxes.

In Georgia, Clarke County voters passed a 1 percent special purpose tax that will be devoted to 29 different capital projects, including the purchase of new library materials.

In New Mexico, two successful statewide bond issues will provide $2.5 million for public library acquisitions and equipment; $2.5 million for school libraries; $3 million for academic-library acquisitions. Successful local referenda will provide $1.8 million for the Albuquerque-Bernalillo Public Library system and $.5 million for public Pueblo libraries in Sandoval County.

In Pennsylvania, library millage issues passed in seven jurisdictions in Monroe County, as well as in Bloomfield Township in Crawford County. Ross Township voted to change its base of support from millage to a formula including population and usage.

In South Carolina, a $2.6 million referendum for a new library in Summerville also passed.

These are only some of the library issues that were affected by elections, but they do provide a cross section of the varied nature of library referenda.

Fees for Services

Fee-based services make up 3.08 percent of the average public library's budget, and in a time of diminishing budgets, every cent counts. Libraries are bound to think of instituting fees for certain library services, but Sally Gardner Reed in *Saving Your Library*[34] cautions against such an action, calling it "The Politics of Making Do."

Justifications for charging for services are discussed in chapter 12 "The Future Is Now: Will Public Libraries Survive?" but Reed does make a valid point when she says that the "institution of fees for 'special services' can set the stage for a continued erosion of the free public library model."[35] She notes that in addition to creating discriminatory service, librarians who charge fees will be inviting questions that will be hard to answer. What constitutes special services as opposed to those deemed basic? How will librarians who charge fees for some services explain the difference to municipal authorities? How will they be able to draw the line when budget makers ask that other library services be supported by fee?

Reed points out that it is simple, and tempting, to consider charging a fee for a service that is being threatened, in order to retain that service and make it self-supporting, but the ramifications are far-reaching. The problem with fees for service is that they effectively put these services out of the reach of some patrons, and this is antithetical to the noble purposes of the profession. The most-cherished and important mission any public library has is to ensure that all members of the community are afforded equal access to the collection they support through their taxes.

The Internet and Library Budgets

Public libraries have seen their technology-related costs skyrocket by almost 85 percent in the last two years,[36] and they are faced with how to handle the cost of becoming their communities' access to the Internet.

Evan St. Lifer in "Public Library Budgets Brace for Internet Costs" says that Internet-related costs are emerging as an essential line item, vying with other basic public library services for an increasingly larger piece of the budgetary pie. Public libraries are reportedly spending an average of $100,213 to provide some form of Internet access to patrons and staff. The average expenditure in FY96 by library size for Internet access was:

Size (Patrons Served)	Average Expenditure
Fewer than 10,000	$ 3,480
10,000–24,999	6,405
25,000–49,999	11,073
50,000–99,999	58,334
100,000–999,999	151,150
More than 1 million	375,000

In his article St. Lifer says that by providing Internet access, librarians have been forced to reevaluate their fiscal priorities, and four out of ten respondents in the *Library Journal* report said they would have to cut back spending in other areas to fund Internet-related initiatives. Every library with a population served of fewer than 50,000 that responded to the survey reported having to cut from their materials budget to fund some type of 'net-based service. While some are cutting from their materials budgets, more are looking toward pursuing funding from outside sources to foot their technology bill—state funding (57 percent), federal government (43 percent), corporate or private philanthropy (27 percent), and individual gifts (13 percent).

An even greater number of public libraries have solicited grants (74 percent), with the average grant totaling $129,240, to help offset the costs of the Internet. The Austin Public Library's Internet access was funded through a $200,000 grant from the Texas State Library. APL had formed a partnership with the Austin Freenet and jointly submitted the application. The grant money was used to fund 52 Internet stations.

"The demand greatly exceeds the number of Internet terminals and we are hoping to find other partners in the community to help us fund additional public access terminals," said Brenda Branch, director of the Austin Public Library. The scenario that the APL is facing is one that more and more libraries will have to confront as the Internet carves out a crucial niche for itself in public library services.

Cooperative Collection Development

Access to information will be the key to future library services,[37] and thus guidance for developing the philosophy and mechanics required for cooperative and coordinated collection development must be available to those considering access beyond onsite collections, and traditional interlibrary loans. Increasing costs of library materials, as well as their storage and retrieval, coupled with the incorporation of new information formats, have caused librarians and administrators to rethink the need for cooperative collection development to cope with inflation and decreasing budgets.

Through the online capabilities of the major bibliographic utilities as well as through individual library systems' online catalogs, cooperative libraries are able to locate needed materials using a shared resource base. With the development of faster and more efficient borrowing and lending systems, any size or type of library can use information through resource sharing. In resource sharing, members agree to divide responsibility for particular parts of their collection development programs, with funding typically coming from the library budgets of institutions that will house the material. Resource sharing will play an increasingly important role as libraries' revenues struggle to keep up with escalating costs of materials on a stagnant or decreasing budget; then, cooperative collection development will be more commonplace.

Funds for Library Construction

Data on referenda for public library construction that was collected by *Library Journal* and Richard B. Hall, of the California State Library, show mixed results for those libraries surveyed, with the outcome in some years turning out less propitiously than in others.

In 1994, although the number of referenda held for library capital outlay and for operating funds was about the same, nearly half of the capital outlay referenda failed. In contrast, the capital outlay campaigns of FY95 were fewer, but out of the 45 campaigns, only 6 failed.[38] An analysis of the data to determine the factors that help make an election successful resulted in the following conclusions:

- Special elections are more successful than general ones.

- Spring is not the best season for libraries to hold elections. Only 79 percent of elections during that season were successful. The success for summer was 83 percent, for fall 86 percent, and for winter 92 percent.

- Having other items on the ballot to compete with the library proposal is not a problem in itself, but if there are other issues that ask for money, or if there are issues that voters feel strongly against, the library usually loses.

The struggle to fund library construction is not one for the faint-hearted. Following are three examples of the campaigns that libraries have had to undertake to pay for library construction.

The campaign by the Kalamazoo, Michigan, Public Library was won in March 1995, in part because the staff and volunteers targeted selected groups—library patrons who had also voted in the June 1994 school board election and the August 1994 primary. The library compared its database listing of adult resident cardholders with purchased voting lists, and this list of fewer than 4,000 names was targeted for additional mailings and phone reminders.

This low-profile strategy drew criticism from the local newspaper, which gave the library negative coverage during the last 10 days before the election, but the library's strategy worked in spite of it. The number of people who voted "yes" was 3,234, out of 5,293.

When the small town of Pelham, New York, applied for a LSCA grant to build its first public library, it was told by the New York Division of Library Development that, according to state guidelines, federal funds could not be used to construct a new library where none existed. Two years later, with the help of the U.S. Department of Education, the Division was persuaded to change its guidelines.[39] The residents of the town of 12,500 people raised more than $1.9 million in private donations through private receptions and neighborhood-oriented affairs so that they could build and equip a library. One such affair, held on November 19, 1994, was called "A Novel Night in November," during which volunteers dressed up as characters from a novel and the home where the party was held was decorated with props appropriate to the novel. More than $100,000 was raised through 40 such dinner parties.

The main library of San Francisco was branded a disgrace in 1957, but it was not until 1988 that voters of the city, backed by a 78 percent bond measure, provided $109.5 million to construct a new main library and to rebuild several branches. The next six years, according to Peter Booth Wiley, were spent overcoming two hurdles.[40]

First, the city was facing a financial crisis. When Mayor Art Agnos took office in 1988, he asked all city departments, including the library, to cut their budgets. In 1994, the Friends of the Library won, by 70 percent, passage of a charter amendment guaranteeing the library system a fixed percentage of the city's budget for the next 15 years. Almost $12 million were added to the library's budget.

The second hurdle involved the equipping of the new library. Now that money was available to build and run the library, would it open with nothing in it? The Friends established the Library Foundation of San Francisco to raise $30 million to equip the new library once it was built. The Foundation got off to a slow start until Steve Coulter, president of the Library Commission and a foundation board member, organized a unique fund-raising campaign.

Because San Francisco has clearly defined neighborhoods and constituencies, Coulter asked various groups, such as gay and lesbian groups and African American communities, to donate funds that would be split between special collections reflecting their interests and the new main library as a whole. Donors grew from 600 to 17,000, and more than $35 million were raised.

Of the fund-raising campaign, Wiley said, "Ultimately, rebuilding the city library was an act of political will, one in which the citizenry carried the day no matter how unfavorable the situation."[41] Perhaps this can be said of all efforts of citizens who endeavor to build libraries for themselves: Where there is a collective will, there will always be a way to fund public libraries.

Discussion Questions

1. Should the federal government play a bigger role in stabilizing funding of public libraries?
2. How are public libraries dealing with the fiscal challenges posed by increasing technology?
3. Are collaborations and resource sharing viable means to easing the increasing costs of materials to libraries? Are there any public libraries that have done this successfully? There are any number of academic and special libraries that have been doing this for some time, but would such means work for public libraries?
4. What role does fund-raising play in the public library's budget? How are libraries undertaking fund-raising?
5. Should public libraries charge fees for services? What are the pros and cons? What are some of the examples of what libraries are charging for, and what is the outcome of that?
6. What role do ALA and other library associations play in the political arena to ensure that public libraries are funded adequately?

Notes

1. "Hard Times for Libraries: Will Budget Cuts Diminish Their Community Role?" *CQ Researcher* 2, no. 24 (June 26, 1992): 563.
2. Ibid., 561.
3. Ibid., 563.
4. Ibid., 551.
5. Evan St. Lifer, "Public Library Budgets Brace for Internet Costs," *Library Journal* (January 1997): 45.

6. Ibid., 45.

7. Ibid., 44.

8. "ALA Washington Office: Library Services and Technology Act Enacted," available: http://www. ala.org/washoff/lstapass.html (Accessed April 9, 1998).

9. Ibid., 3.

10. St. Lifer, "Public Library Budgets," 44–45.

11. "ALA Washington Office: Highlights of the Library Services and Technology Act," available: http: //www.ala.org/washoff/lstahigh.html (Accessed April 9, 1998).

12. "President Signs Museum and Library Services Act," available: http://www.nclis.gov/news/pr96/museum.html (Accessed April 9, 1998).

13. "AB Library Notes," *AB Bookman Weekly* 99, no. 3 (February 3, 1997): 302.

14. Hwa-Wei Lee and Gary A. Hunt, *Fund-Raising for the 1990s: The Challenge Ahead, A Practical Guide for Library Fund-Raising, from Novice to Expert* (Canfield, Ohio: Genaway & Associates, 1992).

15. "How the NEH Works," available: http://206. 161.132. 66/html/how_work.html (Accessed March 1998).

16. "Institute of Museum and Library Services: Legislative Report," available: http://www.ims.fed.us/IMLS%20legislative%20report.html (Accessed March 1997).

17. "National Historical Publications and Records Commission (NHPRC) Home Page," available: http://www.nara.gov/nara/nhprc/ (Accessed April 9, 1998).

18. *Federal Register* 62, no. 52 (March 18, 1997).

19. "NSF: About NSF," available: http://www.nsf gov/home/about/start.html (Accessed March 1997).

20. "The National Library of Medicine," available: http://www.nlm.nih.gov/pubs/factsheets'nlm.html (Accessed April 9, 1998).

21. "Council on Library Resources," available: http://sulc3.stanford.edu/clr/ (Accessed April 9, 1998).

22. Dwight F. Burlingame, "Fund-Raising As a Key to the Library's Future," *Library Trends* 42, no. 3 (Winter 1994): 468.

23. Joseph Leroy Harrison, *The Public Library in the United States* (1894), quoted in Paul Dickerson, *The Library in America* (1986): 2.

24. Dickerson, *Library in America*, 46.

25. Lee and Hunt, *Fund-Raising for the 1990s*, 51.

26. Clyde C. Walton, "Gifts, Bequests, Endowments," in *ALA Yearbook of Library and Information Services: 1985* (Chicago: American Library Association, 1985), 133.

27. Steve Sumerford, "Careful Planning: The Fund-Raising Edge," *North Carolina Libraries* 53, no. 1 (Spring 1995): 3.

28. Ibid., 4.

29. "Hard Times for Libraries," 564.

30. Ibid., 564.

31. St. Lifer, "Public Library Budgets," 45.

32. Saul Amdursky, "Anatomy of an Election," *Library Journal* 120, no. 11 (June 15, 1995): 46.

33. "Referenda Rundown: Library Election Results in a Mixed Bag," *American Libraries* (January 1995): 6.

34. Sally Gardner Reed, *Saving Your Library: A Guide to Getting, Using and Keeping the Power You Need* (Jefferson, N.C.: McFarland), 1991.

35. Ibid., 61.

36. St. Lifer, "Public Library Budgets," 44.

37. Bart Harbe, ed., "Guide to Cooperative Collection Development," in *Collection Management and Development Guides, No. 6* (Chicago: American Library Association), 1994.

38. Richard B. Hall, "Back in the Black: Library Campaigns Pay Off," *Library Journal* 121, no. 11 (June 15, 1996): 36–37.

39. Kimberly S. Blanchard, "Making It Happen: A Small Town Builds Its Own Library," *American Libraries* 27, no. 4 (April 1996): 64.

40. Peter Booth Wiley, "An Act of Political Will: SF's Quest for a New Central Library," *Library Journal* 121, no. 7 (April 15, 1996): 36.

41. Ibid., 37.

12 THE FUTURE IS NOW: WILL PUBLIC LIBRARIES SURVIVE?

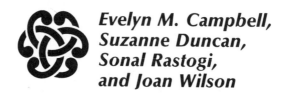

Evelyn M. Campbell,
Suzanne Duncan,
Sonal Rastogi,
and Joan Wilson

Advances in information technology and in the communications industry have changed the way society views and uses information, and this change has had a correspondingly tremendous effect on what is expected from, and demanded of, public libraries today. The traditional uses of libraries and the traditional roles of librarians are being challenged, and over the last decade, libraries and librarians have had to change the way they shape, store, and provide information.

Professional and popular literature abound with predictions of doom for libraries as we know them today—that libraries and librarians will be replaced by computers and databases that will provide users with the information they need. Librarians who have been the traditional gatekeepers of information will be bypassed, and users will be able to go directly to the needed information with a few keystrokes.

Only time will tell whether these predictions will ever become reality. But it is clear that technology has become integrated into the daily life of society, and libraries, because they have always been a reflection of

180

the society in which they exist, must change to accommodate changes in society. Librarians have been forced to reexamine and reevaluate the purposes and the practices of librarianship.

This chapter highlights some of the issues that are affecting librarianship today and proposes some solutions or, at least, an earnest discussion of such issues as the effects of technology on libraries, the role of librarians in the new information age, libraries and customer services in these changing times, collaborations between libraries and other information centers, and how library science programs can help shape the future of libraries.

Technology

This century has seen the advent of personal computers and the enormous technological strides in telecommunications, and these events have forever changed how libraries shape, store, and provide information. The technological advances that have affected libraries include the delivery of information in the form of CD-ROMs and online databases, but what is perhaps having the greatest effect on libraries is the emergence of the Internet and the creation of the National Information Infrastructure.

The Internet

The present Internet grew out of the ARPANET project, which provided the first large-scale demonstration of a new digital communications technology called packet-switching.[1] In 1968 the Advance Research Projects Agency (ARPA) of the Department of Defense provided grants to several universities and corporations to develop a nationwide digital communications medium that was separate from the telephone system. ARPANET linked researchers at different sites and allowed them to share hardware and software resources.

When ARPANET first became operational in 1969, the entire network consisted of four computers, but after the first 10 years of operation, the number of connected computers expanded to more than 100. At this point, ARPANET began to exceed the capacity permitted by its initial design. The original ARPANET protocols were not flexible enough to accommodate the ongoing expansion of ARPANET itself or permit other networks to connect easily into the ARPANET framework.

A new family of message protocols was designed in the late 1970s to address these problems. The most basic of the new protocols are the Transmission Control Protocol (TCP) and the Internet Protocol (IP), which provide the facilities by which computers can exchange messages. Many computer operators quickly adopted TCP/IP as the message protocol for their systems, but other networks also came into existence at this time.

Access to ARPANET was restricted to institutions with defense-related contracts, so universities pushed for independent networks. As a result, CSNET and BITNET were created in the 1970s and 1980s to serve the academic community. Europe also began to create an information infrastructure of its own, based on another protocol called X.25.

Many of these networks were initially isolated from each other because they used different protocols. To communicate between different networks, it was necessary to have one computer linked to two or more networks so that it could serve as a gateway machine. Gateways were developed and operated with mixed results.

When the Department of Defense began to reduce ARPANET support in the mid-1980s, the National Science Foundation (NSF) took over and supported a new networking system called NSFNET, which was available to universities and commercial users. NSFNET became the backbone of an entire collection of networks that is known collectively as the Internet. The Internet has become an enormous global web linking more than 1.5 million computers in more than 50 countries, with data traffic on the NSFNET doubling every year.

SUCCESSES OF THE INTERNET

Computer Professionals for Social Responsibility (CPSR), an organization that examines the effects of technology on society, has been an active participant in setting up the National Information Infrastructure. The organization has noted several successes and effects of the Internet that can be applied to the design of networks in the future.

- The Internet has proven valuable to a large number of users who employ it to communicate with friends and colleagues, share data and software, etc. The best measure of success for any computer system is the satisfaction of the user community.

The explosive growth of the Internet is a clear indication that people find it valuable.

■ The structure of the Internet encourages participation and creative change. The value of the Internet comes primarily from the knowledge and creativity its users bring to it. By making individual contribution easy, the Internet has enabled services to develop and grow.

■ The pricing strategy of the Internet encourages experimentation and growth. For users, universities, or companies, access to the Internet is paid for by the parent organization, not the individual user in the organization. This policy has allowed users to browse the network casually and has generated forms of interaction that could not flourish in an environment of usage or connect-time charges.

■ The Internet is run democratically. Although the Internet requires some central coordination, its loose management structure has demonstrated the value of allowing widespread participation in the process of running the network. Individual users and their institutions often feel a strong investment in the Internet's success because each site derives considerable benefit from being a part of the Internet. Communication on the Internet is also essentially free of censorship.

■ The Internet has demonstrated the value of open, interoperable standards.

SHORTCOMINGS OF THE INTERNET

Despite the Internet's obvious benefits, CPSR has identified several shortcomings that suggest that the Internet is an inappropriate medium to replace public libraries, and that such an action will probably never occur.

■ The Internet is not connected with enough services of general interest to meet the needs of the majority of the public.

■ Individual Internet connections are too expensive, and although service providers allow individuals to dial in to a shared Internet connection, such connections only offer a minimum form of interaction.

- Human-computer interfaces for the Internet are not yet very sophisticated. A large developmental effort needs to take place if extremely sophisticated services are to be offered to unsophisticated users. The Internet is currently most accessible to people who are technically very experienced and knowledgeable.

- Information overload. Users of the Internet should be able to find what they need without being overwhelmed by massive amounts of data, as is currently the case.

- The proliferation of new bulletin boards, discussion lists, information sources, etc., makes it harder for users to locate specific information.

- The Internet lacks sufficient mechanisms to guarantee privacy and security.

Other librarians echo the sentiments of Andy Barnett, assistant director of the McMillan Memorial Library in Wisconsin Rapids, Wisconsin, who believes that the Internet will not replace libraries for several reasons.[2]

- The primary use of the Internet is entertainment and not education.

- The Internet will become increasingly commercial with more entertainment than educational material on it.

- Use will be metered. The vast majority of Internet uses will be metered—the more you use, the more you pay (similar to electricity and so forth).

- What the Internet does best (communication) is not a threat to libraries.

- Ease of use. The Internet is like the Library of Congress without a catalog or shelving system. It is easy to find entertaining stuff but hard to find real information.

- The authenticity problem. Due to persistent security problems, nothing on the Internet can safely be assumed to be authentic. Documents on the Internet may not actually have been written by the person whose name is on them.

- The copyright issues still have to be worked out.

■ Data costs, and good data costs more. The "free" information on the Internet has reliability problems. If you want accurate, reliable information, you pay for that information through the use of gateways and passwords and a running meter. Why pay for information on the Internet when you can get it free at the public library?

■ Surfing is the right metaphor. Surfing is fun, and for some it is cheap, but it is not free. You need specialized equipment and have to know how to use it. You can surf for hours, but you end up back on the beach.

The National Information Infrastructure (NII)

The Clinton administration's vision of a new National Information Infrastructure was first presented in a February 1993 white paper titled "Technology for America's Economic Growth: A New Direction to Build Economic Strength." This was later refined in a report titled "The National Information Infrastructure: Agenda for Action," which was issued in September 1993 by the National Telecommunications and Information Administration (NTIA).[3]

The September 1993 report's executive summary describes the NII as a "seamless web of communication networks, computers, databases, and consumer electronics that will put vast amounts of information at users' fingertips."[4] The summary goes on to say that the NII can help unleash an information revolution that will change forever the way people live, work, and interact with each other.

The government sees the NII as an economic benefit—"An advanced information infrastructure will enable U.S. firms to compete and win in the global economy, generating good jobs for the American people and economic growth for the nation."[5] The CPSR also sees great promise in the NII but views its potential benefits as not being solely economic. The concerns that CPSR has are the same concerns that librarians have, or should have—"The NII must promote the public interest along with private interests. The success of the NII program will depend on the extent to which it empowers all citizens, protects individual rights, and strengthens the democratic institutions on which this country was founded."[6] Some of the concerns that have been identified include the following items.

- The NII may fail to provide universal access. If network connections are not readily available, particularly in rural or economically disadvantaged areas, the NII will fail to serve those communities. The pricing structure may also freeze out individuals and public institutions lacking the necessary resources to pay for access. The NII may also remain out of reach of most nontechnical users unless training programs and well-designed software tools are available.

- A small number of companies may dominate the network and exert undue influence on its design and operation. The NII is an extremely ambitious program that will require substantial investment on the part of private companies who undertake the task of providing the physical infrastructure.

- There is a danger that carriers will control content on the NII. The enormous economic potential of the NII lies in the information and services that the infrastructure carries.

- NII services may emphasize commerce at the expense of communication.

- Public access to government information may be restricted. In recent years more and more public information has been turned over to private companies for distribution. In the absence of pricing regulations, much of this information has become available only to the well funded. If the trend toward privatization continues, the NII will be unable to satisfy its potential as a source of public information.

- The NII may fail to provide a vital public space. Individuals and groups that represent the public interest must be an integral part of the NII design process.

- The NII may be used to justify the elimination of other essential public services. Although increased access to information can benefit and empower everyone in society, it is important to recognize that there are many other problems in society that the NII will not address. For example, making government documents available through the NII does not eliminate the need for reference librarians any more than providing online medical advice eliminates the need for local doctors.

- The NII may fail to protect individual privacy. Using the NII, government agencies and private companies would have unprecedented opportunities to gather and disseminate information about individuals.

What then is the government's expectation of the part that libraries will play in the NII? Surprisingly enough, the Clinton administration sees libraries as playing an important role in the information infrastructure. "As today, the role of libraries in the future will be to advocate and help provide information equity for the public. Libraries will continue to coordinate and facilitate preservation of the records and expressions of the nation's intellectual and cultural life both in traditional and digital formats. Libraries will be sources of free or inexpensive digital information; provide access to an improved flow of electronic government information and worldwide digitized resources; request and be sent copies of remotely stored documents and other publications as allowed by copyright licensing and other agreements."[7]

According to a report by the Committee on Application and Technology, "Putting the Information Infrastructure to Work,"[8] using libraries as gateways to the digital network can help ensure that information is accessible to all and prevent the formation of a society divided into information haves and have-nots. The committee advocates that libraries continue to play their vital role of information safety net for the public by providing access to and promoting literacy of digital materials as they have for printed materials.

The Clinton administration has identified four obstacles to achieving the promise of NII applications in public libraries.

- Technology development. Technologies for digital libraries are still immature relative to the expectations of users. For NII to affect libraries meaningfully, new navigation and retrieval tools will be required to locate, browse, retrieve, and distribute digital information. Moreover, the ability to store increasing amounts of data at steadily decreasing costs is a technological trend that is vital to the massive amounts of data that digital libraries will have to store and support.

- Protection of Intellectual Property. The NII presents three significant new challenges to protecting intellectual property. First, digitization offers an unprecedented, easy, and inexpensive method to produce an indefinite number of perfect copies. Second, information in disparate media can be converted into a single digital stream and can be manipulated easily to create a variety of new works. Third, digitized information can be distributed to and downloaded by thousands of users instantly.

- Data Standards. In order to access resources stored in databases across the globe, standards that specify data description and transmission characteristics will have to be identified and agreed on.

- Education and training. Training on how to use digital libraries on the NII and on how to incorporate these resources into the home and workplace to improve our quality of life and standard of living will be key to attaining the vision.

The results of a national survey of public libraries sponsored by the National Commission on Libraries and Information Science (NCLIS), which indicated that only about 21.1 percent of the responding public libraries are connected to the Internet and 78.9 percent are not, seem to support the argument that public libraries are not yet ready for the information infrastructure. But it is also clear that libraries and librarians have to act now if they are to be active participants in the information age. Librarians must become more than literate about technology, much more than aware of the potential of technology, and much more than passingly familiar with the features and applications of technology.[9] (See also chapters 8, 9, and 11.)

Librarians' Roles

The important role libraries must play in the digital age is recognized by many high-level policymakers. "The role of libraries is critical. Moreover, you will find that librarians around this country are as well informed and as enthusiastic about the national information infrastructure as any group in our entire nation," Vice President Al Gore said in response to a question about libraries at the presentation of the Clinton administration's plan for the development of the National Information Infrastructure (NII) before the Academy of Television Arts & Sciences in January 1994.[10]

Indeed, who are better qualified than librarians to play a central role in the emerging information age? Librarians excel at identifying, acquiring, organizing, housing, preserving, archiving, and assisting in the use of information.[11] And they have been willing to play many roles—as curators, advocates, collectors, organizers, and teachers—and librarianship has always been a dynamic and expanding profession.[12]

One thing is clear—librarians will have to fight for the right to be part of the information age. Although policymakers realize that libraries will play an important role in NII, librarians should be represented at every stage of the planning for the information infrastructure. Librarians must become advocates of public access and must raise their voices over the explosion of information providers and the unorganized, haphazard information currently available.

Librarians are aware of what information technology can bring: unusable formats, high fees, limited preservation, no centralized bibliographic control, restricted physical access, propriety control, market-driven availability, and loss of privacy. To help ensure that information will truly benefit the public, Nancy Kranich recommends several courses of action for librarians.

- Know the issues and the stakeholders. Librarians must educate themselves about the issues that affect their future, including developing an in-depth knowledge about telecommunications regulations at the federal, state, and local levels; about copyright policy; about privacy and national security concerns; and about access to government information. Get to know committees, commissions, and agencies dealing with particular concerns, and form alliances.

- Draft principles. The library community must know where they stand on the issues and they must speak with one voice. They have to get involved with drafting principles that affect the information infrastructure.

- Build consensus. Here again, the need to speak with one voice is re-emphasized. Librarians have to reach a consensus among themselves before they can approach policymakers with their ideas.

- Build coalitions and partnerships. Once librarians agree on a course of action, they must identify those who have similar goals, and form alliances with them.

- Publicize concerns. Bring attention to the issues by contacting local newspapers, visiting editorial boards, drafting press releases, seeking radio and television interviews, writing letters to the editor, enlisting the help of sympathetic influential people, inviting the press to events, etc. Take every opportunity to educate the public.

- Participate in the public policy process. Work to have librarians named to advisory councils at the local, state, and federal levels. Demand a seat at the policymaking table and take an active role in designing the information future.

- Get grants. Libraries must apply for all the grants that are available, and in these times of tight competition, well-conceived projects must be produced by professional grant writers.

- Protect fair use. Librarians must be vigilant about the erosion of fair use, particularly in the digital age when publishers want to put their property on the information highway, but at the same time want to limit public access to it through the charging of fees, etc. Librarians must fight to ensure that users have the right to read, browse, and copy for limited purposes, materials that are distributed over telecommunications networks.

- Set the terms of the discourse. Librarians must not just react to whatever is proposed. If librarians are to save and strengthen our profession and our libraries, we must consider taking legislative action, working with community groups, etc.

Kranich makes a good point when she observes: "We must remain united and look for additional allies. Divided, we cannot make the difference. No one else will stand up with the same conviction, with the same dedication, with the same determination to protect and promote the public's right to know. And if we fail to take a stand, our profession may be absorbed by a marketplace hostile to the ideal and principles of librarianship."[13]

The role of the librarian in the electronic age certainly has changed, and John C. Swan has warned that "this consensus about our endangerment as a species—particularly, a dynamic, respected species with professional standing—is essentially correct."[14] Swan also argues that those who turn their backs on the electronic challenge will be driven farther and farther into the information hinterlands.

Library/Customer Services: Fee or Free?

The core values of librarianship have evolved as a group of ethical principles involving the relationship between libraries and the use of their services, and the universal rights of free expression that each human being possesses. Libraries preserve and provide access to the corpus of recorded human expression. The primary justification for public support of libraries—whether public libraries, or those in public schools, colleges, or universities—has its roots in ideas of the public good. The public good is a social commitment and willingness to provide certain basic services to all members of the society regardless of their means or station.[15]

Based upon that commitment, public libraries have not been willing to charge their users for services provided by what are obviously tax-funded institutions. However, over the last few decades, as library budgets shrank and the cost of library materials escalated, libraries have been forced to reexamine the issue of "charging for services."

Sara Behrman has written that "our institutions are challenged to crowd a host of new services, functions and technologies into buildings with inadequate power supplies, poor communications systems and specialized service points. This reengineering, redefining and, often, remodeling comes at a time when millages are failing due to widespread property tax reform sentiment and federal dollars are jeopardized by a Congress rabid with budget reduction fever."[16]

Librarians have struggled for a number of years with the ethical issues of charging users for services that their tax dollars have made possible. It is an extremely difficult situation for librarians because their own organization, the American Library Association, has stated in its position and public policy statements that "the charging of fees and levies for information services, including those utilizing the latest information technology, is discriminatory in publicly supported institutions providing library and information services."[17]

The majority of librarians, however, make a distinction between overdue charges and fees for services. Overdue charges are levied against a user for failing to comply with a library's circulation policy. One person's failure to return a book on time means that another person who wants the same book will be denied access to it. Overdue fines then are meant to be a method of providing better access for everyone. To those who say that overdue charges present a barrier to the poor, Behrman presents the argument that the poor have complete control over whether they choose to return their materials on time.[18]

To add to the dilemma that librarians have to face in making a decision on whether to charge, the American Library Association has also taken a stand on the charging of overdue fines. In its statement on Library Services for the Poor, it favors "promoting the removal of all barriers to library and information services, particularly fees and overdue charges."[19] Most librarians make a distinction between overdue fines and charging fees for services, but they still cringe at the thought of having to do so. There are other libraries, however, that have identified fee-based services as those that are "value-added" or luxuries—for example, if the information is available free in the library in print form, but the user chooses to obtain the same information from a costly online service, then that counts as a "luxury," and a fee should be charged. Likewise, some libraries provide a fee-based fax service—the material is still available free in the library, but if the user chooses to stay home and have the information faxed to him, that is a "luxury" for which he or she should be willing to pay.

There is, of course, the argument that librarians who make a distinction between "basic free library services" and "value-added services" are threatening the public support enjoyed by libraries, and that fees are a barrier to access because the fee-based services are only available to those who can afford them. This will create a welfare system of library service—making beggars and second-class citizens of those library users who cannot pay for certain services.

Behrman also points out that rather than viewing new services like video and CD-ROM products as a way to inspire additional funding support for the valuable contributions a local library makes to the community, librarians are satisfying short-term funding concerns by generating revenue with these services.

There are those librarians like Marilyn Gell Mason, director of the Cleveland Public Library, who explains her library's policy of charging fees—"Our decision to provide a fee-based service was predicated on our goal to be the first place anyone thinks to go for information at all. Rather than turn people away who want time-consuming and specialized research, we chose to provide the service for a fee. Businesses are the most frequent users of the service, mostly because they would rather pay us than do the research themselves."[20] Why would anyone choose to spend 30 minutes doing costly research when a librarian can do the same research in 10 minutes?

In "The Future Revisited," Mason looks back at the predictions she had made in her 1985 article "The Future of the Public Library." One of her predictions was that within 10 years more than half of the services provided by the public library to users would be to individuals who never come into the library. Mason now admits that although she accurately forecast the direction of future library service, she was wrong about the rate of change. "The real surprise is not the low percentage of external use but the relationship between the growth of the library's electronic library and that of conventional use of the library. Apparently, the more we provide electronically the more people use the library conventionally. Walk-in use of the library is up, the growth curves parallel each other, suggesting a causal relationship between them and electronic services. This reinforces the idea that print and electronic information fill different needs."[21]

Behrman reminds us that public libraries today are the only safety net for those unable to afford access to electronic information. What then are the alternatives to make sure that library services are available to users at no cost? It stands to reason that if libraries are charging fees to make up for limited funding, they would not have to charge for services if the funding problems were solved.

Even in these difficult times, some libraries are thriving and doing so without charging their users. Behrman says that these libraries are successful because of their collaborations with other agencies and organizations, and because they are masters at communicating and marketing their successes.[22]

Collaborations

Collaborations, whether they are between libraries or with other agencies, are avenues that will have to be explored as a solution to the problem of diminishing funding for public libraries. With the decrease in support from governments at the municipal, state, and federal levels, libraries have turned to innovative fund-raising campaigns and partnerships that were never considered before. However, these partnerships must be formed carefully, so that there is no backlash on either the library or the sponsor. The library should never allow itself to be controlled by the sponsor and not the professional library staff.[23]

In the last decade or so, collaboration and partnering have become important elements in maintaining free and equal access to library services and technology. Collaboration also has the potential to open doors to more federal funding opportunities. Behrman says that regional partnerships between libraries, library schools, and private companies have generated foundation support greater than any given to a single entity in the funding equation.[24] Partnerships between libraries and burgeoning community networks offer new gateway services to the public—for instance, libraries should not overlook the fact that an Internet provider might offer free Internet access to the public library, as many have done in cooperation with cities and libraries all over the country.

The Internet must also not be overlooked as a source of collaboration. Kenneth E. Dowlin, in "Distribution in an Electronic Environment, or Will There Be Librarians As We Know Them in the Internet World?" points out that one of the most powerful attributes of the Internet is its ability to foster collaboration.[25] "Networking is a powerful tool for symbiotic collaborations. The electronic milieu is creating new communities all over the world, brought together by common interests. . . . Collaboration is one of the key elements in the creation of knowledge. Thus, the Internet could lead to the development of knowledge through this collaboration."[26]

Dowlin has identified several of the necessary changes that must take place in libraries before Internet collaboration can occur.

- ■ From singular processes to mass processes. Libraries must increase their ability to deal with masses of information.

- Graphic to neographic. The majority of the library's staffing and facilities have traditionally been devoted to the book as the primary vehicle for the preservation and distribution of knowledge even though other media have been in libraries for a while. It is time to consider the library not just a graphic-based institution but one that is neographic (a term coined by Dowlin).

- Retail to wholesale. Libraries have viewed their main function as that of providing information to the ultimate consumer—the user. With the ability to extend access through other institutions and agencies, libraries need to incorporate the concept of also being in the wholesale business. Other agencies can expand the library's abilities to reach currently unserved populations and communities.

- Monodimensional access to multidimensional access. The library has traditionally been a leader in communities in increasing the diversity of access to information and knowledge. To reach the maximum population, the library may need to think in terms of services similar to banking institutions—automated teller machines (automated information machines for the library), etc.[27]

Behrman observes that it is not enough just to collaborate on projects. Public libraries must also communicate their successes to their funders and to their constituents. The community must know the importance of the library and its services. She also asserts that collaboration and partnering with others requires time, energy, a commitment to the vision of success, and a clear sense of purpose. It is not easy, but it is essential.

The American Library Association: ALA Goal 2000

It is informative to consider how the American Library Association views its role in the information infrastructure, and how those views may affect the library world. With the ALA Board's adoption of the ALA Goal 2000 in 1995, the ALA made clear its intention of being a major participant in the new information age.

The five-year plan, which was the brainchild of ALA Executive Director Elizabeth Martinez, set nine essential goals intended to guarantee librarians an essential role in the formation of national information policy. This effort is ultimately aimed at protecting and enhancing the public's right to access the information required for meaningful participation in an information-based society.[28]

The nine essential goals are:

- ALA will have been accepted by the public as a voice and the source of support for the participation of people of all ages and circumstances in a free and open information society.

- ALA will have become an active formal participant in the various national arenas, discussing and deciding the objectives of the information society that affect libraries and their users.

- ALA will have identified and will already be in collaboration with other organizations and groups working for broader public participation in the development of information-society issues.

- ALA will have created a vision statement for broad distribution defining its position and role within the emerging information environment.

- ALA will have an expanded Washington office, a major organization entity devoted to serving as an advocate for the public's intellectual participation. It will have greatly increased its ability to learn about, analyze, share information about, and affect important national information issues as they occur, in addition to tracking traditional library issues.

- ALA will have completed a five-year thematic cycle that has framed the advancement of these issues and coordinated the support of all areas of the Association in preparation for the twenty-first century.

- ALA will have provided training and support to library professionals and members of the public in order to create an awareness of the variety of social and technical issues related to the information society, providing the necessary background for promoting further dialogue at more local levels.

- ALA will have reviewed and adjusted its internal operations as a means of assisting all divisions and units in carrying out the new focus as appropriate to their spheres.

- ALA will have redefined library information education and provided five years of training for professionals to update their skills for the new information age.

Tom Gaughan, in "ALA Goal 2000: Planning for the Millennium," describes the plan as a "sweeping, visionary plan to immediately propel the Association into major-player status in the information society."[29] The plan grew out of a concern that librarians' voices were not being heard, and that the library, once a central institution in the creation, use, and distribution of knowledge, was being pushed to the periphery.

Martinez's intention is to bring the ALA back to the policymaking table: "It is our duty to share what we have learned as one of the major information institutions by claiming a greater voice for our members and our users in the national information discourse."[30] And although ALA Goal 2000 does not claim to answer all the concerns librarians have, it is a step in the right direction and one that, if it succeeds, will make libraries and librarians strong participants in the information age of the next century.

Education: Preparing Librarians for the Future

To meet the changing needs of public libraries, library science programs have had to rethink and redo their curricula in order to produce graduates who are well prepared to face the challenges of the profession. Kate Murphy, in a *New York Times* article titled "Moving from the Card Catalogue to the Internet," wrote that "the field of library science has changed drastically. While it is still a discipline dedicated to finding, filtering, organizing, evaluating and presenting information, it now requires a great deal more technical expertise with electronic information and computer networks."[31] To meet that change, many universities are reinventing and restructuring their library schools—not only their curricula but also their names. Rutgers University led the way in 1982, when the Graduate School of Library and Information Studies merged with the School of Communication Studies to form the School of Communication, Information, and Library Studies (SCILS). Of the 56 ALA-accredited library science programs today, 8 are partnered with other disciplines and professional programs.

And while some 15 schools have closed since 1976, the library science profession is in no danger of disappearing. Prudence W. Dalrymple has pointed out that there have always been fluctuations in the number of educational programs in any profession. Although there are currently only 56 LIS programs compared to 70 in 1982, these fewer programs are producing more graduates—from 1986 to 1996 the number of master's degrees awarded annually in the United States and Canada rose from 3,596 to 5,273, an increase of 1,677, or 46 percent.[32]

The ALA's figures also indicate that total enrollment at schools of library and information science increased by 47 percent from 1986 to 1997. Also, membership in the association increased to 58,112 in 1996 from 42,361 in 1986, a rise of 37 percent. These figures refute any assertion that librarianship is a dying profession; many librarians attribute this new lease on life to the fact that, although LIS programs are producing more graduates than ever before, fewer of these graduates are going into traditional libraries. This has, in turn, created new job opportunities for librarians.

Murphy observes that, although there are no comprehensive job placement statistics for LIS program graduates, officials at ALA have noticed a marked increase in the number of professionally trained librarians pursuing nontraditional, technologically oriented jobs. Companies like Monsanto, Ford Motor, Microsoft, Intel, and CNA Insurance have begun intensively to recruit library and information science graduates to fill such positions as scientific researcher, configuration manager, records management analyst, and graphic multimedia designer.

"Industry has come to realize the competitive advantage of hiring professionals who not only know how to find strategic information quickly, but how to evaluate its validity and present it coherently," commented Leigh Estabrook, dean of the University of Illinois School of Information and Library Science.[33]

This recent increase in job opportunities for LIS graduates can help explain the increase in enrollment in LIS programs, and the increase in job opportunities can in turn be explained by the fact that LIS programs are producing graduates who have been taught most of the skills they need to survive in the information age. It is obvious that these LIS programs are doing something right in the way they have reinvented and restructured themselves.

Dalrymple has noted several trends in LIS programs that might be responsible for the changes in LIS programs.

- Advisory boards and focus groups of employers, faculty, and students keep programs vital and responsive to society's needs.

- Grants, outside government funding, and increased revenues from a host of entrepreneurial initiatives enable schools to deliver high-quality education.

- More than half of the accredited LIS programs have recently completed, or are in the midst of, major curricula reform.

- Instruction is no longer confined to the lecture method; students learn in electronic classrooms and through modular self-paced, computer-based instruction, either on- or off-site.

- Interdisciplinary arrangements with other departments broaden students' perspective and stimulate various joint-degree programs.

- The need to provide increased access to education for traditionally underserved populations (minorities and those living in geographically remote areas) drives the stepped-up recruitment efforts of universities and LIS schools.

There is no need to mourn the demise of the traditional library science school—a new and more viable one has taken its place in producing graduates who are well equipped to meet the challenges of the new millennium.

Conclusion

Technology, which has greatly changed the way librarians do their jobs, will continue to affect libraries in the next century. The librarian who recognizes that technology has become an integral part of librarianship and who rises to the challenges that the new information age has presented and will continue to present, is a librarian who will remain an important, viable force in public libraries, and in libraries everywhere.

The ways or the methods by which librarians do their jobs certainly have changed, but the core values or missions of librarianship have remained the same. Libraries will continue to exist in the next century. They have always represented the community in which they exist, and they will continue to preserve the community in the twenty-first century.

Discussion Questions

1.   What are some trends that doomsayers cite to predict the demise of the public library?
2.   What evidence is there that the public library is likely to prosper and play a vital role in the millenium? Compare the evidence with the trends listed above.
3.   How can the public library use the Internet to assure a bright future for itself? What is the role of the MLS (MIS) education program in promoting the public library?
4.   What must librarians do to assure their survival as a profession and as vital participants in the National Information Infrastucture (NII)?
5.   What are the benefits of charging fees for some library services, and what long-range effects are likely to be experienced from the practice?
6.   How and why must the public library lead the way in collaborative efforts to better serve the total community?
7.   How can new library school graduates influence the static level of salaries and positions in a new century of opportunity? What support groups can you include in your campaign?

Additional Readings

Lamolinara, Guy. "Digital Transformation: Dr. Billington Discusses Future of Public Libraries." *LC Information Bulletin* 55, no. 1 (January 22, 1996): 3–4.

"Libraries for the Future." Available: http://www.lff.org/ (Accessed September 1998).

Low, Kathleen. "The Future Role of Reference Librarians: Will It Change?" *The Reference Librarian*, no. 54 (1996): 145–161.

Mielke, Linda. "Future Directions for Libraries." *Public Libraries* 36, no. 1 (January/February 1997): 11.

Plater, William. "Capturing the Vision of the Future: Keynote Address to the Indiana Library Federation District 4 Conference, September 30, 1994, Husey Mayfield Memorial Public Library, Zionsville, Indiana." *Indiana Libraries* 13, no. 2 (1994): 3–14.

Sager, Don. "Looking Forward: Student Perspectives on the Future of Public Library Service." *Public Libraries* 35, no. 1 (January/February 1996): 27–32.

———. "The Status of State Library Service to Public Libraries." *Public Libraries* 34, no. 6 (November/December 1995): 333–338.

Taylor, Merrily E. "Getting It All Together: Leadership Requirements for the Future of Information Services." *Journal of Library Administration* 20, no. 3/4 (1995): 9–24.

Towey, Cathleen. "Looking Toward the Next Century: Where Are Library Services Headed?" *Public Libraries* 36, no. 1 (January/February 1997): 14.

Whitwel, Stuart C. A., "Is There an Andrew Carnegie in the House?" *American Libraries* 27, no. 1 (January 1996): 91–94.

Woodhams, Helen. "Confusing Personal Preference with Public Good." *Public Libraries* 36, no. 1 (January/February 1997): 10–12.

Notes

1. "Serving the Community: A Public-Internet Vision of the National Information Infrastructure," available: http://www.cpsr.org/cpsr/nii_policy (Accessed April 9, 1998).

2. Andy Barnett, "Top Ten Reasons the Internet Will Not Replace Public Libraries," available: http://www.infi.net/~net/~cwt/top-ten.txt (Accessed Feb.-March, 1997).

3. "Serving the Community," 2.

4. "The National Information Infrastructure: Agenda for Action," available: http://www.cpsr.org/cpsr/nii/ntia_nii_agenda.txt (Accessed April 9, 1998).

5. Ibid., 2.

6. "Serving the Community," 2.

7. "Library Applications of the National Information Infrastructure," available: http://nii.nist.gov/nii/applic/lbr/lbr.html (Accessed January 21, 1997).

8. "Benefits of Using NII Applications in Libraries," Available: http://nii.nist.gov/nii/applic/lbr/lbrben.html (Accessed January 21, 1997).

9. W. Lee Hisle, "Roles for a Digital Age," in *Creating the Future: Essays on Librarianship in an Age of Great Change*, ed. by Sally G. Reed (Jefferson, N.C.: McFarland, 1996), 36.

10. Nancy C. Kranich, "Staking a Claim for Public Space in Cyberspace," in *Creating the Future,* 8.

11. Ibid., 17.

12. Hisle, "Roles for a Digital Age," 33.

13. Kranich, "Staking a Claim for Public Space in Cyberspace," 27.

14. John C. Swan, "The Electronic Straitjacket," in *Creating the Future*, 45.

15. Gordon M. Conable and Carrie Gardner, "Can Intellectual Freedom Survive the Information Age?" in *Creating the Future*, 71.

16. Sara Behrman, "Free and Equal Access to Library Services and Technology," in *Creating the Future*, 244.

17. Ibid., 245.

18. Ibid., 246.

19. "ALA Policy Manual," available: http://www.ala.org/washoff/mission.html (Accessed August 8, 1996).

20. Marilyn Gell Mason, "The Future Revisited," *Library Journal* 121, no. 12 (July 1996): 71.

21. Ibid., 70.

22. Behrman, "Free and Equal Access to Library Services and Technology," 249.

23. John N. Berry, "A Good Deal for Both," *Library Journal* 120, no. 20 (December 1995): 6.

24. Behrman, "Free and Equal Access to Library Services and Technology," 249.

25. Kenneth E. Dowlin, "Distribution in an Electronic Environment, or Will There Be Librarians As We Know Them in the Internet World?" *Library Trends* 43, no. 3 (Winter 1995): 414.

26. Ibid., 414.

27. Ibid.

28. "ALA Goal 2000," available: gopher://alall.ala.org.7...cgoal/41110041.document (Accessed October 23, 1996).

29. Tom Gaughan, "ALA Goal 2000: Planning for the Millennium," *American Libraries* 26, no. 1 (January 1995): 17.

30. Ibid., 17.

31. Kate Murphy, "Moving from the Card Catalogue to the Internet," *New York Times,* January 6, 1997, sec. D5.

32. Prudence W. Dalrymple, "The State of the Schools," *American Libraries* 27, no. 1 (January 1997): 31.

33. Murphy, "Moving from the Card Catalogue to the Internet," D5.

APPENDIX

**Outlook for
Gale Research/*Library Journal*
"Libraries of the Year"
and Other Selected Libraries
in the Twenty-First Century**

CHICAGO PUBLIC LIBRARY

Charlene Chisek

Introduction

In characterizing the Chicago Public Library (CPL) as "Chicago Hope"[1] instead of an Emergency Room (ER), Evan St. Lifer's 1995 article opted for belief in the future, not crisis-management. Furthermore, the subtitle, "A Public Library Reborn," implies reengineering. Of the two popular hospital television series set there, "Chicago Hope" takes the lead in cutting-edge technology. However, technology alone does not render a public library reinvented.

Before evaluating the CPL, the term *reengineering* needs clarification. Then the issues raised by St. Lifer's *Library Journal* article itself will be discussed, including more recent information regarding library hours, partnerships with Gale Research and Microsoft, and ALA Library Service Awards, as well as a branch library's audiovisual system. Next we will examine the CPL web site and finally round out the discussion with comments by Commissioner Mary Dempsey.

Reengineering Definition

According to Russell M. Linden, "reengineering requires us to challenge the fundamental assumptions on which bureaucracies are built and radically redesign these organizations around desired outcomes rather than functions or departments. In the process, it forces us to develop new ways of thinking and of seeing the world."[2] Signs of change can be found in the following.

1. Walls are coming down.

2. Alliances are becoming standard operating procedures.

3. Speedy customer service is becoming a goal.[3]

Although technology does not usher in reinvention, it creates opportunity for continuous improvement and change.[4]

For public libraries, more specific criteria include:

1. using information technology creatively

2. demographics and history of the library

3. philosophy and how it changed

    a. mission statement

    b. vision statement

4. public and staff response to the library's reinvention

5. specific aspects of the library's reinvention

    a. technology

    b. collection

    c. marketing/PR

    d. customer service

    e. performance evaluation process

6. library staff training and education

7. collaboration

Chicago Hope

Turning the Corner?

St. Lifer begins his discussion of CPL by describing the past CPL with 79 branches and 2 regional libraries as "notable for its low staff morale, political interference, indifferent public support, and disgraceful lack of a permanent central library."[5] Commissioner Mary A. Dempsey, a lawyer/librarian selected by Mayor Richard Daley and approved by the Chicago City Council in 1994,[6] tried to turn morale around, with the assistance of Cindy Pritzker, board president and "member of the richest family in Chicago."[7] In addition, CPL had a triad "responsible for helping Dempsey transform CPL: Emelie Shroder, assistant commissioner for research and reference services; Charlotte Kim, assistant commissioner of neighborhood services; and Alice Scott, assistant commissioner, systemwide services."[8]

Undoubtedly, Dempsey won confidence by praising the staff from the beginning. In January 1994, she gushed: "I'm impressed by the enthusiasm and hopefulness of the administration, staff, and even some of the library's biggest critics. I come to this position with great respect for activists. You have the responsibility to listen to your users. I don't believe in preconceived notions."[9]

Furthermore, Dempsey's background bolstered a quest for library funding. As she declared, "I don't know what being politically connected means. If it means knowing elected officials and knowledge of how the state and city operate, then that's a plus for the library."[10] Dempsey, a "regular user of CPL for both popular reading and business reference,"[11] took a pay cut and changed her lifestyle because of her belief in public service.[12]

A Twenty-First-Century Strategy

Dempsey knew, however, that a love of libraries combined with political clout could not reshape CPL. Instead, she relied on her staff's participation to create a library for the twenty-first century. Clearly, Dempsey pays more than lip service to TQM buzzwords like employee empowerment. "Via 21 CPL department reps, each of the library's almost 1,500 full-time employees (FTEs) had a hand in developing the contents of the recently approved Strategic Plan."[13] By asking the administration to focus on specific infrastructure needs, the plan addresses "staff development/training, technology, high-quality facilities, consistent funding, and a more automated book acquisitions and delivery system."[14]

Although Alice Scott describes Dempsey as someone with a vision, the "Chicago Hope" article does not articulate a vision statement.[15] In fact, CPL's undated mission statement on its web site sounds very traditional: "We welcome and support all people in their enjoyment of reading and pursuit of lifelong learning. Working together, we strive to provide equal access to information, ideas and knowledge through books, programs and other resources. We believe in the freedom to read, to learn, to discover."[16]

Furthermore, Mark Knoblauch, a cowriter of the strategic plan, admits that it will only measure the library's success temporarily. According to him, "The big thing the library needs to accomplish is to determine the role of the public library as the way people obtain information changes heading into the twenty-first century. We don't necessarily have all the answers, but we've positioned ourselves to be able to respond to change as it evolves."[17]

CPL Closes for a Day

True to the first priority of the strategic plan, Dempsey closed the entire CPL system on November 23, 1994, for its All Staff Institute Day (ASID).[18]

> Staff could choose up to four hour-long workshops, or tours of individual central library departments, or of the entire Harold Washington Library Center.

- City of Chicago trainers presented workshops on time management, effective listening, creating successful meetings, dealing with difficult people, quality skills, and telephone excellence.

- At the Neighborhood Services Buffet, a daylong poster session, staff rotated 13 presentations on projects and services including: "Motherlink: Family Literacy in Libraries," "Self-check: Library Page Evaluation," and "Multiple Books for Neighborhood School Collections."

- Novelist Rebecca Linz spoke to an overflowing room on the "Power of the Romance Novel." Staff presented three programs on alternative choices to popular authors entitled "John Grisham Is Out and So Is the Librarian."

- In four packed sessions, Chicago Police Department Youth Officers discussed gang culture and answered staff questions about how best to deal with gang members when they use the library.

- Jane Getty, Illinois Library Association executive director, and Southwest Airlines' Tim Kraft, urged staff to "Break Out of Your Box" and expand their approach to customer service. Roger Sutton, editor of the *Bulletin of the Center for Children's Books* and a CPL alumnus, led a discussion on the possibilities of young adult services.

■ The professional exhibits included bookdealers and publishers, city services, library education programs, computer vendors, the H. W. Wilson Co., Baker & Taylor, Ingram, the American Library Association, and the Illinois State Library.[19]

Because of its success, CPL repackaged the popular seminars into monthly workshops called "Back by Popular Demand."[20] In addition, when CPL switched to a new library system, "850 staffers received nine hours of CARL training in three weeks."[21] Once the computer system came online, the CPL found that "despite providing patrons with better access to electronic information, the business, science, and technology staff, for example, has grown from 25 to 32 in five years, and division Chief David Rouse has assigned eight people to work the reference desk where there used to be four."[22]

Resisting Change

Naturally, Dempsey's direction does not have 100 percent support. "The possibility of CPL undertaking a more centralized collection development policy in order to save money and create better quality control . . . is disquieting to librarians who want to ensure CPL's diversity by keeping collection development autonomous at the branch level."[23] The commissioner, however, has gone on record that she is willing to listen to any strong misgivings but not to fear of change.[24]

Diversity: CPL's Treasured Resource

Of course, the city of neighborhoods prides itself on ethnicity, "seen through one of CPL's two regional libraries, the Sulzer, whose patrons speak a staggering 84 different languages. Further, the system has extensive collections in 45 languages, the nation's second largest African American collection at its other regional (the Woodson), and the Midwest's largest Chinese- and Spanish-language collections in Chinatown and Rudy Lozano branches, respectively."[25]

Assistant Commissioner Kim "had the challenge of providing 'high-quality and personal library service' despite waning budgets and surging technology. Kim is on a mission to consolidate and renovate branches—combining storefronts into full-service facilities—while still providing equitable service to patrons."[26]

An example of personal library service is found in Hector Hernandez, head librarian at Lozano, whose "service philosophy boils down to a Spanish proverb: *Haz el bien, yo no mires a quien* (Do what's right, no matter who it benefits)."[27] In May 1996, the Pilsen Together Chamber of Commerce designated him the Pride of Pilsen. Nineteen years earlier, Hernandez had volunteered at Lozano, and in 1995, he became Reforma's Librarian of the Year.[28] Through June 1996, his accomplishments include:

> the formation of a chess club that currently boasts 100 members, several of them regional and national competition champs; literary programs that bring together renowned Mexican authors and aspiring local talent; the transformation of a meeting room into a story room/resource center for parents and teachers, slated to open this fall; and an electronic hookup to the National Library of Medicine and the Illinois Consumer Health Information Network.[29] In response to such customer service, CPL Friends of the Library groups more than tripled, from 14 in 1991 to 50 in 1995.[30]

In regard to branch building, a news release hailed CPL for ending 1995 with 12 newly constructed or renovated branch libraries in 17 months. "The new or improved libraries are full service facilities, a majority of which are equipped with state-of-the-art computer, multimedia, and informational resource access. 'The Chicago Public Library's long term commitment to cultural and educational growth of the City's many ethnically diverse communities will always be a continuing process,' said Library Commissioner Mary A. Dempsey."[31] This building spurt totaled more than $20 million. (The news release did not even put a price tag on 5 of the 12 branches.)[32] On a personal note, having grown up on the South Side of Chicago and perused the shelves of the Pullman Branch in my youth, I rejoiced that CPL spent $2.3 million to restore this once-elegant structure, built in 1927, to its former grandeur.[33]

Bucks for Branches

Beyond the investment in bricks and mortar, CPL entered "several innovative partnerships with the private and public sectors, including the Adopt-a-Branch program, which has yielded more than $250,000 for five branches through 1995."[34] For instance, the Chicago Bulls basketball team contributed $50,000 to the Manning Branch for a "Computer Court" used by 1,000 patrons monthly.[35]

On another front, "the Chicago Community Trust, a city nonprofit fund-raising organization, has contributed $1 million toward the library's Blue Skies for Library Kids program, an effort to turn eighteen branch libraries into community centers."[36] Another page on the CPL web site notes that this program formed

> "community problem-solving" partnerships because of an effective model for planning that directly involves community input. The model, known as the ABC PLUS Team, consists of a team made up of a library administrator, a librarian from the branch, several active community members, and representatives from Chicago Institutions known as "PLUS Team Members." Together the team designs, implements, manages, and evaluates their Blue Skies programs for children and families.[37]

Since 1992, programs have emerged, such as Little League baseball teams, drama clubs, job readiness programs, family math workshops, and library sleepovers. The following changes also occurred:

1. Active neighborhood organization involvement.

2. Increases in users, Friends groups, and volunteers.

3. Cosponsorship with the Children's Museum, the Art Institute, Museum of Science and Industry, Park District, and United Charities.[38]

Nonetheless, the biggest return of all came from Board President Pritzker and the CPL Foundation, which raised $14 million from 1989 through 1994.[39] Pritzker "and her husband donated a million dollars themselves."[40] Originally, the endowment earmarked enrichment of the book collection. Says Pritzker, "No matter how much money we raise, the city still has to give us our operating budget. In other words, we can't be penalized for trying to do better ourselves. The goal is $20 million, so that we can have an endowment."[41] By 1995, the Foundation had expanded to enrich library technology as well.[42]

CPL's Defining Moment

As the jewel of CPL's resurgence, the $145-million Harold Washington Library Center (HWLC) opened in 1991.[43] "The library's architects looked backward and around the corner for inspiration—at the late-19th-century Beaux-Arts style in general and at Chicago's Rookery and Auditorium buildings."[44] For those of us still bedazzled by the prior main library's Tiffany mosaic ceilings, this structure is overpowering at first.

Architecturally, the building sparked debate. According to William F. Birdsall, librarians saw it returning "to the intimidating 'cathedral of learning' stereotype characteristic of the monumental libraries of the nineteenth century. One prominent library consultant was disappointed 'in how libraries and librarians were viewed' in the public debate. She felt the architectural design unfortunately favored the 'romanticized versions of a sacred, silent place.' "[45] In spite of these misgivings, large urban neoclassical library building construction abounds because of "a sensuality that generates an emotional response not derived from professional, bureaucratic, rational instrumentalism. These buildings have what Kevin Lynch calls '*imageability*: that quality in a physical object which gives it a high probability of evoking a strong image in any given observer.' "[46]

Indeed, Pritzker attests to the emotional responses evoked by the building: "People are never lukewarm. They either like it or hate it, and if they hate it they want to be sure to tell you. So I've heard lots of comments: that the structure is too massive for the site, that it's too close to the sidewalk, it's too this or too that."[47]

Once inside, attitudes soften because of

> the details: the light maple woodwork, the arched doorways, the green marble counters. And there has been an attempt to make the library user friendly: Information desks are set up to work almost like triage in a hospital; every floor is equipped with an interactive directory that—with its graphics of little elevators that demonstrate how to move from cookbooks to African art—resembles a video game. And the back of the building will feature a book return with drive-up window.[48]

In socialite style, Cindy Pritzker has grand plans for the "Winter Garden, which sits, airily, like a crown atop the library. A public space that will double as one of the city's most magnificent settings for charity galas, the Winter Garden is a wonder of details: A mammoth greenhouse ceiling of glass and steel tracery tops the three-story space; a maze of intricately laid marble in a bold geometric pattern is on the floor."[49]

One begins to wonder what happened to the library in the Harold Washington Library Center. Shroder, head of HWLC, had the architects design the building "so that heavy floor loads for microform storage and compact shelving are distributed over several floors and the ends of the building, permitting increased storage in these areas. The use of subfloor wiring races has made it easier to redesign the use of interior space and accommodate changes in computer technology."[50] Because the Center was designed as a loft-style structure with no load-bearing interior walls, the administration could make quick post-opening changes such as moving the technical services and library automation departments, adding the Winter Garden and reorganizing the special collections area.[51]

On another personal note, shortly after it opened, I took one of the two daily tours at HWLC and noticed that half the shelves were empty. My friends thought it a sorry sight that the library had no books. Instead, the CPL envisioned increasing a sad collection that had lain stale in warehouselike conditions for almost 20 years. The people of Chicago waited a long time for a new main library and almost forgot it. Once it reopened, however, satisfaction with HWLC spurred collection development and branch revitalization.

Current Trends

Library Hours

Recent articles still bemoan the shortened hours at CPL. In October 1996, Steve Cisler wrote that during the 1995 ALA Annual Conference in Chicago, he passed up the Harold Washington Library Center because of its short and inconvenient 36-hour workweek.[52] However, a more recent article (February 1997) explains that HWLC "opened at the height of the recession in 1991 and faced immediate budget cuts, which restricted hours until January 1994, when the main library and the branches were opened seven days a week."[53] Currently, the web site lists the following hours for Harold Washington:

> Monday 9–7
>
> Tuesday & Thursday 11–7
>
> Wednesday, Friday, Saturday 9–5
>
> Sunday 1–5[54]

Library hours have now increased to 54 a week. One wonders how many urban libraries open on Sunday.

Partnerships

In March 1996, Gale Research announced a two-pronged partnership with CPL, sharing and trading electronic databases and technological know-how to forge a new library/vendor relationship.[55] First, Gale "installed a server linking CPL's Central Library with its 80 branches. CPL is also now connected to the company's Internet databases on businesses and associations, literature and authors, and biographies through GaleNet. CPL is also employing the publisher's electronic Library of Congress cataloging tool, SuperLCCS, and its DISCovering Multicultural America ethnic CD-ROM database."[56] Second, the firm will electronically integrate "the 'unusual resources' in CPL's Jazz, Gospel and Chicago history special collections" into a practical format.[57] Unfortunately, they had not ironed out all the details, and neither party could predict how it would work.

Also in March 1996, Bill Gates announced "a donation of $1 million in software to the Chicago Public Library (CPL), including high-speed telecommunications service (a T-1 line) and networking software as well as multimedia reference and educational software for all 81 CPL branches. Training and technical support is also part of the package."[58] This merges with "a $3-million commitment from the city to support systemwide technology upgrades, and a $10-million fund-raising commitment from its library foundation. The Microsoft gift . . . enables CPL to advance its timetable for purchasing hardware and other software, such as the network version of Gale Research's reference products."[59] By the end of 1996, every branch had gone online; previously, only seven had the connection.[60]

ALA Library Service Awards

In contrast to the emphasis on technology, another news release celebrated the 5 CPL programs garnering Young Adult Library Services Association (YALSA) awards in February 1997, out of 50 winners nationwide. The honored programs include:

1. Junior Volunteers for the Summer Reading Game

2. Bus Painting Project

3. Teen Study Center

4. Knight Moves Chess Club

5. Teen Parenting Course[61]

Previously, the chess club received coverage under diversity at the Lozano Branch. Of the five programs, four belong to Blue Skies for Library Kids, discussed earlier. Although each portrays special innovations, only particulars about teen parenting follow:

> Woodson Regional Library, in response to community concerns, developed a program in partnership with the Illinois Department of Public Aid and Mount Sinai Hospital to aid teen mothers in parenting, nutrition, child development, and how to use the library to become better parents. The classes also focused on literacy, helping mothers learn the importance of reading. The library provided materials for parents and children and through the courses, the young mothers met caring, qualifying adults, who became mentors and teachers.[62]

Automated Auditorium

In June 1996, *Computers in Libraries* documented the Lincoln Park Branch's high-tech auditorium. With a flick of the switch, the librarian can show movies or videos to groups and provide computer training (such as on the OPAC, network, Internet, or home page creation), while community organizations give slide presentations/lectures. According to Scott Drawe, the auditorium seats 90 and can reproduce the computer screen "to a 121-inch image for a whole room to see. We can also project the pictures in a book using the document camera and offer a story reading session to a larger group of children than the normal 30."[63]

CPL Web Site

After praising CPL's web site, Microsoft offered $1 million to speed up its technological thrust.[64] The many news releases and stories already quoted in these pages barely touch the wealth offered by CPL. This lengthy quote from one page sets the tone for CPL's web site.

> The Chicago Public Library is providing leadership to address the information needs of Chicago's children and adults through **Project MIND**, a $10 million three-year initiative of the Chicago Public Library foundation. **Project MIND** will provide the Chicago Public Library with the essential resources to give all Chicagoans equal access to read, to learn and to discover by infusing state-of-the-art technology and training in the use of this technology into every aspect of the Library's services and programs. It is the goal of **Project MIND**—**M**eeting **I**nformation **N**eeds **D**emocratically—to make available the same information, resources, services and technology to all Chicago Public Library branches which serve neighborhoods as diverse as the Robert Taylor Homes, Lincoln Park, Douglas Park and Beverly. This access will be accomplished through the creation of the **Voyager Network,** the Chicago Public Library's dynamic information network which will continue the Chicago Public Library's 120 year tradition of enriching the lives of Chicago's children and adults, many of whom are unable to have the latest information and technologies in their homes.[65]

Initially, the Home Page divides into:

1. CPL Information
   - About CPL & Events
   - CPL Online Catalog
   - Databases
   - Harold Washington Library Center
   - Neighborhood Libraries

2. Chicago & Illinois
   - About Chicago
   - About Illinois
   - Colleges, Universities & Libraries
   - Freenets

3. Subject Guides
   - About the Internet
   - Internet Tutorials
   - CPL Subject Guides to the Internet
   - Search the Internet

The bottom bar offers:

Contents   Search   CPL Home   Comments   What's New.[66]

It is not possible to share every aspect of this rich web site (http://cpl.lib.uic.edu/cpl.html), but some highlights beyond the usual OPAC, accessed February–March 1997, follow.

Welcoming users to the CPL home page, Mary Dempsey stresses its development by the librarians and staff. Almost 80 items from November 1995 to date inhabit the news release page. Among other information, the site provides 1994 use and collection statistics for HWLC.

Local city information abounds—four pages of entries, from finding hot spots by El stop using the Virtual El, to Chicago Area Expressways

Congestion Map, to demographics, to Murder in Chicago (a selected list of mystery fiction with a Chicago setting by CPL prepared by the staff of the HWLC Literature and Languages Division), to quick lists of restaurants by type of food, to Chicago local weather forecast by the National Weather Service, to Yahoo! Chicago.[67] On the Illinois page, job hunters can search for state or national positions, check the winning lottery numbers, and visit Ticket Master's Illinois Event Guide, to name just a few options.[68]

In the Internet section, the CPL staff shines, recommending only the best information with annotations. From online tutorials, for example, comes "Yahoo! Surf School: this is a great site! It's very cleverly done and completely unintimidating. In typical Yahoo fashion, it is clear and fun. It includes useful tips to getting the most out of your surfing experience and improving your system, along with definitions, clarifications, and guidance. It has an added bonus of being quick to load."[69]

Similarly, librarians listed useful resources for typical reference questions, avoiding subscription, sample, or temporary sites. They include, by subject area, Internet links, information homegrown by CPL, and more comprehensive lists.[70] Lastly, the staff selected reliable search engines for their patrons and annotated them (e.g., McKinley: Supposed to be kid safe).[71]

Instead of perusing any more pale portraits of this web site, readers should log on to the CPL home page and surf it!

Dempsey Response

In a telephone interview on March 5, 1997, Commissioner Dempsey responded enthusiastically to the mostly positive "Chicago Hope" article, finding nothing disagreeable. Since the article came out, CPL received another $60 million from the Chicago City Council to construct/renovate more branches. She claimed that no other public library system can surpass CPL's past (15 branches in three years) and future building program.

Obviously proud of the stepped-up staff development and training, Dempsey repeated the statistic that, in 1996, CPL provided 700 hours of training to 5,000 participants, and she mentioned especially reference, children's service, automation, and technology. In the same breath, the commissioner boasted about installing free Internet access throughout the system and about many awards the CPL web site has won.

Unwilling to speak for staff response to her reinvention techniques, Dempsey only offered that they stay really busy and work really hard. Naturally, she realizes that, for some, change presents difficulty, not opportunity.

Finally, the commissioner revealed that, in 1994, CPL revised its long and rambling mission statement, which did not say much, to its current simple and direct approach. However, she bristled at the notion of its being considered "traditional," because the mission statement addresses information and other resources without tying them down to a specific medium. In the new mission statement, CPL stressed its goals of

- Sufficient, well-trained and courteous staff who are rewarded for their competence and creativity.

- Adaptable, state-of-the-art technology that is adequately linked to internal and external users.

- *Safe*, clean, structurally sound, comfortable and inviting libraries.

- Financial resources sufficient to meet current and future demands for library materials.

- Prompt ordering and delivery of materials for all agencies.

- Funding consistent to plan for library development.[72]

Conclusion

In briefly looking back at the concept of reengineering, it is clear that CPL has definitely undergone a number of changes. Examples have proliferated throughout this discussion for each aspect, so this recap will only mention a few.

Although the exterior walls have not come down and, in fact, have blossomed, the HWLC triage information desks, interactive directory, and drive-up window remove internal barriers. Furthermore, one wonders who has not partnered with CPL; the list seems endless—sports teams, museums, parks, charitable groups, vendors, corporations, and others. Although not directly addressed, the goal of speedy customer service probably catapulted Dempsey into jumping on the Internet bandwagon as soon as possible. Also, the web site gets updated regularly, and library hours have also expanded.

Even branch libraries use technology creatively, as at the high-tech auditorium. Recently, the history of the library changed dramatically with the opening of HWLC. Without knowing the particulars of the prior mission statement, however, it is not possible to tell how the CPL has changed from its previous goals. Nevertheless, increased funding reflects the public's continued support for CPL and, indirectly, its reinvention. Unfortunately, attempts to interview the staff and solicit their comments on reengineering were unsuccessful.

Although technology puts CPL in the headlines, some staff members anonymously criticized centralized collection development in "Chicago Hope." As the news release web pages show, CPL markets itself aggressively. As the YALSA awards note, service—not technology—provides the key to library doors. Still, the performance evaluation process represents another unknown.

Library staff training and development seem to be cornerstones in Dempsey's plans for the twenty-first century. The All Staff Institute Day reflects the variety of programs to accomplish those goals that CPL has undertaken and will undertake. As already mentioned, CPL considers "collaboration" its middle name.

Because of a few question marks, CPL does not merit an "A" for reinvention, but it has made a promising start. Dempsey did not falter, like Ken Dowlin in San Francisco, by forcing a virtual library on Chicago before its time. Instead, she personifies the conclusion of John N. Berry's editorial:

> While vision is essential and can carry the program a long way, it is not enough. Unless you share the creation of that vision with all those who use or work in the new facility— unless your vision is a compromise with theirs—you will lose their support as quickly as the new edifice gained their enthusiasm. Vision is one important factor in leadership. It takes much more than that to make a modern library system work well and please the people it serves.[73]

Notes

1. Evan St. Lifer, "Chicago Hope: A Public Library Reborn," *Library Journal* 120, no. 10 (June 1, 1995): 42–43.
2. Russell M. Linden, "Reengineering Government: Advice from the Experts," *Governing* 8, no. 8 (May 1995): 67.
3. Ibid.
4. Ibid., 69.
5. St. Lifer, "Chicago Hope," 42.
6. Leonard Kniffel, "News Fronts: Local Lawyer/Librarian Selected for Top Chicago PL Post," *American Libraries* 25, no. 1 (January 1994): 13
7. Marcia Froelke Coburn, "The Prize Pritzker," *Chicago* (September 1991): 81.
8. St. Lifer, "Chicago Hope," 42.
9. Kniffel, "News Fronts," 13.
10. Ibid.
11. Ibid.
12. Ibid., 15.
13. St. Lifer, "Chicago Hope," 43.
14. Ibid.
15. Ibid.
16. "The Chicago Public Library Mission," available: http://cpl.lib.uic.edu/003cpl/mission.html (Accessed February 22, 1997).
17. St. Lifer, "Chicago Hope," 43.
18. Ibid.
19. "News & Trends: News Analysis: Chicago Public Seizes the Day with Intensive Staff Institute," *Wilson Library Bulletin* 69, no. 5 (January 1995): 11.
20. St. Lifer, "Chicago Hope," 43.
21. Ibid.
22. Peter Booth Wiley, "Beyond the Blueprint," *Library Journal* 122, no. 3 (February 15, 1997): 112.
23. St. Lifer, "Chicago Hope," 44.
24. Ibid.
25. Ibid.
26. Ibid.
27. Beverly Goldberg, "News Fronts USA: SIGHTING The Pride of Pilsen," *American Libraries* 27 no. 6 (June/July 1996): 26.
28. Ibid.
29. Ibid.
30. St. Lifer, "Chicago Hope," 44.

31.   Communications Office, "Chicago Public Library—News Release: Chicago Public Library Ends 1995 with Unprecedented Construction Activity," January 1996, available: http://cpl.lib.uic.edu/003cpl/news/9601constr.html (Accessed February 22, 1997).

32.   Ibid.

33.   Ibid.

34.   St. Lifer, "Chicago Hope," 44.

35.   Communications Office, "Chicago Public Library."

36.   St. Lifer, "Chicago Hope," 44.

37.   "CPL Blue Skies for Library Kids Program," February 1997, available: http://cpl.lib.uic.edu/003cpl/blueskies.html (Accessed February 22, 1997).

38.   Ibid.

39.   St. Lifer, "Chicago Hope," 44.

40.   Coburn, "The Prize Pritzker," 81.

41.   Ibid., 82

42.   St. Lifer, "Chicago Hope," 44.

43.   Coburn, "The Prize Pritzker," 85.

44.   Ibid.

45.   William F. Birdsall, *Myth of the Electronic Library: Librarianship and Social Change in America* (Westport, Conn.: Greenwood Press, 1994), 68.

46.   Ibid.

47.   Coburn, "The Prize Pritzker," 84.

48.   Ibid., 85.

49.   Ibid.

50.   Wiley, "Beyond the Blueprint," 111.

51.   Ibid.

52.   Steve Cisler, "Weatherproofing a Great, Good Place: The Long-Range Forecast for Public Libraries: Technostorms, with Rapidly Changing Service Fronts," *American Libraries* 27, no. 10 (October 1996): 46.

53.   Wiley, "Beyond the Blueprint," 113.

54.   "Welcome to the Harold Washington Library Center," December 1996, available: http://cpl.lib.uic.edu/001hwlc/001hwlc.html (Accessed February 22, 1997).

55.   Michael Rogers, "Library Journal INFOTECH: Industry News: Chicago PL and Gale Research Form Partnership," *Library Journal* 121, no. 8 (May 1, 1996): 21.

56.   Ibid.

57.   Bridget Kinsella, "News: Gale Research, Chicago Library in Online Partnership," *Publishers Weekly* 243, no. 18 (April 29, 1996): 20.

58.   Evan St. Lifer and Michael Rogers, "*LJ* News: Microsoft Gives CPL $1M in Software," *Library Journal* 121, no. 7 (April 15, 1996): 13.

59. Beverly Goldberg, "News Fronts USA: Gates Gives Chicago PL Million-Dollar Connection," *American Libraries* 27, no. 5 (May 1996): 19.

60. Ibid.

61. Francisco Arcaute, "Chicago Public Library—News Release: Library Wins ALA Library Service Awards," February 1997, available: http://cpl.lib.uic.edu/003cpl/news/970219yalsa.html (Accessed February 22, 1997).

62. Ibid.

63. Karen Commings, "Libraries of the Future: High-Tech Learning Centers: Chicago Public Library, Lincoln Park Branch," *Computers in Libraries* 16, no. 6 (June 1996): 18.

64. Goldberg, "News Fronts USA," 19.

65. "The Chicago Public Library Foundation Project MIND: Meeting Information Needs Democratically," available: http://cpl.lib.uic.edu/003cpl/projectmind.html (Accessed February 22, 1997).

66. "Welcome to the Chicago Public Library," available: http://cpl.lib.uic.edu/cpl.html (Accessed February 22, 1997).

67. "About Chicago," February 1997, available: http://cpl.lib.uic.edu/004chicago/004chicago.html (Accessed March 1, 1997).

68. "About Illinois," February 1997, available: http://cpl.lib.uic.edu/004illinois/004illinois.html (Accessed March 1, 1997).

69. "Online Tutorials," February 1997, available: http://cpl.lib.uic.edu/007internet/tutorials.html (Accessed March 1, 1997).

70. "Information by Subject," February 1997, available: http://cpl.lib.uic.edu/008subject/008subject.html (Accesssed March 1, 1997).

71. "Search the Internet," January 1997, available: http://cpl.lib.uic.edu/011search/011search.html (Accessed March 1, 1997).

72. "Chicago Public Library Strategic Plan: Guiding Principles: Vision Statement," received from Commissioner Mary Dempsey in 1997.

73. John N. Berry, "Editorial: 'Vision' Is Not Enough," *Library Journal* 122, no. 3 (February 15, 1997): 84.

APPLETON PUBLIC LIBRARY

Fran White

Appleton, Wisconsin, is a small town (pop. 66,000) located 30 miles south of Green Bay. Situated on the Fox River, the town counts paper production among its primary industries. Lawrence University, established in 1847, is an important institution in the city. Although the town was originally settled by northern Europeans, many diverse ethnic groups have made Appleton their home. These groups include the Hmong people, Hispanics, African Americans, and Native Americans.

It is clear, based on the number of institutions, businesses, and private individuals who have home pages on the World Wide Web, that information and technology are motivating forces in Appleton. The Mission and Vision Statements of the Strategic Plan, written by the Board of Trustees of the Appleton Public Library in 1995, reflect these values.

> **Mission Statement**
> The Appleton Public Library provides the community with educational, informational, and recreational library services and materials in an accessible, economic, efficient, and timely manner.

> **Vision Statement**
> The Appleton Public Library will serve to meet the ongoing and changing educational, informational, and recreational needs of the community through access to traditional library resources and emerging technologies. A dedicated,

sufficient, and highly qualified staff will work together with the Library Board to develop and implement clearly focused and shared goals. The library will provide a safe, pleasant, and efficient environment in an aesthetic and convenient facility. An expanded funding base will sustain current operations and support anticipated growth of service to the community.

The library's primary roles will be formal education support, independent learning, reference and information, and children's door to learning.

The library will be a leader in providing delivery of ideas and information as part of a strong regional community network with links to educational institutions, businesses, governments, community agencies, and other libraries. This network will incorporate human, electronic, and material resources that will enrich and benefit the community.

The Appleton Public Library is poised to enter the twenty-first century. The community began to recognize the changes that were occurring in society, both economically and in terms of information delivery, in 1985. It was at this time that the Appleton Library Foundation was established, "making a difference and providing the 'edge of excellence' for the Appleton Public Library." The Foundation set an endowment goal of $1 million in 1989 and is currently within $100,000 of that goal. The city provides funding for library operations, but Foundation funds are used to enhance the collection and provide cutting-edge technologies. The far-sighted citizens who established the Foundation realized that municipalities alone would not be able to bear the burden of bringing public libraries into the twenty-first century. Coupled with this creative financial outlook is an openness to new developments in technology and in the forms of information available to society. The library collections consist of books, maps, videos, pamphlets, magazines, tapes, and compact discs. Information is accessible to Appleton patrons through interlibrary loans, online databases, CD-ROM databases, special equipment for patrons with disabilities, microforms and readers, and Internet access.

The director of Appleton Public Library is Terry Dawson. Dawson has been at Appleton since 1978 but has been director for slightly less than a year. Appleton has a library staff clearly committed to moving into the new millennium with cutting-edge technology and enthusiasm for growth. The combination of community support, financial support, and a dedicated staff puts APL in an excellent position for entering the twenty-first century. The library and staff have been constantly reinventing themselves, particularly in the last decade.

Director Terry Dawson shared his opinions on Appleton's reinvention in a recent e-mail exchange.

1. To what creative uses have you put information technology?

For the public, we have our online catalog. Not very innovative anymore, but it surely was when we started it up. We've had dial access to the catalog for years, but it is now available through the Internet and therefore much more accessible. Currently the catalog, and our shared database, is a service of the Outagamie Waupaca Library System and includes the holdings of more than 20 libraries. The most recent innovations in the catalog are:

1. inclusion of the Information Access "General Reference Center" with indexing and full text of magazines, and

2. the ability for patrons to place holds and review their account information.

Our in-house public access Internet workstations (currently there are five), and our web page are other innovations. We were the first public library in Wisconsin to put up a web page.

We have a number of stand-alone CD-ROM databases for the public.

Our LAN supports both Macs and Wintel machines. It is heavily used by staff for file sharing and e-mail. The most innovative use of the LAN and Internet from a service point of view has been our service desk workstations. At our reference, media, and children's desks, we have Pentium machines which, under Windows 95, are simultaneously running:

1. an Internet browser

2. a telnet session into our online system, to access the catalog, general bibliography records, and patron information

3. B&T Link (networked CD-ROM database)

4. WISCAT (state union catalog on seven networked CD-ROMs)

In addition, we have a FirstSearch authorization and password at each of the public service terminals. In sum, this puts tremendous information resources at the fingertips of our public services staff.

2.   Do you have any data on the demographics of the community served by the library? If you do, would you share them with me? What are your library's hours?

I don't know how much you want, but briefly, our municipal population is about 68,000, and the area for which we serve as the primary public library is a population of about 100,000.

Hours:
Monday–Thursday	9:00 A.M.–9:00 P.M.
Friday	9:00 A.M.–6:00 P.M.
Saturday	9:00 A.M.–5:00 P.M.
Sunday	1:00 P.M.–5:00 P.M.

Summer Hours:
Monday and Thursday	9:00 A.M.–9:00 P.M.
Tuesday, Wednesday, Friday	9:00 A.M.–6:00 P.M.
Saturday	9:00 A.M.–1:00 P.M.
Sunday	CLOSED

3. Has your philosophy changed as we get closer to the new century? Has your mission statement changed? Has your vision statement changed?

Philosophy and mission have not changed appreciably. We did not have a vision statement until about two years ago. As such, our vision statement, like our goals and strategies, does include technology.

4. What is your "reinvention?" What areas are you reinventing—technology, collections, tech services, marketing, performance evaluations, job descriptions, collaborations/partnerships? Any other areas not listed?

I'm not sure of the extent of the reinvention per se. Just as our mission has changed only a bit, I don't think libraries are doing anything much different from what we've always done. The way we do it has certainly changed, though. We are given new tools, new opportunities, and more ways to do what we've always tried to do.

The development of the MARC record format and the use of shared online cataloging systems goes back decades. Surely, these have led to a profound reinvention of the way we catalog materials, and ultimately to the online public catalog and the demise of the card file. These reflect a substantial change in the way society stores and moves information, but we may have reinvented library service more substantially even decades earlier when we committed ourselves to reference and readers' advisory service, or children's programming.

Certainly technology means new tools, new skills, new job descriptions, and more carpal tunnel surgeries. But I'm not sure that we've changed what we do, except that we've become more formal educators. Who's teaching people how to use the new information resources and tools? For many, the answer is "the public library."

5. What is the response of the public and your staff to this "reinvention?"

That varies across the human spectrum. Future shock occurs everywhere, but on the whole, the response is quite positive. We get a lot of good feedback on our services and technologies. But Nicholson Baker is everywhere.

6. Do the changes require additional staff and librarian training or continuing education?

Sure, and we wrestle with that. Many people are highly self-motivated and will perceive their own needs and teach themselves the skills to meet those needs. Others will never do anything until someone shows them how (or would prefer to get someone to do it for them). Such is life. Mostly, people like to learn; I particularly hope that no one who wants to work in a library finds foreign the need for continuous learning under any circumstances.

7. Which came first, the vision of the "reinvention," or the new technology/automation which facilitated it?

The vision of service came first. The tools at hand lend themselves to development of new visions of ways to provide the service.

At a recent meeting of our Library Board's policy committee, we came to consensus that the basis for all policy is "core values." The Board asked me to present a list of our core values. With the help of a number of people on the staff, I drafted the list, which follows:

Appleton Public Library Core Values

Why we exist:
Libraries exist to collect, organize, preserve, and make available the cultural record.

In order to do this:

Libraries promote learning.

Librarians operate libraries according to fundamental values of access and service.

Librarians operate libraries according to ethical principles, including:

> respect for privacy
> respect for intellectual property
> placing organizational goals ahead of personal goals
> preservation of intellectual freedom

Librarians operate according to the scientific method.

Librarians develop expertise in organizing, cataloging, and indexing.

Public libraries in democratic societies have a special role of making all kinds of knowledge from all points of view available to all parts of society.

Here at the Appleton Public Library:

We balance educational, informational and recreational library services according to community needs.

We exist as a public library in Wisconsin and as a department of the City of Appleton.

We have a special role in collecting, preserving and making available the unique cultural record of this community.

We provide access for the public in this community.

We work cooperatively with other organizations to promote learning and literacy.

We are strongly oriented to customer service, but are committed to efficiency and economy.

We believe that technology provides us with important tools to fulfill our mission.

Bibliography

Appleton Public Library. Available: http://www.apl.org/pages/plan.html (Accessed February 1997).

ATLANTA-FULTON PUBLIC LIBRARY

Lisa S. Payne

The Atlanta-Fulton Public Library opened in 1938 in a building now known as the Central Library. In 1985, after passage of a $38-million bond referendum, AFPL embarked on one of the nation's largest library building programs. This program thus far has doubled the amount of branch space. Today, the AFPL has grown to include 30 branches, a MARTA www.ci.austin.tx.us/adadocs/library/lbkiosk, a research library, and a bookmobile.

The AFPL serves a population of more than 720,000 people and houses 3.5 million items, with 1.8 million items in circulation. According to the *World Almanac*, it is ranked, by population served, as one of the top 50 libraries in the United States and Canada. The mission of the AFPL Central Library and its branches is to "provide materials, information and program events to meet public need, for independent learning, formal education support, reference, early childhood education, popular materials, and research."

These needs are met through a variety of materials, programs, and methods. Materials include books, phonograph records, audio disks, 16-mm films, videos, framed prints, databases, and CD-ROMs. Programs include story times, art exhibits, films, and classes. There are many different ways to access information through the AFPL. There are reference desks in each library for walk-in help. A computerized catalog, called CARL, provides circulation information on all materials owned by the AFPL.

There is a central reference desk for telephone inquiries, which is capable of responding to short-answer questions. I called the desk and found the librarian to be very helpful. I did have to wait about five minutes to be helped, but I did not think this was an excessive amount of time to wait at a busy reference desk at midday. An answering machine gave interesting information while I waited. I learned that this reference service is available on Mondays 10–5, Tuesday–Thursday 10–8, Friday–Saturday 10–5, and Sunday 2–6. Calls are normally limited to five minutes. I was on the phone with the reference librarian for at least 10 minutes, so the librarians must also feel that a limit of five minutes is not realistic.

Another way to access information is through the computer and the Internet with a system called Passport. In 1993, the AFPL conducted a user survey, and of the patrons surveyed, 31.6 percent said that reference was the most important role of the library, while 30.7 percent said that educational support was more important. Only 27.5 percent believed that having popular materials was the most important. The majority of patrons thought that either reference service or educational support was the most important role of the AFPL. The AFPL has responded to these patrons' needs with new technology.

In evaluating the AFPL's move toward the twenty-first century, technology is the first thing that comes to mind. How has the AFPL progressed with technology, and is it continuing to do so creatively? From the information available it appears that the AFPL is heading in the right direction, even if it is at a slow pace. The AFPL has a computerized catalog, CARL, that can be accessed via a personal computer. Along with CARL comes the Passport system. In 1984 Passport was introduced to all patrons via branch access or home PC access. Passport is a wonderful, valuable tool that offers 20 menu items for patron reference. The librarian I spoke with, Ann Frazier, said that more menu offerings are in the works. The menu currently offers CARL along with several other catalogs. In addition, Passport offers a periodicals index, *Books in Print*, an index to the *Atlanta Journal and Constitution*, a community bulletin board, the Auburn Avenue Research Library catalog, an encyclopedia, a corporate index, more than 350 full-text periodicals, and several other helpful reference tools. Thus AFPL's Passport system has taken technology and put forth a valuable resource with unlimited potential for patrons.

I asked if there were any disadvantages to the Passport system. Frazier replied that although it has been a huge success, a few kinks need to be worked out. One problem is that increased usage has caused the system to get slower, especially in the afternoon peak hours. This has created frustration for both patron and librarian. However, she did mention that the current memory is being upgraded to combat this problem. She also said that if the patron chooses to access by modem instead of the Internet, the directions can be cumbersome and confusing. She cautioned patience, because the information is worth the time it takes and the frustration experienced. Although Passport system is accessible to people around the country, certain menu items are available only to cardholders of the AFPL. This seems logical because, after all, these patrons pay for the Passport system with their tax dollars.

Another way the AFPL has embraced technology to move forward is through the Atlanta-Fulton Public Library/High School Partnership for the Internet. This innovative program was begun in November 1994 and currently serves more than 290,000 patrons. The program's purpose is to help the library fulfill one of its missions to support formal education (K–12) and adult independent learning "by providing user-friendly, equitable access to government, medical, education, and life skills databases via the National Information Infrastructure (NII)." The NII has been called the national data highway of the future. By working with and offering access to the NII, the AFPL has made a giant leap into the twenty-first century. By combining access to the Passport system along with the NII, the AFPL offers a new dimension in access for reference and research by students and patrons of all ages.

Some of the database topics offered are electronic reference desk, business and economics, government agencies, career and job market resources, geography, history, travel, health and nutrition, science, fine arts and recreation, and school resources. Access to the NII has been offered along with Passport at all the AFPL branches. This program, however, allowed the AFPL to go further and reach more people. There are now workstations with Passport/NII access in 21 schools.

The AFPL provided the training and ongoing support to the staff in the school media centers where the workshops are located. The AFPL staff also provides special promotions, contests, and meetings to encourage the students to make use of the program and thereby increase participation. An average of 77 school Internet sessions take place daily with few problems. The branches have averaged 113 sessions daily. Plans are being developed to expand the program into Atlanta's middle and elementary schools.

Another way the AFPL is using technology to reach people is through television. The library presents 24-hour programming on a cable channel appropriately called the Library Channel. This is a wonderful way to attract potential patrons to library programs and services. It also offers an innovative way to serve patrons, such as shut-ins, who may be unable physically to go to the library. The AFPL also uses the technology of the telephone to offer Tele-Librarian. This feature offers patrons the opportunity to renew their library books for another loan period.

The AFPL is making the most of all forms of technology to improve access and services to patrons. Not only is the AFPL using technology to move forward, but it is also focusing on the community by offering services and materials that are more relevant to its core population. Atlanta historically has had a large minority population whose needs have been ignored until recently. The AFPL is now reinventing itself by focusing more on the diversity of its patrons and the surrounding communities. One shining example of this is the Auburn Avenue Research Library on African American Culture and History.

The Auburn Avenue Branch opened on May 14, 1994, and is the second public library in the nation to open with a mission to serve as a repository for literature and materials on African American history. The collection is noncirculating and includes 23,000 books, 2,000 periodicals, 181 African American newsletters, and 1,600 vertical files along with microforms, oral history tapes, photographs, films, and videos that document the lives of significant African Americans. "The library is not just for African Americans; it's for everyone to come and feel what it is like to be black in America," said Fulton County Commissioner Emma Darnell. Unfortunately, with this incredible resource comes some problems. Budget cuts and lack of funding have been detrimental to this $10-million state-of-the-art library. The library director, Julie Hunter, has had to set aside some goals, such as digitizing the collection, as well as passing by an opportunity to purchase rare items that would strengthen the collection. The branch's hours are also reduced because of budget cuts. AFPL gets an "A" for opening the Auburn Branch, but a "C" for support. What good is an incredible research library if there is no money to staff it or to develop its collection?

AFPL gets a low grade in staff support at the other branches as well. The county government has forced the AFPL to leave 22 percent of 545 staff positions vacant and to limit the purchase of new materials (AFPL has lost 40 percent of its purchasing power). This has resulted in shortened hours, elimination of a main reference desk, and reduction of some services—for example, business reference and homework help. The population served by AFPL has risen 15 percent, but staff and services have still been cut. Ron Dubberly, AFPL director, states that "the staff is working much harder and is greatly stressed." With all of the technology and special programs being offered, AFPL has a head start going into the twenty-first century. If budget cuts and reduced staffing continue to be an issue, however, AFPL may find itself back in the dark ages.

Bibliography

American Library Directory, 1996–97. 49th ed. New Providence, N.J.: R. R. Bowker, 1996.

Atlanta-Fulton Public Library. Available: http://afplpac.as.public.lib.ga.us (Accessed March 1997).

Atlanta-Fulton Public Library/High School Partnership for the Internet. Available: http://afplpac.as.public.lib.ga.us.

Chepesiuk, Ron. "Schomburg of the South: The Auburn Avenue Research Library." *American Libraries* 27 no. 2 (February 1996): 38–40.

Goldman, David, and Pam Perry. *Insiders Guide to Metro Atlanta.* Macon, Ga.: Macon Telegraph, 1996.

McCormick, E. "Cuts, Politics Hobble Atlanta Library System." *American Libraries* 27 no. 10 (November 1996): 14–15.

AUSTIN PUBLIC LIBRARY:
1993 Library of the Year

Evelyn M. Campbell

Library advocates advise that the surest way to maintain funding for public libraries is to build community political support by working closely with community groups and local government. The Austin Public Library, winner of the 1993 Library of the Year Award, practices this concept.

John N. Berry, in his June 15, 1993, article in *Library Journal*, said, "Good government is central to what they practice at the Austin Public Library" with the library creating close bonds with the government and the people of the city of Austin. Since the award four years ago, some of those programs have been discontinued because of limited resources in the library's budget, and others have been transferred to other city departments and are flourishing. However, the effects of some of those programs that no longer exist are still being felt today and are still benefiting the city.

One such program was the City of Austin Creativity Program, which began in 1990. It was based on a book written by City Manager Dr. Camille Cates Barnett, and it consisted of an eight-hour fun workshop in which videos, exercises, puzzles, and interactive discussions were used to encourage participants (city employees) to overcome obstacles to creativity, to look for new ways of solving problems, to take risks, and to change their paradigms. The fun workshops were offered every Friday for three years, and approximately 3,000 city employees were trained.

Downsizing and resource reductions forced the cancellation of the program in 1994, although it was effective and popular. "Many of the concepts that were taught resulted in changes throughout the city. Many of those changes still continue, such as employees feeling empowered to take risks and be innovative," said APL Director Brenda Branch.

She described a problem-solving session she had with employees of the Public Works Department who were brainstorming how to improve relations between divisions. As a result, the employees created a customer bill of rights and an employee bill of rights that greatly inspired the workforce.

Branch has taught the fun workshops outside of Austin. "I have taught this fun workshop at several library conferences around the country, and it is always well received," she said.

Other programs that were named in the Berry article have also been discontinued or transferred. Project Walking Books (which brought materials to Austin's elderly and homebound) was eliminated because the Austin City Council felt that the program was not cost-effective. The VICTORY Homework Centers (homework centers at branches in "youth-at-risk" neighborhoods) have been transferred to the Austin Independent School District's Continuing Education Division. The Employee Learning Program was transferred to the City Human Resources Department, where it is flourishing with better funding. The Job Information Center (which included counseling; assessment and training; referrals to other agencies; books, computers, and software for writing résumés; and regular seminars and workshops) was considered redundant and was discontinued.

The Quality Resource Center has remained funded, although at a lower level. The collection at the QRC consists of several thousand books, videos, audiocassettes, and periodicals on quality-related issues. QRC also has an IBM and a Macintosh computer with high-quality software that enables users to create fishbone diagrams, gantt charts, pareto charts, flow charts, and other types of high-quality processes. The Greater Austin Quality Council has archived its annual Quality Award applications at the QRC so corporations who are applying for the award can see what other organizations have previously submitted.

Another program that began in 1989 and is still going strong today is the City of Austin Workplace Literacy Program, which has been renamed the Employee Learning Program. Since its inception, more than 561 employees have been matched with fellow Austin employees and have successfully learned how to read. Branch said that on the latest employee survey, 96 percent of the Workplace Literacy students said their job performance had improved.

Branch gave an example of how the learning program changed the life of one man. "The student that I tutored back in 1989, who was a custodian and didn't even know the alphabet, is now a court stenographer in the Municipal Court. He went on to get his GED and his life has been transformed," Branch said. "He tells me, he used to hide at parties because he didn't know what everyone else was talking about. Now he loves to go to parties and talk to people because he reads the paper and can discuss current events. He has much more self-confidence because he doesn't have to rely on his wife to fill out forms for him anymore. There are hundreds of stories like this."

A new service the APL has initiated that it hopes will touch other lives is the Spanish Information Line, so Spanish-speaking citizens can feel comfortable asking for information. Another new service that the library has introduced is providing public access to the Internet. "There is an overwhelming demand for this service," Branch said. "It has transformed the job of every APL employee in some way, but it is incredibly popular, and demand will only increase."

APL's public access to the Internet was funded through a grant from the Texas State Library. APL formed a partnership with Austin Free-Net and jointly submitted the application. Approximately $200,000 was received to fund 52 Internet stations—2 at each branch library, 5 at the central library, 8 at the Community Internet Training Center at the Riverside Drive Branch Library, and 2 at a neighboring community library in Cedar Park.

The city has hired a technician to troubleshoot the Internet stations, and Free-Net has recruited hundreds of community volunteers to assist library customers with the Internet stations and to provide training. "The demand greatly exceeds the number of Internet terminals, and we are hoping to find other partners in the community to help us fund additional public access terminals," Branch said.

Like public libraries all over this country, APL has faced uncertainties in its budget and in staff, but it has managed to add new programs, open additional branches, and expand hours of operation. In the 1986–87 period APL had 251.6 full-time employees; by 1989–90 it had dropped to 209.025 FTEs, but in 1993–94 it went up to 269.475 FTEs, and in

1997 the figure was up even more with 287.83 FTEs. In 1993–94 APL's budget was $10,111,587; in 1996–97 it was $11,641.637.

It is to the library's credit that it has continued to add new programs, and that it has been able to add new branch libraries and to extend the hours of others, even in a time of staff and money shortages. In 1993 Berry said this of the APL, "It is truly a Library of the Year and library for the long haul" and what he observed then, is still true today.

Bibliography

Austin City Connection. Available: http://www.ci.austin.tx.us/adadocs/library/lbfacts.htm (Accessed February 14, 1997).

Austin Public Library. Available: http://fox.co.net/ident/acplib.html (Accessed February 14, 1997).

Berry, John N. "Library of the Year 1993: Austin Public Library." *Library Journal* 118, no. 11 (June 15, 1993): 33.

"Nothin' But 'Net: Austin Public Library's Internet Newsletter for Kids with Connections." Available: http://www.ci.austin.tx.us/adadocs/library/lbkids2.htm (Accessed February 14, 1997).

THE ENOCH PRATT FREE LIBRARY AND CYBRARY

Crista Lembeck

Since 1994, the Enoch Pratt Free Library (EPFL) in Baltimore, Maryland, has billed itself as a library and "cybrary." In fact, the subtitle of the 1994–95 annual report is *Library & Cybrary: A Whole New World.*[1] The inclusion of *Cybrary* in the EPFL's process of self-definition and reinvention indicates Pratt's vision of the future, and its role in that future, of the public library within the local community and the world. Enoch Pratt Free Library is indeed reinventing itself with the advent of new technology and the twenty-first century. While EPFL is a *Library* and *Cybrary* approaching "a whole new world," Baltimore is also the "City That Reads." This is significant in evaluating whether EPFL has indeed reinvented itself. The ability for a public library to reinvent itself rests on a variety of influencing factors, including the environment in which the library exists. Not only do the library director and staff need to be creatively committed to the potential for reinvention, but the community must also be dedicated to supporting its public libraries, and the economic, political, and social environments (both past and present) surrounding the library must be conducive to the concept of reinvention.

Past

EPFL has had a progressive history of inventing and reinventing itself over the past 114 years of its existence. Enoch Pratt, the founder and benefactor of Baltimore's public library, stated in 1882, when the library was founded, that the library "shall be for all, rich and poor, without distinction of race or color, who when properly accredited, can take out the books if they will handle them carefully and return them."[2] This concept was progressive in its own right, but there was more:

> Baltimore accepted the gift and its citizens eagerly voted their approval in October 1882. The perceptive Mr. Pratt had a proviso. Although the Library became the property of the city, its management was to be entrusted to a self-perpetuating Board of Trustees. Enoch Pratt served as its president until his death in 1896. In effect, the city government was committed to the continuing support of its new acquisition, but could exercise no partisan political influence over it.[3]

The library was to be funded from public monies (after the initial donation and creation by Pratt himself), and use of the library would be free to everyone. Later, between 1900 and 1914, EPFL was unique in its approach to offering services to Baltimore's immigrant communities (discussed in Amy Begg's "Enoch Pratt Free Library and Its Service to Communities of Immigrant Residents of Baltimore During the Progressive Era, 1900–1914"[4]). Begg concludes:

> Professional librarians who worked with Baltimore's immigrant communities worked to orient their patrons to American life and culture. These professionals were motivated by a perception that librarians should serve as Progressive reformers, encouraging recent settlers in America to strive for success in this country. The efforts of Baltimore's Pratt Library staff suggest that they perceived success as achievable through awareness of the prevailing culture, obtained through books made available by a public library.[5]

Clearly, EPFL has been reinventing itself to meet the needs of the citizens of Baltimore throughout its history.

Present

Carla D. Hayden, the library's director, states, "In the last decade of the fifteenth century, explorers traveled west, gazed out across new lands and seas, and realized they had discovered a whole new world."[6] She parallels the excitement and enthusiasm of a long-ago era of exploration of the geographical world with the current eagerness to explore and experience new territory through the advent of technological advancements and cyberspace. She sees libraries as instrumental in the process of leading people through these new territories. "In the last decade of the twentieth century, as we travel into cyberspace, public libraries are guiding their customers into new worlds as amazing and awe-inspiring as any discovered five hundred years ago."[7] Hayden also is confident that "using the Pratt Library as a navigator, [we] can set [out] toward the twenty-first century."[8]

Although EPFL has never received *Library Journal*'s prestigious Library of the Year Award (in fact, Pratt has not even been a "Library of the Year Special Mention"), Carla Hayden, the director of EPFL, was recognized as the 1995 Librarian of the Year by *Library Journal*.[9] A successful library, one that is prepared to lead the way for its patrons into the twenty-first century, requires a combination of visionary individuals and a dedicated, supportive community. Enoch Pratt has benefited from both. As with Austin Public Library in Texas, "A unique quality of this outstanding library is the very close bonds it has created with the government and the people of the city that it serves."[10] Hayden has been instrumental in "creating a new model for libraries in the old Eastern cities,"[11] and Baltimore's motto is "A City That Reads!" In fact, Baltimore rallied to support its beloved library and succeeded in fending off significant budget cuts in 1997 through a combination of "a 24-hour readathon in one of the central library's show windows,"[12] public testimonies, cards and letters, articles, editorials, and media attention.[13] "Enoch Pratt Free Library officials credit an outpouring of support from Baltimore library advocates for averting Mayor Kurt L. Schmoke's plan to close 10 of the library's 28 branches."[14] Pratt spokeswoman Averil Kadis pointed out that "Pratt recently hired a development officer and observed that, ironically, 'the brouhaha has put us in a good position to ask for funds by publicizing the library's precarious finances."[15] Thus, EPFL is a library that serves its community, and its community supports EPFL.

Carla Hayden decided to take the position of director at Baltimore's EPFL in July 1993. The drawbacks were obvious and plentiful. Taking on this position was, as John N. Berry, editor in chief of *Library Journal*, stated, "a daunting challenge,"[16] and "by taking the job Carla D. Hayden faced huge professional and career risks."[17] The challenges and risks for Hayden included facing the deteriorating physical conditions of the library's facilities—"EPFL has 28 branches but no new buildings since 1971, although there have been some renovations. Two working branches currently in use were built in 1890."[18] She also faced a shrunken budget, reduced hours of service, and "personal sacrifice, leaving her hometown and family roots . . . and turning down an offer to become Director of the Chicago Public Library, her hometown library, itself already reborn with its great new central building and its program to revitalize branches."[19] But Hayden was not to be discouraged. She envisioned the potential for the future of EPFL while keeping an eye on the past.

In fact it was Enoch Pratt's glorious history that attracted Hayden to the position:

> She knew of the EPFL's many decades as the leading inno-
> vator among America's big urban libraries. She could recite
> the honor role of leaders from EPFL who changed the face
> of U.S. librarianship. She knew the scope of Pratt leader-
> ship, from reaching out to the Baltimore community with
> exemplary branch service and new and innovative children's
> libraries to the enlightened policy and practice that under-
> girded what was, at the time, a new style of administration
> and governance.[20]

Hayden became instrumental in the reinvention of EPFL, but she did not do it alone. The EPFL's annual report for 1994–95 focuses on the "achievements that have marked the progress of [their] journey as [they] plan for the future."[21] These achievements required support from all areas affecting EPFL, from the patrons, to Hayden herself, to the board, and on up to the mayor of Baltimore:

> A $20.7 million, 1997 fiscal year budget allocation for the Enoch Pratt Free Library was approved by the mayor and city council of Baltimore, nearly matching the 1996 budget of $20.8 million. During the course of the negotiations, the library secured a promise from Mayor Schmoke that he would meet with the Pratt board and develop a plan for stable funding for the next three years, allowing the library to continue with implementation of its three-year strategic plan.[22]

EPFL's three-year strategic plan was not geared solely to the future. Hayden and her staff began implementing innovative programs almost immediately. The confirmation of its secure budget allowed EPFL to move forward with exciting plans, of which many libraries (in particular, urban libraries) can only dream. Some innovative programs that EPFL currently sponsors fall into the following categories: "for Children and Youth, for Baltimore Communities and Neighborhoods, for Lovers of Books and Reading, in Information Technology, in Public and Private Partnerships, and in Managing Resources and Raising Funds."[23] Broken down into detail, these categories include the following progressive programs designed to provide Baltimore with access to the future now, and to lead the way into the twenty-first century:

> **For Children and Youth:** A Whole New World: Electronic Information Literacy project underscores EPFL's continuing commitment to services for children and youth. "Working with children who might otherwise be denied the opportunity, the program trains nine-to fourteen-year-olds to gain access to information through the Internet, communicate with children world-wide, use educational databases, and enhance their communications, comprehension, and writing skills."[24]

> **For Baltimore Communities and Neighborhoods:** "The Pratt Library is an active contributor to the revitalization of City neighborhoods benefiting from the federal Empowerment Zone grant awarded to Baltimore. Involved in the planning from the moment the grant proposal began taking shape, Pratt has been asked to play a variety of roles in the grant implementation over the next four years. . . . As plans

develop, 'Village Centers' in each Empowerment Zone community will be connected electronically with Pratt's information resources. In the meantime, information on the grant and its implications are provided at all Pratt public service agencies."[25]

In Public and Private Partnerships: "In establishing partnerships with other organizations, community groups, and government agencies, the Pratt Library explored new worlds in the choices it made. Working with the Police Department and Commissioner Thomas Frazier, branch libraries incorporated Community Oriented Police Services (COPS) in June. Under the rubric 'Coffee for Cops,' the program calls for a reserved space in each branch which police officers on the beat can use as a work station to write reports, make job-related telephone calls, or just relax for a few minutes. The officers have access to the library's information resources, computers, fax machines, restrooms, and coffee maker. For branch managers and staff, the arrangement establishes an authoritative adult presence in the library at a time when there is concern about building and personal security. For the police force, it provides an opportunity to get to know the neighborhoods and their residents in a pleasant, nonthreatening environment."[26] Berry credits EPFL ingenuity for solving "two problems with one program."[27]

Future

Enoch Pratt Free Library has a three-year strategic plan. In fact, Carla Hayden refers to this plan as the library's "compass" toward the future. Again, requiring integrated support, Hayden, along with her staff, the board, public officials, and the general population of Baltimore, has reinvented EPFL with "a new model from past glory."[28] The future efforts of the Pratt Library will be concentrated in the following areas:

- youth services and education support
- community and economic development

- technology
- collection development
- human resources
- facilities
- funding and marketing

Obviously Hayden, the EPFL staff, the board, and the city of Baltimore have a broad view of the role of their public library in the future. The library's three-year strategic plan does not focus solely on technology and the electronic-digital-virtual worlds of cyberspace. There is an emphasis on supporting and improving on existing and traditional services, as well as an eager embracing of new technological developments and advancements that promises an exciting future for EPFL and the citizens of Baltimore. EPFL is reinventing itself for the twenty-first century without attempting to ignore or deny its glorious past.

As John N. Berry states:

> What Baltimore needs now, what these times demand and EPFL must become, is a new kind of urban library designed to deliver information to the right people and places to solve nearly intractable current inner-city problems. Hayden and her team would reinvent EPFL, would try to make it the new model of effective urban librarianship. They would respect and try to re-create the spirit of its past, but what would be restored at EPFL would be the willingness to risk change and innovation that marked its glory years and the pride triggered by that leadership.[29]

Evidence of this willingness to risk change and innovation exists in the announcement made February 5, 1997, that the Enoch Pratt Free Library had awarded a $655,000 contract to SIRSI Corporation of Huntsville, Alabama, for a sophisticated information software system that will project Pratt customers into the twenty-first century almost four years before 2001. Installation was planned by June 1997. " 'The SIRSI project is a prime example,' said Dr. Hayden, 'of the new direction in which our library is going. Not only will it give our customers state-of-the art information services, but the cost will be shared by the City and the Pratt Library Board of Trustees.' "[30]

"The simple mission statement that graces the three-year strategic long-range plan for EPFL created by Carla Hayden and her team tells precisely what is expected of a modern, urban library. EPFL's purpose, it says, is 'to provide access to information resources, staff, and services that respond to the pursuit of knowledge . . . by the people of the City of Baltimore and . . . the State of Maryland.' Information, education and knowledge are the business of EPFL."[31] EPFL's mission statement does not appear to contain new and revolutionary concepts in and of itself; however, when we examine the ways in which EPFL is approaching the access to information resources, staff, and services in the pursuit of knowledge, we become acutely aware that EPFL has reinvented and positioned itself to become a new model for the public libraries in our urban areas.

"The plan's vision statement promises to put the grand old Pratt back in the leadership of American libraries by the year 2000. In two and a half short years Carla Hayden and her staff have taken giant steps toward fulfilling that plan. That is why she has been named *LJ* Librarian of the Year for 1995."[32]

A key to EPFL's and Hayden's success in reinventing the public library for the twenty-first century lies in Hayden's view of the importance of libraries in communities, and the role that they can play in revitalizing our urban areas: " 'If you want people to own homes, you have to have public services like good schools, cleanliness, and good libraries to support property values. . . . We now see ourselves not only as a city agency but more like a city utility,' said Hayden, elaborating on her vision for EPFL. 'We are the information utility, but we are like the streets.' "[33] If everyone envisioned the role of our public libraries as being as important as maintaining our streets and picking up trash, every public library in the country could be prepared for the twenty-first century.

Ultimately what EPFL has done is reinvent itself for the present with one eye looking back on the past and one eye looking toward the future. This is evidenced in EPFL's and Hayden's accomplishments during the past three years. To summarize, Hayden's

> vision was to reinvent EPFL as a new model for urban public librarianship while respecting and recreating the glorious history of the library. In partnership with the community and the library board, Hayden worked to get the city of Baltimore to add $1.2 million to the library's budget. Grants

> and private donations have totaled nearly $10 million during her tenure. Saturday service has been restored to nearly all locations of the library, in response to community needs. . . . The newly created EPFL Information Access Division was awarded a state contract to operate Sailor, a statewide electronic network serving public libraries and their users. The same department will be used to streamline such library functions as collection development and processing. . . . Also initiated during Hayden's administration are an electronic literacy program for children; increased mobile service to day care centers, camps, apartment buildings, and senior centers [along with] Student Express [and] multimedia homework centers for middle and high school students.[34]

If we consider Dr. Charles R. McClure's "Possible Public Library Roles in the Electronic Environment,"[35] EPFL, through its physical branches and its web site, is already a Network Literacy Center, a Liaison for Government Information, a Center for Electronic Life-Long Learning, a Global Information Access Center, a Community Information Organizer and Provider, an Economic Development Center, a Global Switching Station, and an Electronic Twenty-Four-Hour-a-Day Reference, Referral, and Reading Center. The future for EPFL and Baltimore is now.[36]

Notes

1. *Enoch Pratt Free Library Annual Report 1994–1995, Library & Cybrary: A Whole New World*, 1–18.

2. Averil Jordan Kadis, "Enoch Pratt's Gift: From Town Library to State Resource Center," April 1996, available: http://www.pratt.lib.md.us/index.html (Accessed February 20, 1997).

3. Ibid.

4. Amy Begg, "Enoch Pratt Free Library and Its Service to Communities of Immigrant Residents of Baltimore During the Progressive Era, 1900–1914," March 1996, available: http://www.h-net.msu.edu/~urban/comm-org/begg/pratt. html (Accessed March 6, 1997).

5. Ibid.

6. *Enoch Pratt Free Library Annual Report 1994–1995*, 2.

7. Ibid.

8. Carla D. Hayden, "Director's Welcome Message," available: http://www.pratt.lib.md.us/index.html (Accessed February 20, 1997).

9. John N. Berry, "Librarian of the Year 1995: Carla D. Hayden, Enoch Pratt Free Library, Baltimore," *Library Journal* 121. no. 1 (January 1996): 18–36.

10. John N. Berry, "Library of the Year 1993: Austin Public Library," *Library Journal* 118, no. 11 (June 15, 1993): 30.

11. Berry, "Librarian of the Year 1995," 36.

12. "News Fronts: Pratt Supporters Derail Plan to Close 10 Branches," *American Libraries* 27, no. 7 (August 1996): 13.

13. "Pratt $20 Mil. Budget Secure, Reduction Threats Overcome," *Library Hotline* 25, no. 26 (July 1996): 1.

14. "News Fronts," 13.

15. Ibid.

16. Berry, "Librarian of the Year 1995," 36.

17. Ibid.

18. Ibid., 37.

19. Ibid., 36.

20. Ibid.

21. *Enoch Pratt Free Library Annual Report 1994–1995*, 2.

22. "Pratt $20 Mil. Budget Secure, Reduction Threats Overcome," 1.

23. *Enoch Pratt Free Library Annual Report 1994–1995*, 1–18.

24. Ibid., 3.

25. Ibid., 5.

26. Ibid., 10–11.

27. Berry, "Librarian of the Year 1995," 38.

28. Ibid., 36.

29. Ibid.

30. Averil Kadis, "SIRSI Press Release," February 1997, available: http://www.sirsi.com/Preleases/enoch.html (Accessed March 6, 1997).

31. Berry, "Librarian of the Year 1995," 38.

32. Ibid.

33. Ibid.

34. "Enoch Pratt's Carla Hayden Is '*LJ*' Librarian of the Year," *Library Hotline* 25, no. 3 (January 1996): 1–2.

35. Charles R. McClure, John C. Beachboard, and John C. Bertot, "Enhancing the Role of Public Libraries in the National Information Infrastructure," *Public Libraries* 35, no 4, (July/August 1996): 232–238.

36. Enoch Pratt Free Library, available: http://www.pratt.lib.md.us/index.html (Accessed February-March 1997).

BROOKLYN PUBLIC LIBRARY

Kevin Smith

The Brooklyn Public Library serves the informational needs of 157 ethnic groups in Brooklyn, New York. For four hours on Sundays, 10,000 to 12,000 people use the Brooklyn Central Library. In a given year more than two million people patronize this institution.[1] The Central Library, with its 5.2 million items, is the hub of the Brooklyn library system, which includes 58 branches. With patron numbers of that magnitude, one can only imagine the extent of the entire system.

In 1892 the legislature of the state of New York approved the Brooklyn Public Library. Four years later, on November 30, 1896, a resolution passed by the Brooklyn Common Council established the library. Originally the system was to be a network of small libraries spread throughout Brooklyn without a large central library. As Brooklyn grew, however, a central library became necessary. Construction began in 1912 but was not completed until 1941; apparently, building funds were scarce because of the two world wars that intervened during construction.

The philanthropy of Andrew Carnegie, "America's patron saint of libraries," of course, aided in the spread of branch libraries. From 1901 to 1923, Carnegie contributed $1.6 million to the Brooklyn Public Library. When building his libraries, Carnegie had in mind the millions of immigrants newly arrived in America. His hope was for the libraries to be community centers. The neighborhood library could be a place for new Americans to learn about their new culture without losing their native one.[2] Originally, 21 "Carnegie Libraries" were built, but only 18 remain today.

From the beginning the Brooklyn Public Library has been firmly grounded in neighborhood library service. A little more than 100 years ago, in December 1897, the first Brooklyn branch library opened. It was housed in Public School Number 3, which is now part of the Bedford-Stuyvesant section of Brooklyn. This original branch had segregated reading rooms for men and women. It was also one of the first libraries to have open stacks where readers were free to browse. Before the spring 1900, Brooklyn had opened six branches. The precursor of a bookmobile was also in place, known as a "traveling library department."[3]

One of the most impressive displays of information technology at the Brooklyn Public Library is its Business Library. It has existed since 1943 and is the only public library devoted exclusively to business reference information on the East Coast. Allegedly, the Brooklyn Business Library is the largest in the country. The reference collection contains more than 100,000 volumes, and the circulating collection has 30,000 books. In addition, the business collection includes CD-ROM databases, magazines, and newspapers. Users from around the globe patronize the Brooklyn Business Library.[4]

The Business Library has three unique features. First, there is the Small Business Information Center (SBIC), a resource center for starting and maintaining a small business. The librarian who staffs the SBIC is a specialist in small business information. At the SBIC, patrons can arrange to consult experts from the Service Corps of Retired Executives (SCORE) free of charge. The SBIC's collection contains books and CD-ROM titles specifically addressing small business interests.

Second, there are Reference Services at the Business Library. Patrons can inquire about investment and industry information. Those who cannot come in person or access the LAN may telephone a request. Librarians, however, can only answer three inquiries per person.

Third, there is the Business Library LAN. Patrons may access the business LAN 24 hours a day and use a variety of CD-ROM databases. These databases include the Brooklyn Public Library Catalog, National Trade Data Bank, New York City Census Summary, Zip Code Population, County Business Patterns, ABI/Inform, and Newspaper Abstracts.

According to its Internet web page, the vision statement of the Brooklyn Public Library is as follows, "The Brooklyn Public Library will be a vital center of knowledge for all, accessible twenty-four hours a day, and will be a leader in traditional and innovative library services which reflect the diverse and dynamic spirit of the people of Brooklyn."

With patronage consisting of 157 different ethnic groups, diversification is essential to the Brooklyn Library. The spirit of Andrew Carnegie is apparently still present in the library system as each branch strives to be a cultural center for the community it serves.

Recently, the Brooklyn Public Library acquired a new executive director, Martin Gomez. Revitalizing the library and enhancing its public service for the twenty-first century is his mission. Gomez's administration stresses three top priorities. The first is to strengthen the commitment of providing top-quality library service to young people. Second, the BPL wants to put every public library in Brooklyn online for Internet access. Third, the BPL plans to address the language and informational needs of new Americans who have recently immigrated to Brooklyn.[5] This last priority is very reminiscent of Andrew Carnegie's dream.

Age-specific library service is the central element of Gomez's plans. He believes that specialists provide better library service than generalists.[6] His reintroduction of specialist librarians overturns 20 years of generalist librarianship. According to Gomez, in the 1970s, two factors contributed to this trend. First, severe budget cutbacks forced the library to seek a more economical means of staffing. In addition, there was a lack of children's and young adult librarians.[7] Ultimately, Gomez wants age-level specialists again to take part in library management. This shift in philosophy may leave some generalists a little dismayed.

"Sleeping giant" is the term Martin Gomez affectionately uses when describing his new charge.[8] He realizes the libraries' great potential in better serving the plethora of community diversity. Compared to its sister libraries, New York Public and Queens Borough Public, Brooklyn had been lagging behind in technology. Gomez, however, has made great efforts to rectify the situation. The library board actually handpicked him in 1995 to resurrect the antiquated but noble library. Again, ethnic diversity is a major concern for Gomez. His grand plan includes making the Brooklyn Public Library the national model for serving the immigrant community.[9]

Establishing an identity of its own is another goal Gomez has for the library. Many times the Brooklyn library is mistaken for its relative across the East River. Ironically, however, when it comes to lobbying New York City for funds, it is necessary for the three libraries to present a unified front.[10]

Solidarity is a term that does not describe the library board, staff, and elected officials. At the moment, the three groups do not have a shared vision. During his tenure, Gomez intends to correct this and give the library and its associates a sense of common direction. Reflecting the Brooklyn community, Gomez plans to create a more ethnically diverse senior staff. Including new staff members—45 percent of the present staff—in management decisions is another facet of Gomez's mission. The administration of the Brooklyn Public Library has commendable ideals as it desires to be one spirit serving a heterogenous society.

When I telephoned the Brooklyn Public Library and asked about its reinvention, no one was able to comment. Every attempted inquiry was immediately referred to the marketing department, which, of course, gave only positive, well-rehearsed responses. It must be noted that the attitudes of those to whom inquiries were directed were not very appealing.

Notes

1. Brooklyn Public Library web page, available: http:/ /www brooklyn.lib.ny.us (Accessed March 1997).
2. Ibid.
3. Ibid.
4. Ibid.
5. Lillian Gerhardt, "Leadership from Brooklyn PL," *School Library Journal* 42, no. 10 (October 1996): 4.
6. Ibid.
7. Ibid.
8. Evan St. Lifer, "One Big City, Three Great Libraries," *Library Journal* 121, no. 10 (June 1, 1996): 49.
9. Ibid.
10. Ibid.

BROWARD COUNTY LIBRARY: 1996 Library of the Year

Melanie Carlson

The Broward County Library (BCL) in Broward County, Florida, won the 1996 Gale Research/*Library Journal* Library of the Year Award. In so doing, the BCL proved that an adaptable, industrious library can offer something for everyone, by providing programs that benefit the user, the funder, and the library itself. BCL did this by gathering support from a wide range of voters and by building unique partnerships with groups of private businesses, public agencies, nonprofit institutions, and individuals.

Background

Broward County is located to the south of Palm Beach County and to the north of Dade County, Florida. The county includes the cities of Fort Lauderdale and Hollywood and is home to more than 1,382,000 people. Today, the median age in the county is 41 years old.

BCL opened in 1974 with two city libraries (Hollywood and Fort Lauderdale), 100 employees, and a budget of $1.5 million. Today, the budget has increased to $29 million with 2 main libraries, 3 regional libraries, and 29 branches spread throughout the county. A bookmobile also visits 30 neighborhoods. The library is governed by the county under the Department of Community Services. BCL's director is Samuel Morrison, who began with the library when it opened in 1974. He left in 1987 to work at the Chicago Public Library but in 1990 returned to Broward County, bringing with him a vast amount of urban experience that has given him the background for the innovative programs he has initiated. Morrison began his career with a federal LSCA (Library Services and Construction Act) project to bring library services to migrant workers picking citrus in Central Florida. This, together with his urban Chicago experience, has helped make the Broward County Library 1996 Library of the Year.

BCL has achieved its successful goals by using the following methods: developing programs that benefit users; implementing new and creative ways to provide that service; and encouraging, rewarding, and developing the staff with educational incentives and learning programs. The BLC mission statement includes the following:

> "Free, convenient, and equal access to information in useful formats" in "environments that foster lifelong learning, personal enrichment, and a literate society; strengthening information cooperation through resource sharing and actively promoting library services, programs, and materials to the community."

Partnerships

Promotion and cooperation are two of the keys to BCL's success. Cooperation refers to its partnerships with nearly 500 businesses such as banks, airlines, brokers, travel firms, and religious groups. It also has educational connections involving school boards, universities, community colleges, schools, as well as organizations of teachers and/or educators. These partnerships are enacted by negotiating "deals" so all parties can benefit. One of the first partnerships was with its Friends of the BCL. This partnership helped to build the BCL building on the campus of the Broward County Community College. This cooperative effort so impressed the community that it brought more opportunities into the system.

Another cooperative partnership is in its BCL Business Resource Center. This center has not only been enhanced by the county but also by private donors, including a local bank. The center provides information resources and counseling for small businesses. It is seen as a great opportunity to promote economic development and growth in the county.

Another successful BCL partnership is found in the operation of a professional library for educators that includes a full range of print and electronic resources in education. The library also maintains the Florida Diagnostic and Learning Resources System, a library for parents, teachers, and agencies that works with exceptional children. In the works is a plan for a new combined middle-school library and public library branch similar to the community college campus concept.

Technology

BCL promotes itself as a Broward Information Gateway (BIG). SEFLIN (Southeast Florida Library Information Network) is yet another partnership; it is an independent, electronic network that combines 13 consortium libraries of various types, headquartered at BCL. SEFLIN Free-Net carries information on local groups and activities, government information, and the Internet and e-mail in a three-county area (Dade, Broward, and Palm Beach). Private, public, and academic libraries are members. Each library pays a standardized amount to SEFLIN in return for access. Resource sharing is also provided. Soon World Wide Web access will be available. Two library kiosks in local malls give the public links to the Internet as well.

BCL provides the Technology Center, which SEFLIN helps finance. The center offers a training facility for the school board and library staff. It also provides a place where the public can work on computer terminals. Through an arrangement with local vendors, new software and hardware packages can be previewed and tested by patrons. Training classes will be offered in the future.

To help fund these programs, BCL, and its BIG services, has offered a credit-card size "BIG" card that works not only as a library card but as a debit card as well. Money is deposited at an add-value station that credits the card. Patrons can then make computer printouts or photocopies without having to carry cash. Revenue from this card will also be used to finance expansion of library technology.

Minority Programs

BCL and its partnerships have implemented two creative programs that benefit the county's minority population, 14 percent of which is African American and 8.4 percent Hispanic. In the 1970s, one of the branches opened with a focus on Spanish-language materials. Today, eight libraries have an almost-complete core collection of materials in Spanish. The collection includes reference materials, adult fiction and nonfiction, children's materials, and periodicals. BCL hopes soon to expand this program into 24 branches.

Another program envisioned by BCL is the African American Research Library and Cultural Center. Although still in the planning stages, it will provide all the services a regular branch does, including research, collections, exhibit areas, and rooms for performances and small dance troupes.

Training and Education

As stated earlier, BCL has achieved its successful status by encouraging, rewarding, and developing staff education. Florida is home to two library schools: the University of South Florida in Tampa and Florida State University in Tallahassee. Both schools offer classes at the BCL Fort Lauderdale branch. The county reimburses employee tuition at the end of the program. The Broward Public Library Foundation allocates money annually to employees as an incentive to earn an MLS. The Friends offer interest-free loans, so employees can pay the tuition before they are reimbursed on graduation. Employees also qualify for interest-free loans to pay for books. Almost 24 employees have completed an MLS while working full-time at BCL. Undergraduate education is also encouraged, and approximately 60 employees are working toward that goal. BCL tries to encourage other staff members to further their education as well, which in turn promotes better library service.

The Broward County Public Library has grown and developed rapidly since its opening in 1974. Its creative community-partnership relations and its goals to provide programs that benefit the patron, the partners, and the community as a whole have resulted in its achievement as the 1996 Gale Research/*Library Journal* Library of the Year.

Other libraries working toward similar goals should look to BCL as an example of how a community works together to benefit its citizens.

BCL's home page is: http://www.co.broward.fl.us/library.

Telephone Interview with a BCL Librarian

I recently spoke with a reference librarian at the main library of Broward County Library in Fort Lauderdale, Florida. When I had read the article on BCL, I was amazed at the number and variety of services and programs Broward County offered to its patrons, especially the payment of full tuition for any library employee who completes the MLS program. My first question to the librarian was whether all employees took advantage of this wonderful opportunity. She replied that a large number of their employees do take advantage of this, either pursuing an MLS or in some type of undergraduate study. My interviewee had not done so, she explained, because she was close to retiring (three years) and did not feel it was necessary to her career. She did stress several times to me that an MLS is getting to be a requirement nowadays for advancement in the library field. Broward County does use professionals as well as paraprofessionals at the reference desk. She is a paraprofessional library associate, and she said she has probably gone as far as she can go without the MLS. She was also very encouraging and kept telling me to finish my MLS.

I next asked her about all the technology and programs offered by the library. She said they were wonderful and told me that a whole floor was filled with computers and PCs for the patron. When asked if the librarians received training when new products were introduced, she said that the library is heavily committed to training and continuing education, and she can attend any training classes she would like. Indeed, her supervisor is very supportive of this.

My final question was about job opportunities for librarians at the Broward County Library. Here she discussed the first negative aspect. She told me that recently a librarian in the humanities department had retired and was not going to be replaced. She said that, even with all the wonderful technology and services provided, like everywhere else, tighter budgets meant leaner staffs. The reference librarian was interesting and helpful, and I am glad I had the opportunity to talk with her.

Bibliography

Berry, John N. "Library of the Year, Broward County Library." *Library Journal* 118, no. 11 (June 15, 1996): 28–31.

"Broward County Library Premiers 'BIG' Card." In "The Weekly Newsletter," *Library Hotline* (February 26, 1996): 1.

De la Pena McCook, Kathleen, and Paula Geist. "Hispanic Library Services in South Florida." *Public Libraries* 34, no. 1 (January/February 1995): 34–37.

"Florida Library Homepages." In *1996 Florida Library Directory with Statistics*. Tallahassee, Fla.: Florida State Library, 1996.

BROWN COUNTY LIBRARY:
1994 Library of the Year

Suzanne Duncan

Located in Wisconsin, Brown County Library (BCL) was named Library of the Year in 1994. It consists of one main library, eight branches, and a bookmobile. This library serves more than 200,000 people, including the large Hmong and Native American populations in the community.

The library can trace its origins to the donation of a library building by Mr. Kellogg to the city of Green Bay in the 1900s. Approximately 24 years ago, a consolidated county system was created. The Kellogg building needed replacement, and the Brown County Board of Supervisors decided to develop a consolidated city library system. This system has allowed for a focus on services rather than on funding concerns in the library system, according to Pat LaViolette, director of the system.

According to LaViolette, the library's mission is "being involved in the life of the community, embracing the life of the community, . . . [and] think[ing] often of the community." The goals the system follows are "budgetary and other goals that are broad based enough that any time an opportunity presents itself, the library can move toward it." Being able to react quickly and redirect resources when the opportunity presents itself is important to the library system.

"The involvement and empowerment of the library staff and the willingness of the director and staff to experiment with organizational change are two key factors in the choice of BCL as Library of the Year" for 1994. It uses "its services, facilities, and programs as models for other government and nongovernment agencies demonstrating how effectively and efficiently government can operate." The BCL has made community involvement and coalitions a goal and part of its mission. The library has a Recycling Hotline that improved government service and proved to be cost-effective for the county. The questions received by the solid waste department were added to the library's telephone reference and community information service line.

The BCL has an extensive volunteer program. These individuals go to local jails, nursing homes, and senior centers and also serve as "reading buddies" with at-risk third graders. The community Quality Center in Green Bay was created when local business leaders wanted to place all the materials they had on Total Quality Management in a central location. Those materials are now accessible to the whole county. The library was also one of the first government agencies to adopt TQM.

Pat LaViolette attributes her library's uniqueness in many ways to the types of librarians she has. Brown County Library has Level I, II, and III for its librarians. A Librarian I is not required to have a Masters in Library Science (MLS). The person must have a background in the field related to the work area and three to four years of experience in that field; for example, the Children's Department has many trained and qualified teachers. This has widened the focus and services of the departments involved. This practice, especially in the Children's Department, has given the library high visibility in the community.

LaViolette has recently started hiring Librarian IIs who must have a masters but not necessarily an MLS. She also looks for people already well connected in the community. These individuals have a personal philosophy of giving back to the community. She believes that this gives more exposure to the library and ties it deeper to the community. The staff of Brown County Library is given the environment needed to empower themselves. LaViolette has no worry about her staff members overextending themselves, and therefore, she places no limits on them. She believes that individuals who empower themselves are strong over-achievers who have learned how to self-regulate. LaViolette indicated that her library is always reinventing. "When you're at the point you think you should be at, it's time to retire." The library is constantly changing and always looking for new opportunities, she says. The library must become part of these opportunities.

The day I interviewed LaViolette she was just getting her e-mail account set up. The rest of the staff already had e-mail. This was revealing in two ways. One was the fact that she was one of the last people in her system to get e-mail. The second was that technology was not mentioned by John N. Berry in his article on the 1994 Library of the Year Award.

The library has just installed DYNIX (a library automation system) and now has a Wide Area Network (WAN). The library currently spends only 17 percent of its budget on technology. LaViolette does not believe that the library can simply focus on technology; a balance is needed. Considerations between print and electronic media range from which gives the greatest access to the largest number of people to how they will improve service and provide more (or less) privacy to the patron. A major role with technology is that of teaching. Children, high school students, and adults are comfortable with technology. Individuals between 50 and 60 need more encouragement to use modern technologies in the BCL.

LaViolette went into some detail on a joint venture with local schools and the University of North East Teaching College. About two years ago, the superintendent of the Green Bay School Board wanted to start sharing resources. The superintendent used his influence and got other superintendents and the university to join with him and the BCL. From their collaboration the North East consortium was created. The vision of the consortium is to allow anyone coming into any type of library (public, academic, or school system) to be able to determine where any information is held anywhere in the county. This information would then be delivered to the location of the user. This is one of the first resource-sharing endeavors of this type in the state.

The governor of Wisconsin recently presented his vision of resource sharing for the state and, unfortunately, completely left out the state's public libraries. LaViolette has sent a letter to the governor providing him with information on the consortium and encouraging him to include public libraries in the vision.

At the time of the interview, the Internet was only available on two terminals at the central library and one branch. The goal was to have access at all branches and to have more terminals at central library by the end of 1997. Internet access was initiated by the library but is now driven by student demands.

While Brown County Library continues to integrate itself in the community, it does not give technology the priority that many other public libraries have given it. The library does have a web page, but it provides no useful information about the library: for instance, it does not include the hours of operation, types of services, programs offered, locations of branches, and important phone numbers. Brown County Library is a library for its community. An individual who is not in the area would have a hard-to-impossible time finding out anything about this library. In the ever-increasing shrinkage of the world through technology, BCL may one day be a small community library in the global community.

Bibliography

Berry, John N. "Library of the Year 1994: Brown County Library, Green Bay, Wisconsin." *Library Journal* 119, no. 11 (June 15, 1994): 30–33.

Brown County Library. Available: http://www.dct.com/org/bcl (Accessed April 9, 1998).

LaViolette, Pat. Interview by author. March 7, 1997.

PUBLIC LIBRARY OF CHARLOTTE & MECKLENBURG COUNTY: 1995 Library of the Year

Diane Wagner

During a booming economy in 1891, prominent citizens of Charlotte City organized the Charlotte Literary and Library Association, a subscription library housed above a bookstore. Although it was understood that the public would have access to the collection, control of the library was transferred to the school commissioners in 1901. Also in 1901, Andrew Carnegie donated $25,000 for a library building in Charlotte with the conditions that the city would furnish the site and that taxpayers would support the operations. The building was dedicated July 2, 1903. The first public library in the state to serve African Americans was opened as an independent institution in 1905 under the Carnegie Library's 1903 charter. The Brevard Street Library for Negroes became a branch of the Charlotte Public Library in 1929 and remained in use until 1961.

Eventually, with expanded services and increased circulation, additional space was critically needed at the main library and four branches. In 1952 a $1.6-million bond issue was approved by Charlotte and Mecklenburg County voters, and a new main library was built on the site of the razed Carnegie building. Nine branch buildings were also constructed at that time.[1]

Today the Public Library of Charlotte & Mecklenburg County (PLCMC) is reinventing itself for the twenty-first century. What services have been rethought and redesigned for a radical improvement? Where did it begin? Who has done it? What types of operations have been reinvented to better serve the world?

264

The PLCMC currently serves a population of 581,000, and approximately 60 percent of the county residents have a library card.[2] With an annual circulation approaching 5.7 million in 1996, circulation reached nearly 10 items per capita. However, according to an article in *Library Journal* (September 15, 1993), the *Charlotte Observer* reported that PLCMC was not flourishing in the early 1980s. Although it was one of Charlotte-Mecklenburg's oldest cultural institutions, the solitary, passive entity was not visible and did not have the clout to get the money it needed to regain its position as an innovative leader. An entirely different public library in tune with the community is in existence today with increased visibility, public funding for new projects, new technology, and private funding for many programs. With 22 branches including a business and a law library, PLCMC now uses a proactive approach entirely different from that taken 20 years ago.[3]

What brought about the drastic change? A visionary marketing strategy with an emphasis on fostering relationships has garnered community support to save the library. It came alive as one of the most innovative and dynamic libraries in the country by striving to be a major community asset. Helen Ruth Fleming, former marketing and development director for PLCMC, wrote in the same *Library Journal* article, "Libraries, vital components in this new age of information delivery and technology, are part of the cultural fabric of every community. Librarians should investigate how they can position their institution to be a major community asset. The possibilities are endless, because access to good information is at the core of every business's strategic plan, every child's education, every banker's prospectus, every writer's story, every composer's music, and every journalist's article."[4]

Change also was encouraged when board members began looking toward the future, seeking new, proactive leadership to direct the library and using techniques of strong marketing and fund-raising. In 1983 the PLCMC appeared on a bond referendum for library renovation funds for the first time in 30 years. The board chairperson helped establish the Friends of the Public Library, and community support was sought to increase visibility and establish a political awareness for passage of the library bond issue.

How has the philosophy of the library changed, and how has this affected programs and politics? In 1989 with the reopening of the renovated main library, a new philosophy emerged, incorporating a focus on continuous improvement from the Total Quality Management program.

Surveys showed that the library was popular, but Robert E. Cannon, executive director of libraries, wanted a real change. At that time a 10-year plan (currently redone nearly every two years) was drafted. Tremendous amounts of training by experts on customer service as well as trainers in communication ensure that the new outlook continues to provide excellent service.[5] When I recently spoke with Cannon, he mentioned that $35,000 is budgeted annually for training. Although this amount does not represent an increase, a former $40,000 position has been modified to provide a full-time technology trainer in the system who offers courses to the staff and furnishes the workbooks and textbooks used for the training.

I asked if there were any changes in the mission statement to reflect the reinvention of the library. Cannon's reply was that the way to approach work has changed, although the mission statement itself has not. The first paragraph of the mission statement reads:

> The Mission of the Public Library of Charlotte & Mecklenburg County is to make available to all residents, by convenient and free access, a wide variety of expertly selected library materials and resources for the public's educational and informational needs; to promote the enjoyment of reading and books, lifelong learning, citizenship and the appreciation of the world's cultural achievements.[6]

How has the staff responded to the reinvention of the library? Awards programs such as "Doing It Right," a program where staff members are rewarded for effective work with patrons, have changed staff attitudes toward library users. The suggestion-award program has encouraged employees to submit improved methods of conducting business. When I asked Cannon if performance evaluations had undergone changes to reflect the reinvention of the library, he replied that the current method has been used for years, and because everyone has been pleased with it, there has been no change. Pay and work plans are individualized with eight ranges of pay for the 400 employees.

How has the public responded to the reinvention of the library? Cannon believes that in order to survive, libraries must be seen in a new light by the community. To change the way information is provided while coping with restrictions on funding, the institution and its services must be marketed aggressively. Programs and activities are reported in the media nearly every day, and the increase in library usage since Cannon has been director is 80 percent.

The most important aspect of the library's successful reinvention is the high-quality customer service. A Service Excellence program includes customer service training for all public service staff members, reader's advisory workshops, and recognition for employees providing outstanding service to patrons. The Main Library remains open during most holidays. Renewal and hold notifications via telephone reduced mailing costs by $100,000 in 1992, while making it easier for patrons to use library services. A popular service in one branch allows patrons who do not like to wait for bestsellers to rent them for two weeks with a $2 charge.

The second part of the plan was to identify the goals of PLCMC, and as a result, a strategic plan for the next 10 years was developed. To gain the public and private support needed to accomplish their goals, programs and services were identified featuring topics of interest to the community. Areas chosen because of visibility potential included children's services, international business, information technology, and uptown revitalization efforts.

The NOVELLO Festival of Reading, a four-day literary marathon, was created in 1991. It has grown as a major annual cultural event with broad-based support from the literary, political, and business communities. Well-known writers, such as Anne Rivers Siddons, Ferrol Sams, Dori Sanders, Charles Kuralt, Valerie Sherwood, Maurice Sendak, James Stewart, and Gloria Houston have participated by discussing, signing, and selling their books.[7]

Additional coverage of all library activities has been a result of the community involvement with NOVELLO, and many more corporations have become involved with PLCMC. The success of NOVELLO, winner of a Southeastern Library Association program award in 1994, led to the library's involvement on Chamber of Commerce committees and other cultural organizations. By cosponsoring the Uptown Hotline, a 24-hour-a-day number with information about uptown activities, the PLCMC ensures the inclusion in the hotline of important library events.[8]

After building relationships with leaders of the international community to secure their suggestions and support, the International Business Library was opened in 1994 to meet the information needs of more than 320 foreign firms in Charlotte as well as U.S. companies and institutions with overseas operations. A goal of PLCMC is to "have the most extensive international business collection among public libraries in the Southeast."[9]

To what creative uses has PLCMC put information technology? Its Virtual Library is designed for the entire community. Using professional staff members and volunteers, free hands-on training is available to provide access to online services. New technical employees have replaced some regular professional and clerical positions. The regional free-net, Charlotte's Web, was developed by the library along with the school system, a local community college, a university, a television station, and other agencies. Start-up funds included state and local allocations in addition to a $450,000 federal National Telecommunications and Information Administration matching grant. The web provides continuous access to information and communication services through home PCs and public access terminals, 74 of which are installed in library branches. Free and equal access is part of the PLCMC commitment to reach out and serve anyone.[10]

I asked Cannon if the collection has been changed along with the reinvention of the library. His response was that $250,000, 10 percent of the budget for materials, is being spent on videos and CD-ROMs now. He thinks that, although most of the budget continues to go to traditional library service, new and old technologies must coexist.

In 1995 PLCMC was named Library of the Year by Gale Research/ *Library Journal.* The purpose of the award is "to offer media recognition and a financial reward to the library that most profoundly demonstrates creativity and leadership in serving its community."[11] A panel of librarians throughout the United States and *LJ* editors select the winning library based on three elements: "service to the community; creativity and innovation in coping with the changing needs of the American public as demonstrated by either specific community programs or a dramatic increase in library usage; and finally, the leadership role the library plays by creating programs that can be emulated by other libraries."[12] The winning library receives a $10,000 grant from Gale Research, Inc.

In the June 15, 1995, issue of *Library Journal*, John N. Berry wrote, "The key is not just in accepting change, it is in welcoming it, taking the risk to predict it so you can be part of it, even launching it and then shaping it as it progresses. That combination of qualities and the results of that high-risk approach to running a library made the Public Library of Charlotte & Mecklenburg County (PLCMC), headquartered in Charlotte, N.C., the obvious choice to be the Gale Research Inc./*Library Journal* Library of the Year for 1995."[13]

The commitment to a unique vision by the governing authority, a staff willing to experiment with change, and management that forces change so that the library does not just react to it ensure that library service will be better than ever. PLCMC wants to be the "library of the future" characterized by change producing better library service.

Voter support is necessary for these programs to flourish. With a budget of $15 million, bond issues have been passed to continue the library's expansion. Three new branches recently were opened to meet the needs of a growing population, and renovations for branches in the inner city were completed.

Fleming writes, "With the increasing competition for dollars, the winners are going to be the highly visible institutions with strong reputations for serving the needs of the community. Institutions that deftly build alliances with other educational and cultural organizations—as well as with the business community—will make their dollars go further. Never forget people give to people, and people can only support causes they know about. Building relationships is the name of the game."[14]

According to the *Five Year Plan*, this is the vision for PLCMC.

> In the year 2002, envision a modern public library system consisting of a Main Library, five regional and seventeen branch libraries, a public law library, an African-American resource collection, and a library by mail service, all linked together through the use of the most modern computer systems and daily delivery service.

> Envision a public library system that is totally oriented towards meeting the information and service needs of the clientele, with the best library collections, programs, services and question answering capabilities in the state, region, and nation. Envision complete library information services via computers to the home.

> Envision a public library system that promotes and enjoys increased public use and high demand. Reading itself is promoted heavily and readership by all age groups has been shown to increase markedly. Envision a library system

> that is considered the most cost effective in the nation, with the highest level of per capita giving, highest level of non-tax revenues; the highest level of economic return for the cost of the services provided.

> Envision a public library system which features and incorporates the best of library and other technologies to quickly meet user demands for services and information. Picture buildings which have been designed and built with the utmost care; beautiful, but functional buildings that will contribute to the cultural wealth of the citizens of the city and county.

> Envision a library system that more aptly and aggressively contributes to the solving of the problems of the community, like meeting the information needs of isolated older adults, or young adults, illiterate adults, or children who have not experienced a positive exposure to the joys of books and reading, especially in economically deprived areas.

> Envision a public library system that is linked to millions of computers throughout the world, so that information and the sharing of it can be fast, sure and complete.[15]

PLCMC's *Ten-Year Plan* states, "It is a goal of The Library to be the most innovative, creative, and forward looking public library system in the country. . . . The library seeks to continuously improve . . . and become one of the best, if not the best library system in the nation."[16] This library exemplifies a total commitment for improvement through continuous change and is the institution to examine for those interested in building the library of the future. This also is why PLCMC won the American Library Association and *Information Today*'s "Library of the Future" award for 1996.

Notes

1. "History of PLCMC," available: http//www.plcmc.lib.nc.us/ (Accessed February 18, 1997).

2. John N. Berry, "Public Library of Charlotte & Mecklenburg County," *Library Journal* 120, no. 11 (June 15, 1995): 35.

3. Helen Ruth Fleming, "Library CPR: Savvy Marketing Can Save Your Library," *Library Journal* 118, no. 15 (September 15, 1993): 32.

4. Ibid.

5. Berry, "Public Library of Charlotte & Mecklenburg County," 32–35.

6. "Mission Statement," *Five Year Plan (Draft)*, available: http://www. plcmc.lib.nc.us/find/fiveyear.htm#financ (Accessed February 18, 1997).

7. Wilda Williams, "Writers in Residence: Booking Authors in Libraries," *Library Journal* 118, no. 3 (Accessed February 15, 1993): 140.

8. Fleming, "Library CPR," 34–35.

9. Ibid.

10. Berry, "Public Library of Charlotte & Mecklenburg County," 33.

11. "Nominations Sought for Gale/*LJ* Library of the Year," *Library Journal* 117, no. 5 (March 15, 1992): 18.

12. Ibid.

13. Berry, "Public Library of Charlotte & Mecklenburg County," 32.

14. Fleming, "Library CPR," 35.

15. "The Public Library of Charlotte & Mecklenburg County in the Year 2001," *Five Year Plan*, available: http://www.plcmc.lib.nc.us/find/fiveyear.htm#financ (Accessed February 18, 1997).

16. Berry, "Public Library of Charlotte & Mecklenburg County," 35.

KALAMAZOO PUBLIC LIBRARY: 1994 Special Mention Library of the Year

Joan Wilson

Kalamazoo (Michigan) Public Library received an honorable mention in the 1994 Library of the Year Award sponsored by Gale Research/ *Library Journal*. This article explores why KPL was considered outstanding and whether it has continued to distinguish itself. Finally, is KPL reinventing itself?

History and Demographics

According to KPL's brochure, "All You Need to Know," the following is a thumbnail sketch of the library's history:

> 1860 School district inherited a tiny collection from a disbanded township.
>
> 1872 Kalamazoo Public Library opened to all residents, not just students.
>
> 1893 First permanent home built for the library, corner of South and Rose.
>
> 1896 Children's Room created, one of the first ten in the country.

1990 Voters created the district library, with a separate board of trustees.

1995 Voters supported a millage to fund building and renovation program.

KPL serves the residents in the school district and city of Kalamazoo and the townships of Oshtemo and Kalamazoo. In Michigan, there are six classes of district libraries. The smallest, Class I, serves 0–3,999 people. KPL is in the largest class, Class VI, that serves 50,000 and over. The following are statistics from the Library of Michigan's 1996 *Michigan Public Library Statistical Report.*

Library Service Population:	119,487
Total Operating Expenditures:	$5,199,647
Staff	$3,577,421
Books/Print Materials	$380,578
AV/Non-Print Materials	$55,543
Subscriptions	$32,749
Electronic Format	$47,199
Electronic Access	$157,084
Other Operating Expenditures	$949,073

Philosophy

The library brochure, "All You Need to Know," includes the library's mission statement: "The Kalamazoo Public Library is committed to providing open access to quality services which respond to the informational, cultural, and leisure needs of people within the library district, in a fiscally responsible manner."

Reinventions

Saul Amdursky, KPL's director, discussed the benefits brought about by KPL's becoming a district library on April 2, 1990, in a January 1993 *Library Journal* article, "Gaining Independence at the Kalamazoo Library." Some of the benefits listed:

- avoided imminent financial crises
- gained an independent board
- staff received more equitable treatment
- gained freedom to plan own future
- became eligible for additional revenue
- improved service to community

Among the changes put in place were automation of all library services, an online public access catalog, and a CD-ROM tower. The main library, which had not been changed since 1959, underwent physical renovations.

In a June 15, 1995, *Library Journal* article, "Anatomy of an Election," Amdursky described in detail KPL's success in winning an election that increased its millage from 2.8074 to 4 mills. Between 1992 and 1994, research was done to determine the needs of the community and the library. Research was also done to determine the level of commitment by the community to increased financial support.

In a telephone conversation with Amdursky, he told me that the research did not actually take two years. During that time, the voters determined how the public schools would be funded. Once the method of financing was established, KPL moved quickly to ask the voters for an increase in funding.

Collaborations

In order to win the election to increase the millage, Amdursky described in the June 15, 1995, *Library Journal* article how the staff, trustees, Friends of the Library, community leaders, and neighborhood associations worked together. The Friends of the Library provided most of the money. More than $8,000 was raised for the campaign. Among those who helped was the president of a large marketing firm, who offered his work pro bono. The theme of the campaign was "Reach for Your Future."

Public and Staff Response to Reinventions

Amdursky mentioned in the closing paragraph of his January 1993 article in *Library Journal* that gaining control of the library's destiny by becoming a district library was not an easy task and that enemies may have been made. He did not go into detail about this. He did, however, describe some of the challenges, such as establishing a business office, that had to be met as a result of becoming independent. He emphasized that the benefits received from that independence had been worth all the challenges that had to be faced.

In the June 15, 1995, *Library Journal* article, Amdursky described how the staff compared the library's patron database with the list of those who had voted in the last election. The staff developed a campaign database from names that were on both lists. The goal was not to get people to vote—the goal was to get the people who voted to vote "yes" in the election that would increase the millage for the library.

During the telephone interview, Amdursky talked about the negative reactions of some residents and the local newspaper, the *Kalamazoo Gazette*, toward the low-profile campaign to win the millage increase in March 1995. One example of the negative reactions was that of an unidentified individual who stated in the *Kalamazoo Gazette*'s February 28, 1995, "Voice Vote" section that there was no need for the increase since books were not as important anymore.

Staff Training

In a telephone interview with Chris Price in the administration section, he told me that previously, in addition to in-house training, the library paid for staff members to attend computer workshops offered by local colleges. However, because of KLP's increased use of automation and technology, a technical trainer was added to the staff a year ago.

Creative Uses of Technology

One strong example of KPL's creative uses of technology is its home page on the Internet at http://www.kpl.gov/home.htm. Before I had talked with anyone at KPL, I felt that I knew the library and the community it served. At the site, there is information concerning an issue that is important to the local residents, the future of the Kalamazoo Mall. There are articles from the *Kalamazoo Gazette* covering both sides of the issue. There are also photographs showing the progress of the construction and renovation projects going on at the Main Library and all the branches.

Evaluation of Performance

James Fish was one of the members of the panel that judged the 1994 Library of the Year Award. At the time he was the director of the San Jose Public Library. He has just recently become the director of the Baltimore County Public Library. In a telephone interview, he said that everyone on the panel was impressed by the outstanding quality of KPL's work. It was his opinion that KPL should have received an award for its presentation alone. He described it as slick but not gaudy. He also remembered that it was a close call between the winner and KPL.

In my opinion, Kalamazoo Public Library has always had its focus on the community it serves and continues to reinvent ways to meet the needs of that community. From opening the first of 10 Children's Rooms in the country in 1896, to gaining independence from the Board of Education, to getting a "yes" from voters to increase funding, KPL's leadership has shown excellence in service to its patrons.

Bibliography

Amdursky, Saul. "Anatomy of an Election." *Library Journal* 120, no. 11 (June 15, 1995): 46–47.

———. "Gaining Independence at the Kalamazoo Public Library." *Library Journal* 118, no. 1 (January 1, 1993): 61.

———. Telephone interview by author. March 5, 1997.

Berry, John N. "Brown County Library: Library of the Year." *Library Journal* 119, no. 11 (June 15, 1994): 30–33.

Fish, James. Telephone interview by author. March 11, 1997.

Kalamazoo Public Library. *All You Need to Know.* Kalamazoo, Mich.: Kalamazoo Public Library, 1997.

Michigan State, Library of Michigan, Federal Program Division. *Michigan Public Library Statistical Report.* Lansing: Library of Michigan, 1996.

Price, Chris. Telephone interview by author. March 5, 1997.

"Voice Vote." *Kalamazoo Gazette,* February 20, 1995, late edition, sec. A7.

THE NEW YORK PUBLIC LIBRARY

Lisa Crisman

The New York Public Library was founded in 1895 and continues today as one of the most extensive library systems in the world. Centered in a massive urban area with an incredibly diverse population, this library system is striving to meet the demands of changing technologies and community involvement. A history of public and private partnerships is helping the library continue its mission to serve as one of the world's largest research institutions as well as one of the world's largest public library systems.

The NYPL includes the boroughs of Manhattan, Staten Island, and the Bronx and began with a generous endowment of $2.4 million "to establish and maintain a free library and reading room in the city of New York." By incorporating this fund with the two semipublic Astor and Lenox Libraries, the New York Public Library system was founded in 1895. Thirty-nine branch libraries were added with a Carnegie Foundation grant in 1901. The main New York Public Library building was dedicated on May 23, 1911, and opened with more than 1 million volumes. At this time the annual circulation for all libraries in the system is 11.6 million, and the city boasts 2.1 million registered library card holders.

As the city has grown, the NYPL has also grown, adding branches and items to the collection. There are four main research libraries in Manhattan, which contain 38.8 million items including 11.8 million books. The New York Public Library for the Performing Arts contains a collection focusing on dance, drama, music, and film. The Center for the Humanities includes the Berg Collection of rare books. The Science, Industry and Business Library supports open access to information in education, research, and entrepreneurial activities. The Schomburg

Center for Research in Black Culture, located in Harlem, concentrates on the rich heritage and contributions of African descendants. In addition, the NYPL system includes the Andrew Heiskell Library for the Blind and Physically Handicapped, the Early Childhood Resource and Information Center, and the Nathan Straus Young Adult Center.

The branch system of the NYPL manages 82 libraries in the boroughs of Manhattan, Staten Island, and the Bronx. The branches serve patrons from varying ethnic and economic backgrounds. To accommodate the diversity of its population, the branches offer a variety of services with some acting as Centers for Reading and Writing that include computers for instruction and tutoring for adult new readers. One branch is a multi-media language-learning center for adults that assists non-English-speaking citizens. Additional services include a Directory of Community Services staffed by library personnel and available online, career opportunity information for youth and adults, children's and young adult services, and Books by Mail available to homebound patrons of all ages who reside in the NYPL area.

While performing these traditional library services, the New York Public Library is also looking to the future. Each of the branches and main research libraries has online access through the catalog with additional databases for 2,600 periodicals and more than 1,000 full-text sources. The research libraries have a separate catalog (CatNYP) for items within the research collections. The branch libraries are connected by the LEO system, which is accessible from home computers as well. The LeoLine allows patrons to renew books, review items on their record, cancel holds, and assess fine totals. This service is available in English and in Spanish. LEO also contains an easy-to-use Kid's Catalog and an online entrance to the research libraries systems.

Two examples of how the NYPL is looking toward the next century are the renovations of its branches and through CLASP, the Connecting Libraries and Schools Project. One example of the rejuvenation of a branch library is the City Island Branch in the Bronx. Funding was raised through a cooperative effort by the city council, borough funds, and state funds, with additional construction funding from the library system. Included in the renovation was money for new books, expanded reading rooms, Internet access, and space for public programs. The adult and young adult collections were expanded, and a new children's area was added with funding for new programs to meet the needs of these growing numbers of patrons. Disability access was added as well as a community room that holds up to 45 people. This renovation project was accomplished with support from the community and shows the library's commitment to its service mission to connect libraries and their neighborhoods.

One of the most exciting ongoing programs is CLASP. Originally a three-year pilot program funded in 1991 by the DeWitt Wallace-Readers Digest Fund, the program was such a success that it has expanded and is now a cooperative effort including the Brooklyn and Queens Public Library systems. The mission of the program is to make reading and books an integral part of children's lives. Its three goals are:

- collaboration between New York City schools and public libraries

- encouragement of family reading and family literacy

- to increase community awareness and use of public libraries

One of the first accomplishments of the program was to issue NYPL library cards to all children in public and private schools. The program also includes visits to schools and libraries, parent workshops about involvement in education, teacher workshops, family literacy/ reading programs, and summer reading programs. Extensions of the program are classes in introduction to technology, after school and weekend programs, and involvement with community organizations. The emphasis is on people, in the library, in the schools, and in the community. Through far-reaching programs like CLASP, the New York Public Library is ensuring its place in the community and in the information age by promoting a literate public that is fully aware of the benefits of an active library. Programs such as this also contribute to the economic future of the city.

In keeping with the information age and interest in the World Wide Web, the New York Public Library sponsors an active web site that connects the community and the world with its services and its collections. Links on the site cover various topics related to the library. "On-Lion" is an education web site for children and young adults with links to fun sites, research sites, reference sources, and books. There are tips for parents and educators and connections to announcements of programs and performances. The Performing Arts Library building contains a performance space with an active schedule that is available online. Archives of press releases about the library and its programs are also available.

The New York Public Library is involved in the publishing of a variety of items, all available for ordering online. They cover topics from exhibit catalogs to music reference to black history. In keeping with its tradition of promoting reading and literacy for the community, the library sponsors the Helen Bernstein Book Award for Excellence in Journalism. This award is one of the largest monetary literary awards given annually.

In an age when many large urban libraries are closing branches, limiting hours, and reducing collections, the New York Public Library remains viable. Although it has also been affected by budget concerns, shorter hours in branches, and personnel constraints, the NYPL is looking toward the future, to another century of service to its incredibly vast and diverse community. By balancing the introduction of new technologies and the support of research centers with its commitment to the promotion of reading and literacy with community involvement, the New York Public Library is guaranteeing its existence well into the twenty-first century.

Bibliography

"CLASP: Connecting Libraries and Schools Project." New York: New York Public Library, n.d.

"It's Your Library: A Guide to the Branches of the New York Public Library." New York: New York Public Library, n.d.

The New York Public Library. Available: http://www.nypl.org (Accessed April 10, 1998).

New York Public Library Main Branch and Jefferson Market Branch visits, April 1, 1997.

REDWOOD CITY PUBLIC LIBRARY: 1992 Library of the Year

Sonal Rastogi

The Redwood City (California) Public Library, awarded Library of the Year for 1992 by Gale Research/*Library Journal*, shows a historical touch in terms of its architecture. The library was relocated into an old firehouse, the oldest building in town, but the architect carefully preserved the original architecture while adding 40,000 square feet of space. "The result is a library that is a landmark both in Redwood City and for librarians from all over the nation." With the renovation, new ideas and innovation came through according to the library director, Jane Light, who stated in John N. Berry's 1992 *Library Journal* article about Redwood's award that "the new building brought a great flowering of creative energy. We developed a new strategic plan, a new mission statement. We were able to actively address changing community needs."

Redwood City is a diverse, rapidly changing community of 66,000, with a growing Hispanic population that accounts for 25 percent of the Redwood City population. The library has been successful in catering to these changing needs. Sally Reed, director of the Norfolk Public Library, stated in an interview that the two major roles of public libraries are 1) to provide access to information by adapting to the changing community needs, and 2) to teach the community. When we evaluate the Redwood City Library in terms of these two roles, we can comprehend the outstanding performance of the library.

For any library to perform these roles effectively, the mission statement—especially as it relates to the population to be served by the library—needs to be addressed and developed. Redwood City Public Library has efficiently addressed the community needs—that is, changing population—and developed an appropriate mission statement in 1989 that reads:

> The Redwood City Public Library actively addresses changing community needs by providing current, accessible materials and information services for children and adults in a professional and helpful manner.

The reflection of the mission statement can be seen in the words of the director, Jane Light, who reported, "Every time I see a shelf empty of a title, I buy ten more copies, whether it's a résumé book or gardening tome. We have a fine collection with popular stuff in some depth. We can be without a book, but not without a résumé book." The director's assertion shows the library's commitment to buying collections designed to meet the user's (public patron's) needs. Needs assessment or community analysis is a valuable mechanism in developing an appropriate collection, and Redwood City Library has done this effectively and successfully. Because 55 percent of the children enrolled are Hispanic, most of the library's collection is geared toward serving this specific population. In addition, during a recent three-year period, the library tripled the size of its Spanish-language collections.

In terms of providing customer service, the Redwood City Library has been quite successful in carrying out its outreach/extension services for special populations—by providing a Kurzweil machine for visually impaired patrons and by offering telenews, a recorded-news service by telephone for patrons who can no longer read newsprint.

Children's services have been greatly emphasized, and the librarians visit each elementary school classroom to read stories as well as provide information about library services. Bilingual librarians visit the classes with a high enrollment of Spanish-speaking students. Excellent outreach service can be seen in the library's TOPS program (Time Out for Parents), which provides free child care for parents who use the collections on Saturday mornings. This program also won the Public Library Association Achievement Citation in 1991. Senior services are also given in the form of monthly lectures, for example, "Touch Me,

Wrinkles Aren't Contagious," and "The Aging Eye." ESL programs have been provided for the Spanish-immigrant population.

Training for staff is an ongoing and continuous activity, as Light says: "We simply can't take things for granted that people will be self-renewing." All the staff is encouraged to participate in planning and problem solving in regular meetings in each work unit and for the entire library. Training is also provided in-house by experienced staff members—Ned Himmel, head of reference service, provides the Effective Reference Performance training developed by Transform Inc. to Redwood City staff members who regularly work at branches or at reference, adult, or children's services; Chuck Ashton, head of the Children's Services, provides training for adults, volunteers, and family workers on how to select books for children, tell stories, make puppets, and accomplish related activities.

I had a telephone interview with Mary Mcgrath, document specialist, who feels strongly about Berry's 1992 article. She said that the library has always been in the process of reinvention and with the upcoming changes has adapted well to this reinvention in view of the changing population. When asked about how she feels about the library's coping with the technological changes, she stated, "We were on GEAC system (library catalog) but with the ongoing changes in the different database systems, we are on DYNIX (library catalog) presently. We have adapted to this transformation like any other library." She wholeheartedly agrees with Berry's article in that by being in the practicing area of the profession—working on the reference desk—she can well assert that the customers are given the highest importance and they "always go smiling." She also mentions that the patron suggestions-complaints are well received and implemented.

Redwood City Library is a part of the Peninsula Library System consortium and shares its resources with the other member libraries. It has an informative web site, which provides data on the library's operating hours and those of its branches—Fair Oaks and Schaberg. It also provides information on various subject matters—art, business, genealogy, government, history, job, travel—all highly appropriate for the public library patrons.

The Redwood City Library has fulfilled all the criteria for the winning library—"outstanding service to the community; creativity and innovation in coping with the changing needs of the library's public; the library's role as a leader in the field," as defined by Gale Research. The library services have received considerable approval from the citizens, who in return, have voted for a generous support of $50 per capita per year for the library. Personally, I feel that the Redwood City Library is in every way reinventing itself and moving toward a successful future for its incredible services to the community of Redwood City, California.

Bibliography

Berry, John N. "Redwood City Public Library." *Library Journal* 117, no. 11 (June 15, 1992): 32–35.

Mcgrath, Mary. Telephone interview by author. March 10, 1997.

Redwood City Public Library. Available: http://www.pls.lib.ca.us/pls/rcl/rcl.html (Accessed October 4, 1997).

Reed, Sally. Telephone interview by author. February 3, 1997.

SAN FRANCISCO PUBLIC LIBRARY

Whitney M. Berriman

On April 18, 1996, San Francisco's new Main Library opened its doors to the public. The seven-floor, 376,000-square-foot building contains 32 miles of stacks—12 open and 20 closed. (There were 19 miles of stacks in the old facility.) The airy, open new structure was designed by James Freed, of Pei Cobb Freed, to accommodate the future incorporation of additional communications technology.[1] The Main Library will house more than 1 million books, 5 million government documents, and other materials. According to one report, "The children's center alone is larger than any of the existing 26 branch libraries."[2]

There are differing opinions as to the "feel" of the new Main, as it is called. According to critics, "That elusive sense of community, of the library as a place for . . . the fellowship of readers" is just not sensed by some who have visited the new facility.[3] Ken Dowlin, the recently ousted library director, has described this new library as "the mall of the mind," which some feel is an apt description, particularly because Dowlin views library users as "online information shoppers."[4]

The San Francisco Public Library (SFPL) web page notes the new Main Library's technological advances. The visitor to this site is informed that "as the primary resource of free information for San Francisco, the new Main Library is 'wired' for the 21st century, constructed with expanding technology needs in mind."[5] The library is designed to meet patrons' technological needs. There are reading tables with outlets to enable patrons to plug in laptop computers. In addition, there are more than 300 public access catalog workstations available. This enables patrons to access the Internet as well as thousands of other online resources.

286

Currently, 64-bit technology is used at the SFPL as opposed to the web world norm of 32-bit technology. Dowlin explained this technology affects SFPL because "at any of 1,100 workstations in the new library, they can have the latest technology, even capable of full-motion video."[6] When asked his opinion of what ultimate effect the "web world" will have on libraries, Dowlin replied,

> The web world is a new medium. It can do everything, or almost everything, all previous media did. That means full-length movies, text, high-resolution video—the works. The 64-bit machine gives twenty times the clarity or resolution of the current 32-bit one. We have 14 digital media workstations now.[7]

Data Research Associates (DRA) is the automated system used at SFPL. Dowlin explained that, at SFPL, the "basic organization is through the computer."[8] According to Dowlin, before acquiring the automated system, SFPL had no union catalog, which meant that one had to go to 27 buildings to locate every item in the collection. The SFPL staff has "inventoried and loaded MARC-level cataloging for 2.5 million books," he noted.[9] The catalog is online and thus is available to anyone with a personal computer and a modem.

According to its mission statement, the SFPL is "dedicated to free and equal access to information, knowledge, independent learning and the joys of reading for our diverse community."[10] This mission is reflected in the library's five-year plan. One example is the goal to keep the Main Library open at least 60 hours per week with computer access available 24 hours a day. SFPL also plans to "double the size of its book collection within 15 years."[11] Community participation is encouraged by the SFPL.

With all of the changes occurring at SFPL, one may wonder how the staff is coping. According to Ken Dowlin in an interview from early last year, the library added 280 new staff members. The staff at that time totaled 630 full-time equivalents; however, the "payroll lists over 1,200," notes Dowlin.[12] Forty percent of the SFPL staff is composed of librarians. At one point, when asked how staff has reacted to the changes, Dowlin replied,

> I can't really assess that yet. We have to train everyone to get them all knowledgeable about the Internet world, and there's a fire evacuation system in the new building. They have to learn how to adjust the new ergonomic chairs, all kinds of new things. For the first time in history, we have hired a training coordinator.[13]

Later, in an interview approximately four months after the opening of the new Main, Dowlin and SFPL's community relations chief, Marcia Schneider, "agreed that they had not seen the staff under so much stress since the earthquake of 1989."[14] According to the goals listed within the five-year plan, "the staff will have the expertise required to collect, preserve, organize and disseminate information and knowledge. The Library will provide its staff with an atmosphere, training and resources necessary for personal development."[15] This remains to be seen.

I noted that one of the many controversies surrounding the SFPL centers around the use of "affinity groups" to raise funds for the library. These affinity groups consist of more than 17,000 individuals from the following groups: African Americans, Chinese Americans, Filipino Americans, Latino Americans, and the gay and lesbian community. In addition, there are other groups who support the Children's Center, an Environmental Center, and the Center for Rare Books.[16]

Dowlin explained that the "library will have a center for each group. They will be celebration centers, not separate collections. We don't want to ghettoize the library, and some groups were adamant about that."[17] There is concern that there may be a trend developing regarding "the private sector's growing influence over the public library."[18]

Another controversial issue facing the SFPL is fee-based service. The SFPL's fee-based research service is called Library Express. It is Dowlin's contention that the SFPL only charges "for convenience."[19] In his opinion, "Policies for this kind of thing must be shaped by professional leadership working with the community."[20] According to Dowlin, "One of the biggest parts of Library Express is local history. The marketplace just can't do that."[21]

What does the public have to say about SFPL? Dowlin reported that, according to a survey of library users, 63 percent of the respondents want libraries to have computers. With a response of 80 percent each, the predominantly African American and Chinese American portions of the city were adamant that their neighborhood branch libraries have access to computers. Dowlin explained, "Those and other city communities expect access to technology from libraries; they will depend on it."[22] He stated that "one of the things I learned in San Francisco is that neighborhoods are passionate about their branch libraries."[23] The public's perception of libraries' roles has changed over time. Dowlin felt "there has been a big shift."[24] He noted:

> The library is now seen as a communications center. In the past, the public viewed libraries as repositories. This is the most significant shift in recent library history, even though we will retain that depository role. The archiving role will move higher in priority.[25]

As for public opinion of what libraries should be in the future, Dowlin claimed, based on his findings, that "most people went retrograde. Trying to get them to project into the future was difficult."[26]

In an attempt to address the required questions for this project, I contacted Eleanor Shapiro in the SFPL Community Relations office. Shapiro consented to an extremely brief interview. The following is the result of our exchange.

> **WB:** To what creative uses has the SFPL put information technology?

> **ES:** We have over 50 CD-ROMs for our children's collection. There is also an ongoing digital library project involving our historic music collection. We have a comprehensive community database to meet the social needs of the citizens. The adult CD-ROM collection ranges from small business start-up to buying a car. Also, FirstSearch is available at every workstation.

> **WB:** What do you think constitutes reinvention for the 21st century as opposed to regular upgrades?

> **ES:** Our library is so new, it's hard to say at this time. We've just upgraded so what we have now will carry us into the next century.

> **WB:** How is the library changing its philosophy and how will this affect programs and policies?

> **ES:** Well, with the City Librarian [Ken Dowlin] who initiated this project gone, we're heading in a new direction. So, everything is unsure at this time.

> **WB:** Who is currently in charge?

> **ES:** Kathy Page is now acting City Librarian.

As stated earlier, this interview was brief at Shapiro's request. Also, since the SFPL is in such a precarious position, it was difficult to determine the direction in which the library is headed. Much of the library's future will depend on the person who is permanently appointed to the City Librarian position.

It appears that since Dowlin's departure, the SFPL is currently in limbo. With the new state-of-the-art building and the advanced technology, the library appears to be in a position ultimately to handle whatever the future holds. Under Dowlin, the library allegedly went over budget. The SFPL needs a strong leader to take over the role of city librarian. Under effective leadership, the library will have the ability to serve current and future users' needs. The SFPL is a forerunner of the library of the future—not a "problem child" but a "blessed institution."

Bibliography

Berry, John N. "A 'World-Class' Library: *LJ* Interviews SF City Librarian Ken Dowlin." *Library Journal* (April 15, 1996): 32–34.

Kniffel, Leonard. "Criticism Follows Hoopla at New San Francisco Library." *American Libraries* (August 1996): 12–13.

"San Francisco New Main Sets April 18 Dedication." *Library Hotline* (March 18, 1996): 1.

"San Francisco Public Library Mission Statement and Five-Year Plan." Available: http://sfpl.lib.ca.us/drafil/mission.txt (Accessed February 27, 1997).

"San Francisco's New Library Opens to Fanfare, Criticism." *Library Hotline* (April 29, 1996): 1.

Shapiro, Laura, et al. "A Mall for the Mind." *Newsweek*, October 21, 1996. 84–86.

Wiley, Peter Booth. "An Act of Political Will: San Francisco's Quest for a New Central Library." *Library Journal* 121, no. 7 (April 15, 1996): 36–37.

Notes

1. Laura Shapiro et al., "A Mall for the Mind," *Newsweek* (October 21, 1996): 85.
2. "San Francisco New Main Sets April 18 Dedication," *Library Hotline* (March 18, 1996): 1.
3. Shapiro et al., "A Mall for the Mind," 86.
4. Ibid.
5. San Francisco Public Library, available: http://sfpl.lib.ca.us/drafil/century.txt (Accessed April 9, 1998).
6. John N. Berry, "A 'World-Class' Library: *LJ* Interviews SF City Librarian Ken Dowlin," *Library Journal* 121, no. 7 (April 15, 1996): 32.
7. Ibid., 33.
8. Ibid.
9. Ibid.
10. "San Francisco Public Library Mission Statement," http://sfpl.lib.ca.us/drafil/mission.txt (Accessed April 9, 1998).
11. Ibid.
12. Berry, "A 'World-Class' Library," 33.
13. Ibid.
14. Leonard Kniffel, "Criticism Follows Hoopla at New San Francisco Library," *American Libraries* 27, no. 8 (August 1996): 13.
15. "San Francisco Public Library Mission Statement," http://sfpl.lib.ca.us/drafil/mission.txt (Accessed April 9, 1998).
16. *Library Hotline* (March 18, 1996), p.2.
17. Berry, "A 'World-Class' Library," 32.
18. *Library Hotline* (April 29, 1996), p. 1.
19. Berry, "A 'World-Class' Library," 34.
20. Ibid.
21. Ibid.
22. Berry, "A 'World-Class' Library," 33.
23. Ibid., 32.
24. Ibid., 33.
25. Ibid., 34.
26. Ibid.

INDEX

293